John Torrey Morse

Famous Trials

The Tichborne Claimant, Troppmann, Prince Pierre Bonaparte, Mrs. Wharton, The meteor, Mrs. Fair

John Torrey Morse

Famous Trials

The Tichborne Claimant, Troppmann, Prince Pierre Bonaparte, Mrs. Wharton, The meteor, Mrs. Fair

ISBN/EAN: 9783337165239

Printed in Europe, USA, Canada, Australia, Japan

Cover: Foto ©ninafisch / pixelio.de

More available books at www.hansebooks.com

Famous Trials.

THE TICHBORNE CLAIMANT.

TROPPMANN.

PRINCE PIERRE BONAPARTE.

MRS. WHARTON.

THE METEOR. — MRS. FAIR.

BY

JOHN T. MORSE, Jr.

BOSTON:
LITTLE, BROWN, AND COMPANY.
1874.

Entered according to Act of Congress, in the year 1874, by
LITTLE, BROWN, AND COMPANY,
In the Office of the Librarian of Congress, at Washington.

CAMBRIDGE:
PRESS OF JOHN WILSON AND SON.

PREFACE.

LATE in the summer of 1873, in a moment of weakness, I made a reckless promise to the editors of the "American Law Review" to furnish them with an article on "the Tichborne Case." When I came to undertake the task I at first stood aghast at the labor which it promised to entail; it seemed the work of weeks merely to read the materials in the columns of the London daily papers. It soon became apparent that the only way to write the article was to compile a much longer account than the editors of the Review could use and then to compress and curtail that narrative within the necessary limits. The strange fascination of this greatest and most remarkable of all trials, ancient or modern, took such powerful possession of me as I proceeded with my reading and the sketch as written in its first and fuller form seemed so much more adequately to convey the interest of the case than could any brief article, that I finally resolved to publish the result of my labors in its original shape.

The manner in which I have been obliged to write the account has inevitably produced numerous blemishes in it, from an artistic point of view. The significance of many matters was only developed by degrees in the progress of the trial; but the rearrangement and amending of the perspective which each mail from Europe, bringing new papers and fresh material, continually rendered desirable, could be done very imperfectly or sometimes not at all, by reason of the fact that the earlier sheets were already in the hands of the printer. Of the defects in the construction of the account, due to this cause, I am painfully aware. Especially will they be apparent to any lawyer who may be at the pains to peruse the volume. I must trust to the singular attraction of the wonderful cause itself to render my pages agreeable in spite of their faults. For myself, I must say that the most exciting novel I have ever read has failed to hold my attention with so close a grasp as has been exerted by the records of this prosecution. If my narrative gives a clear and intelligible sketch of the proceedings I hope it may derive such an interest from them as will serve in part to hide, or at least to obtain an excuse for, its faults of execution.

The accompanying articles have been from time

to time contributed to the "American Law Review." The trials of Troppmann, Prince Bonaparte, Mrs. Wharton, and Mrs. Fair were, at the times of their occurrence, sufficiently notorious throughout the United States to justify the expectation that even now, though two or three years have elapsed since they took place, some persons may find pleasure in reading them.

The "Meteor" case involved questions of such importance that, though less popular in its character, it has been thought worth preserving.

JOHN T. MORSE, JR.

16 PEMBERTON SQUARE, BOSTON,
    March 14, 1874.

CONTENTS.

	PAGE
PREFACE	iii
TICHBORNE	5
Opening for the Crown	9
Testimony for the Crown	47
Opening for the Defence	80
Testimony for the Defence	94
Closing for the Defence	123
The Chief Justice's Charge	174
The Verdict	232
TROPPMANN AND BONAPARTE	235
I. Troppmann	235
II. Bonaparte	256
MRS. WHARTON	274
THE METEOR	310
MRS. LAURA D. FAIR	335

TICHBORNE.

On Wednesday, April 16, 1873, in accordance with an ancient, honorable, and truly British custom, the Lord Chancellor "entertained the judges, sergeants, and Queen's counsel at breakfast, at his private residence in Portland Place." This hospitable and pleasing ceremonial having been duly performed, his Lordship and guests proceeded to Westminster Hall, and passed in procession to their respective courts. A large crowd, which had gathered for the purpose, witnessed this august spectacle. Perhaps the popular interest was rendered greater than usual by reason of the fact that the case of the Tichborne claimant was to be called for trial a week later in the Court of Queen's Bench. No sooner had the judges taken their seats, and opened in due course the Easter term, than a sort of warning gun was fired by Dr. Kenealy, Queen's Counsel, chief advocate for the defendant. He applied, on behalf of his client, for a rule against Mr. George Routledge, of the well-known publishing firm of Routledge & Sons, to answer for an alleged contempt, in publishing a book the year before, entitled "The Tichborne Romance," in which, as the doctor said, the claimant had been called an impostor and a liar, and had been otherwise held up to contempt. After much argument the judges somewhat reluctantly granted the rule, refusing, however, a request to make it returnable before the trial. The Chief Justice read the counsel a severe lecture on the impropriety of opening such a discussion on the eve of these criminal proceedings, the purpose too evidently being to arouse sympathy for his client, and to enable him thus indirectly, if the expression may be allowed, to draw the first blood. But as the great cause advanced and feeling upon both sides waxed daily warmer and warmer, these processes for contempt were very near being themselves brought into contempt, so very often were they requested and so often also granted. Newspaper editors especially were summoned from all parts of the kingdom to receive severe admonitions, to pay fines, to make public apologies. They had a good many comrades in misfortune, however; and before the end of the matter Mr. Whalley, a member of Parliament, and friend and supporter of the claimant, actually found himself fast within the walls of a gaol, in default of payment of a fine imposed for contempt. As for the rebuke administered by the Chief Justice to Dr. Kenealy, such entertainment soon became a part of the regular order of each day's proceedings.

The trial began on Wednesday, April 23, 1873, upwards of a year having elapsed since, on March 6, 1872, the defendant had been committed to New-

gate, by the Lord Chief Justice of the Common
Pleas, on charges of forgery and perjury. This
was a trial "at bar," in the Queen's Bench, an
occurrence so rare, that it was called to mind that
the latest instance of it had occurred forty years
back, in the case of the Mayor of Bristol. It is by
no means every defendant, even though accused of
weighty crimes, who obtains such a distinction.
The purpose sought to be secured by the arrangement was, the empanelling a special jury, which
could not have been had in the Central Criminal
Court, where the defendant had been indicted.
Neither could it have been had in the Queen's
Bench, under the count for forgery, because that
was a felony. Whence it happened that Dr. Kenealy, who dreaded a special jury and much preferred
to take his chance with twelve ordinary men, requested the Court to order a trial for the greater
crime first. But the Court refused, saying that
the prosecution was entitled to select the count
upon which it would proceed. At the trial of the
civil cause, Tichborne in ejectment *v.* Lushington,
Chief Justice Bovill had made some remarks on
the aristocratic character of the jury, and indeed
no less than three members of Parliament were
originally drawn upon it. This special jury was
summoned by an officer of the Court, called the
Master, instead of by the sheriff, and was "mixed"
of "tradesmen" and "gentlemen."

It is pleasant to deal with all these fine old-
school distinctions. The flavor of a rich mediævalism
thus far in our account has been very strong, and

we hope has not escaped the gratified senses of our readers. This picturesquely mottled array of jurors numbered at first forty-eight; each side then struck off twelve. We can imagine Dr. Kenealy making a deadly onslaught upon a dozen irreproachable "gentlemen," and Mr. Hawkins, Q. C., on behalf of the prosecution, eliminating as many low-bred "tradesmen." The remaining twenty-four were unchallengeable, and they were called in turn until, from such of them as had no sufficient excuse for non-service, the panel was filled.

The indictment ran against "Thomas Castro, otherwise Arthur Orton, otherwise called Sir Roger Charles Tichborne." Mr. Hawkins and four other barristers appeared for the prosecution, in the stead of the Attorney-General; the Chancery Solicitor for the Treasury sat with them. Dr. Kenealy and Mr. McMahon appeared for the defendant. The claimant himself entered the court-room, accompanied — countenanced would be an improper phrase — by Mr. Guildford Onslow, a member of Parliament. It was then suggested that one or two jurors were subject to proper exceptions. One of them was said by Dr. Kenealy to have had some trouble with the trustees of the Defence Fund. He acknowledged that he had passed round contribution boxes for the Fund; and for this reason he was then allowed to retire: a permission of which he availed himself with undisguised pleasure. Mr. Hawkins seized the occasion for the happy remark that now, at any rate, this juror was in the wrong box; and his audience were obliging enough to laugh at the

pun. A like gentle and refreshing rain of wit continued to fall at frequent intervals throughout the proceedings, only occasionally appearing to turn into biting hail when it came from the redoubtable lips of the Chief Justice. In this country, at least in the higher tribunals, a staid and dignified decorum is practised, which usually precludes attempts to enliven the court-room by any displays of indifferent humor in such a forced and illegitimate manner. But throughout this trial, no person — whether upon the bench, among the learned counsel, on the panel of the jury, or in the witness-box — seems ever to have an idea occur to him of a real or supposed droll character, without at once giving vent to it, and generally, it must be added, finding his little comicality, however humble, to be very well received. To an American lawyer this is quite a striking and novel feature in the conduct of the cause.

Mr. Hawkins opened for the Crown. Of a speech which occupied six full days in the delivery, it can be possible here to give only the briefest sketch or "argument." The defendant was charged with having committed perjury at the trial of the civil cause, in which he had appeared as plaintiff, in three main particulars: First, he had sworn that he was Roger Charles Tichborne, heir to the Tichborne estates, whereas in fact he was not this person; second, he had sworn that he was not Arthur Orton, whereas in fact he was Arthur Orton; third, he had sworn that he had seduced

Roger's cousin, Kate Doughty, now Lady Radcliffe, in making which statement under oath, he had sworn to a most foul and abominable falsehood. Of course, in supporting these assertions, he had uttered a multiplicity of subordinate perjuries. The Crown now would seek to prove perjury in each one of these three matters, and thereby would introduce new elements of interest into the case; for whereas in the previous suit in ejectment the defence had only sought to prove that this claimant was not the person he represented himself, and had confined itself to suggesting, collaterally as it were, that he was Orton, it was now to be positively proved that he was Orton.

Mr. Hawkins first presented a sketch of the life of Roger Charles Tichborne, to the point at which all record of that life ceased, or was supposed to have ceased until the claims of this defendant to be that person were preferred. The family was of the Catholic faith. Sir James Tichborne had married a French lady of the noble family of Bourbon-Conti, whence it came to pass that they lived much in Paris; Sir James, indeed, appears to have been one of those British exotics who can flourish and live happily only in the air of Continental Europe. Their son Roger was born in the French capital, January 5, 1829, and thereafter continued to live there, becoming familiar with the streets of that metropolis, having a series of French tutors, learning French as his mother-tongue and the language of his daily life, hearing no Eng-

HENRY HAWKINS, Esq., Q.C.
(Leading Counsel for the Crown.)

lish from his mother, and almost none from his father, taught to confess, and admitted to the bosom of the Holy Church. Later he was sent to the Catholic seminary at Stonyhurst. Here his French was so far from being forgotten that it continued to be the language which he always spoke from preference. His morals were represented by the counsel as being most diligently cared for upon this establishment. Indeed the pupils of Stonyhurst were said to have been walled around and guarded against any knowledge of vice or impurity with such sedulous and minute attention, that the entrance of wicked thoughts into their minds seemed to be little short of an actual impossibility. This garden of astonishing juvenile virtue and moral loveliness was the only school to which Roger ever went, save a short attendance, of only fourteen days, at the seminary of M. Dupanloup, near Paris. Such education as he ever had — and scandalously little it would have been accounted for the son of any person above the degree of a pauper — was finished when he left here. Soon afterward he entered the army, as a cornet in the Sixth Carabineers.

One of the earliest exploits of his budding manhood was to fall in love with his cousin, Miss Kate Doughty; and this unfortunate passion it was that proved to be the first step in the chain of events which has just culminated in the verdict of the jury in this cause. For, though the young lady returned her youthful lover's affection, the parents were of a different mind. In despair at the interposition of this obstacle, which was, or at least which seemed to be insurmountable, Roger resolved to seek consolation or forgetfulness in foreign parts. He does not appear to have been a particularly estimable young man. Mr. Hawkins had his own reasons for seeking to represent him as a pure-minded gentleman. But one, if not the chief, objection to him in his love affair was, undeniably, his very strong propensity for drink. He was not particularly intelligent, nor did his general cultivation do much to supply his native deficiencies or to enable him to do credit to his rank and social position. Accordingly, when he made his proposition to absent himself for a long period, he is not shown to have encountered any very grave opposition from a family and friends who doubtless felt that they could endure his absence with fortitude, if not with pleasure.

In February, 1853, he went over to Paris, to bid his mother farewell, and at this parting interview he gave her a lock of his hair. After her death, this memento was deposited in the Court of Chancery. What a strange collection of articles, so many souvenirs of tender but defunct affections, becoming in the lapse of a few years incomprehensible to all living men, yet still carefully treasured, do those dusty old Chancery crypts contain; receptacles only less multifarious than the renowned recesses of the moon! So the ambrosial curl of the scapegrace Tichborne heir was mustily filed away and formally docketed in Chancery when his mother died, and no surviving mortal cared to keep it longer as matter of sentiment, and it was valuable only for use in these causes. On the fourth of March, the wanderer sailed from Havre for Valparaiso, whither he came in safety. For some time he remained in South America, writing to the family at home with much frequency and regularity kind and affectionate letters, though apparently he was not troubled with home-sickness, for he ever expressed himself much pleased with his roving life. He sent home portraits of himself, — in which, however, he hardly thought they would recognize him, because he had become so " like a red-skin Indian." These portraits Mr. Hawkins promised should be produced to the jury. But the defendant denied having ever sent any thing of the sort. Further, as indicative of the pleasing humor of the youth, the real Roger, it may be mentioned that he sent to his friend Gosford (of whom more hereafter) a little skeleton in a bottle. This also the defendant ignored, and it certainly was not a natural occurrence to imagine.

In April, 1854, Roger sailed in the " Bella," from Rio Janeiro, for New York. He was put on board by a gentleman who would be called as a witness by the government. A letter written by him, just before his embarkation, shows his intention at this time to have been to prolong his stay from home for two or three years longer. And here, said Mr. Hawkins, ends the true and veritable history of Roger Charles Tichborne. Some four or five days after the " Bella " had sailed, her long-boat was picked up at sea; but she never was heard of again.

No person who sailed on board of her ever was heard of again. The underwriters paid the insurance on the ship and cargo. The will of Roger Charles Tichborne was proved, and the executors acted. "One poor, crazy, misguided soul alone refused to believe that her first-born son was dead." But nothing was heard from him who had previously been so regular a correspondent, who had a handsome allowance awaiting him in the hands of his bankers, and who had never before manifested any indifference in respect of so interesting a matter. Eleven long years rolled by in slow succession, in silence and oblivion, when "suddenly, in Australia, a butcher came from the shambles and announced himself as the long-lost heir." That butcher was the defendant in this cause. That butcher was Arthur Orton. The life of the real Tichborne had ended when the "Bella" went down in April, 1854; and it was now necessary to present the narrative of the life of this Arthur Orton, this person still in being, and now before the Court and jury.

It was a difficult task to trace the wanderings of a man of Orton's character and condition in life through so many and such distant years; but the counsel thought he had accomplished the feat with tolerable success.

Arthur Orton was born June 1, 1834, being therefore the junior of Roger Tichborne by about six years. He was the youngest son of a respectable shipping butcher, who lived in London, at 69 High Street, Wapping. He was but poorly educated, learning to read and write and acquiring a smattering of arithmetic, just enough to aid his father a little in his business. The boy was afflicted with Saint Vitus's dance, and when about fourteen years of age he was sent a sea voyage for the good of his health. This defendant had mentioned that he had had Saint Vitus's dance, which, though true of Orton, was not true of Roger Tichborne. Orton, accordingly, took passage, in 1848, from Antwerp, for Valparaiso, arriving there in November of that year. The captain of the ship in which he sailed is dead, but his wife is living, and will appear as a witness in the cause, to testify her belief that this defendant is Arthur Orton. Two months later he was at Valparaiso again, and this time deserted his ship and went inland to a small town called Melipilla. There he became acquainted with a family of Castros, who treated him kindly, and afterward he is found assuming the name of Castro. He picked up also a smattering of Spanish, showing that he stayed in the place for some little time. The dates of Roger's letters, as Mr. Hawkins contended, showed that he could not have been to Melipilla at all; certainly not long enough to pick up the least knowledge of Spanish. Indeed, Tichborne was far from quick at learning. In February, 1851, the defendant again sailed for home, under the name of Joseph Orton, but bearing the seaman's number of Arthur Orton. He arrived in safety, made his way forthwith to 69 High Street, and in the circle of his old acquaintance was dubbed "fatty," or sometimes "bullocky," Orton, on account of his great increase in size. He weighed thirteen stone and was but eighteen years old. At this time his heart was somewhat touched by the charms of a damsel of Wapping, named Mary Anne Loder; with her he " kept company." But erelong he became restless, slipped the chains of affection, deserted the fair Mary Anne, and in December, 1852, embarked on board the ship " Middleton," bound for Hobart Town.

The history of his adventures in Australia was traced with a degree of minuteness which seems extraordinary, in view of the difficulties which must have been encountered in the undertaking. On first arriving at Hobart Town he set up in trade as a butcher. While there, he met a family of Jurys, connected with him by marriage, and at first saw a good deal of them; but, having borrowed £14 of one of them, he opportunely disappeared, just before his note of hand for that sum fell due, and did not afterward renew the acquaintance. Mrs. Jury would be called to swear to the identity of the defendant with Arthur Orton. He was in service at Gippsland and afterward at Wagga-Wagga. At the latter place an old acquaintance from Hobart Town, one Hopwood, met him, and hailed him as Orton; but he replied: " I am not Orton: I am Castro. Come and have a drink." January 29, 1865, he married a servant-girl, describing himself as Castro, born in Chili, and thirty years old: just the age of Orton, but six years less than the age of Roger. He lived with his wife at Wagga-Wagga for a time, in a state

LADY TICHBORNE.

of extreme poverty. He had been leading a disreputable life. According to his own account of himself, he was at one time a horse-breaker, at another time a butcher: he refused to say whether or not at another time he was engaged in certain highway robberies, in company with his supposed double, Arthur Orton; but he was caught, and accused of horse-stealing; and he acknowledged having been very intimate with two notorious bushrangers and highwaymen, Morgan and Tote, of whom the former was shot in 1865. Yet in all his adventures and intimacies he said that he had never mentioned to any person, not even to his wife, that he had been wrecked, and saved from drowning. This secret, for what imaginable reason could not be suggested, he kept locked in his own bosom, jealously guarded from all the world, until later in this year, 1865.

At what time the plan that "this slaughterman" should set up as Roger Charles Tichborne was first concocted, says Mr. Hawkins, it is impossible to say precisely. The inception of such dark plots is usually wrapped in some degree of secrecy. But the way in which it came about was this: the Dowager Lady Tichborne, possessed with the idea that her son was still alive, though for no good reason that she or any one else could suggest, in the year 1863 advertised for him in the "Times." Previously she may be supposed to have been held in check by her husband, Sir James; but he died in 1862, and she was left free to follow her singular bent. About the same time one Cubitt, in Sydney, Australia, opened a "Missing Friends' Office." He advertised it freely, and Lady Tichborne saw the advertisement. Forthwith she wrote to him. Cubitt at once made public the knowledge that an heir to the Tichborne estates was wanted. One Gibbes, a lawyer in the neighborhood, was at the time engaged in putting Orton, *alias* Castro, through insolvency. One day he saw his client smoking a pipe, upon which he observed the initials " R. C. T." Straightway the shrewd man of the law turned upon the smoker, told him that his secret was out, that he was indeed the long-lost heir, Roger Charles Tichborne, and that if he did not disclose himself, then he, Gibbes, would do so. So Gibbes wrote to Cubitt announcing the discovery, and Cubitt wrote to Lady Tichborne, conveying the glad news of the resurrection; and the Dowager, much pleased, hastened to reply. Several letters followed. In her correspondence she artlessly gave divers facts in the life of her son, which she intended should be used in identifying the person claiming that honor. This information, however, obviously came to hand very opportunely for use for a quite different purpose. It gave valuable hints, some of which were improved, and others, strangely enough, were lost. And now the initials R. C. T., seen nowhere for eleven years, reappeared at the foot of the defendant's letters. Strange to say, however, they were invariably accompanied by a peculiar mark, ·)(·, which had always been used by Arthur Orton, after the Spanish fashion. Gibbes suggested to the defendant that it would be becoming in him to write

to his mother; and defendant, who had been in
no hurry to do so, but had for a long while been
willing to occupy the position of third party and
allow the correspondence to be conducted by others,
at last accepted this advice, and wrote an affectionate epistle, whereof the grammar and the
spelling would have made the hearts of most
mothers ache sorely; but the sentiments were
noble.

This agreeable communication was as follows: —

WAGGA WAGGA, Jan. 17 66.

MY DEAR MOTHER: — The delaye which as taken place
Since my last letter, dated 22d April 54 Makes it very
difficult to commence this Letter. [The "delay" since
the "last letter," of which the date was so accurately given,
was nearly twelve years! The affectionate writer's embarrassment was certainly not unnatural under the circumstances.] I deeply regret the trouble and Anxiety I must
have cause you by not writing before. But they are known
to my Attorney and the more private details I will keep
for your own Ear. Of one thing rest Assured, that though
I have been in a A humble condition of life, I have never
let any Act disgrace you or my Family. I have been A
poor Man and nothing worse. Mr. Gibbes suggest to me
as essential that I should recall to your memory things
which can only be known to you and me, to convince you
of my Identity. I don't think it needful, My Dear Mother,
although I send them, Mamely, the Brown Mark on my
side And the Card Case at Brighton. I can assure you
My Dear Mother, I have kept your promice ever since.
In writing to me please enclose your letter to Mr. Gibbes,
to prevent unnecessary Enquiry, as I do not wish any per-

son to know me in this Country. When I take my proper position and title, Having therefore made up my mind to return and face the Sea once more, I must request to send me the means of doing so, and paying a few outstanding debts. I would return by the Overland Mail. The passage Money and other expences would be over Two Hundred pound, for I propose Sailing from Victoria, not this colonly And to sail from Melbourne in my own Name. Now to enable me to do this my dear Mother you must send me " —— [The rest of the letter is missing.*]

Unfortunately for the sufficiency of these brief and mysterious suggestions, there had been, said Mr. Hawkins, no brown mark on Roger's body, and no card case had ever occurred at Brighton. But worse than this even were the defendant's statements, made at this time to sundry persons that he was in the army only thirteen days, and was then "bought off;" that he went to school at Winchester, whereas Roger went to Stonyhurst, &c. But the poor Dowager was satisfied, out of her inner consciousness, so to speak; and, even

---

* It may be remarked here that the letters of Lady Tichborne contain many proper names spelled with small initial letters; on the other hand, the letters of the claimant show a frequent needless and improper use of the capital initial. The former custom might naturally follow a French education: the latter could never be expected to do so; it is an English habit. But, as will be seen hereafter, most of the education which Roger had — indeed all that he had when he was forming his orthographic habits — was French. His family customarily used the French language. His mother's errors, therefore, would naturally have been perpetrated by the son, whereas he, in fact, fell into exactly the opposite kind of blunder. I have not seen in any report of the trial that this suggestion was made in behalf of the prosecution.

before she had received the foregoing tender first letter from her son, in February, 1866, she wrote to her " Dearest Son Roger."

After some delay, the defendant, as appears from his letter, had prepared to return to England. But, before doing so, he deemed it proper to make his will. It was a most unfortunate piece of forethought. In that document he disposed of property at Cowes, Isle of Wight, where the Tichbornes had no property; of property at the Hermitage in Dorsetshire, whereas there was no such family seat in that county; but there was a farm called Hermitage in Surrey, which had been acquired by the family after Roger left; of which, said Mr. Hawkins, some loose rumor might have reached the defendant's ears, and which he had perhaps confounded with Upton in Dorsetshire, which also belonged to the Tichbornes, but which was not referred to. Then he mentioned estates at Ryde, I. W., where the Tichbornes owned nothing. He named three executors: J. Jarvis, of Bridport, a friend of Arthur Orton, but unknown to Roger Charles Tichborne; Sir J. Bird, "of Herts, Baronet," who was shown by investigation to be a wholly fictitious personage; and his mother, "Hannah Frances." " He did not even know his mother's name!" said Mr. Hawkins. The Dowager's initials, " H. F.," had been learned from the correspondence; but her real name was Henriette Félicité. The name Henriette had indeed been signed to one letter; but this had apparently been overlooked. Invention was easier than investigation. This was an unfortunate slip of memory, and altogether the will had so bad a look that its absurdity and manifold errors were acknowledged *ex necessitate*, and it was sought to be explained away and was averred to be a fraud and to have been falsified on purpose. The purpose was to deceive and mislead a banker at Melbourne into making advances to the claimant, as will be set forth more fully hereafter. .

Passages in one of the Dowager's letters in May, 1866, disclosed the fact that the Tichbornes were adherents of the Roman Catholic faith. The defendant's marriage had previously been celebrated only in a Wesleyan Chapel. But upon receipt of this information as to the family creed he was forthwith married again in a Catholic Chapel, and wrote forthwith to his " dearest mama," " and may the blessed Maria have mercy on your soul." " Roars of laughter" followed this announcement. He was first married as Castro; but the second nuptials were by the name of Tichborne, which, however, he very carelessly spelled with an extra *t*, thus, Titchborne. He also at one time inserted the initial D for Doughty, into his name, writing it R. C. D. T., which was erroneous.

Having found his way back to England by the route of New York, this defendant, Sir Roger Charles Tichborne! went whither?—not to Tichborne Park, not to see any of Roger's relations or old friends; but he repaired straight to No. 69 High Street, Wapping! His father, George Orton, however, was dead; another family occupied the house. So the wanderer turned aside to a public-house hard by, and there made inquiries about the Ortons. The landlady answered him, and looking fixedly at him exclaimed, "Why, bless me! you are rather like an Orton yourself!" "Oh, no!" he said, "I'm not an Orton: I'm only a friend of the family." Soon after he communicated with the sisters of Arthur Orton, using the feigned name of Stephens, and opening the correspondence by a sham letter of introduction. The letters written to him were destroyed, or not forthcoming. But the contents could be inferred in part from his replies; in these he denied being Arthur Orton, from which it was obvious that his correspondents had suspected his identity with their long-absent brother. They wrote, asking for pictures of their brother's wife and children. The defendant in return sent pictures of his own wife and children. Sir Roger Charles Tichborne was sending to the sisters of Arthur Orton the likenesses of his own wife and children as being the likenesses of their brother's wife and children! Singular circumstance! yet not more singular than his feeling any interest in the Ortons whatsoever. Beyond all this, however, it was discovered that he sent money to some of them; even made a regular allowance of five pounds per month to one of them. But later, in view of the gross imprudence of such conduct, he sent his gifts in a feigned name, as coming from one "Bland."

The next morning, after this nocturnal tour of inspection, he again returned to inquire about the sisters of Arthur Orton, Mrs. Jury, and Mrs.

Tredgett. He was directed to a Mrs. Pardon, whom he found. He sent in to her the card of a Mr. Stephens, a fellow-passenger of his in the ship from Melbourne, whose card he had secured. Mrs. Pardon again charged him with being an Orton, and a second time he denied the impeachment. Such disagreeable accusations, however, were to be shunned, — he took the warning; and this appears to have been his last open visit. He left a letter, dated at Wagga-Wagga, June 3, 1866, purporting to come from Orton to his sister, and to introduce Stephens. It was signed

ARTHUR ORTON

) : (

M

The letter was evidently composed for the purpose of deception; and was not written when and where it purported to be. For Stephens never saw the defendant until he was on shipboard, crossing the ocean to England. So soon as Mrs. Tredgett opened the letter she uttered an exclamation which Mrs. Pardon heard, but which the rules of law made inadmissible in evidence.

Soon after, a letter, written by the defendant "in a feigned hand," said Mr. Hawkins, was received by Mrs. Pardon, as follows:—

DEAR MADAM,— would you kindly inform the lady for whom I left a letter with you that if she will comicate with me at once she will hear something to her advantage. Please send what information she can conserning Miss

Loader and her own family. And what became of her brother Thomas chilldren.

I remain yours respecful
W. H. Stephens.

Address R. C. T., Post Office, Gravesend.

The letter or letters received by him in reply were not forthcoming: he said, doubtless with truth, that he had destroyed them. But their contents may be in part inferred from his reply. He had evidently been suspected by Mrs. Jury and Mrs. Tredgett of being their brother Arthur. He wrote this time also " in a feigned handwriting," —

Gravesend, 7 Jan. '67.

Dear Madam, — I receved your kind letter this morning and very sorry to think you should be so much mistaken as to think i am your brother, your brother is a very great friend of mine and whom i regard as a brother. And I have likewise promised to send him all the information I can about his family I cannot call on you at present but will do so before long. I sent your sisters a likeness of your brother wife and child this morning I should have sent you one but i have only one left which i require for Copying. I have likewise *one of himself* which i intend to get some copy of I will then send you some of each My future address will be R. C. T. Post Office liverpool Liverpool. Hoping to have the pleasure of making the acquaintance of my friends sister before long I remain your respectfully

(Signed) . W. H. Stephens.

When first shown these letters at the civil trial, the defendant denied having written them and said they were forgeries. But being hard pressed by the Attorney-General, in cross-examination, he at last admitted their authenticity and deliberately acknowledged his falsehood. He had been induced to utter it, he said, because the truth " would injure him in his case."

The matter of the address at " Liverpool," too, was significant. It was not his real address; and, being asked why he gave it, he returned frivolous and evasive answers, until at last he said, " I gave that address, though I was not going to Liverpool, because I did not want to be bothered with them." He was anxious to get the coveted information about his family, and then to have done with them. Nearer acquaintance would be awkward. Already they suspected him: they might hunt him up at Gravesend; so they were put off the track by the sham direction of " Liverpool."

These visits to Wapping, so grossly imprudent as they were, he had instinctively seen fit to conceal, even from his own attorney. At the time he made them, indeed, it was not fully certain that he might not be admitted to be the person whom he claimed to be; and no investigation had coupled him with Orton. It was his own guilty conscience which led him at first to practise such concealment. But afterward he felt obliged to deny them with especial emphasis, when rumors began to get about that he was Arthur Orton. He then wrote, October 20, 1867, to his firm friend Rous: —

We find the other side busy with another pair of sisters for me one of them been to see Mr. Holmes, they had been three days at them and they are quite sure of success. Only there is this difference which they cannot make out. The Brother of these young women is very dark; and very much marked with the smalls pox very much about the face. But they are still very sure I am him. I wonder who I am to be next. The man they think I am is still living at Wagga Wagga under an assumed name. They say I was born in Waping I am glad they have found a Respectable part of London for me. *I never remember having been there.* But Mr. Holmes tell me it a very respectable part of London.

(Signed)   R. C. D. TICHBORNE.

He did not remember having ever been there! on his cross-examination he said: "Probably I took care not to mention my visits there." The double at Wagga-Wagga with the " assumed name," mentioned in this letter, was never heard of in any more definite shape during the trial. Defendant said he knew Arthur Orton, that he saw him in 1866, indeed, that he brought over a letter from him. " But where was Arthur Orton? Was he dead? Then where was the proof of his death? Was he alive? Then let him be produced! Where was Arthur Orton, if he was not sitting there? It would be no avail for witnesses to come forward and say that they had seen some one who was called Arthur Orton, and who was not this man. Perhaps this man who had borrowed other men's names might have lent his own." The defendant himself had said that Orton had changed his name to Alfred Smith, " because he had done something not in accordance with the law." Orton had been charged with bush-ranging, which is *australice* for the plain English phrase "highway robbery;" but whether defendant was in his company he had upon interrogation refused to say.

A knowledge of localities was all-important. The claimant must have some knowledge of the estates which he claimed. Therefore soon after his arrival, after he had been to Wapping, he went to the Park. He went down to Alresford in the neighborhood of Tichborne, and scouted around the place, but very surreptitiously. He did not make himself known to the family, yet he put "R. C. T." on his trunks. He did, however, secure much useful information from Rous. This person now kept a public-house, but he had been the clerk of one Hopkins, the old attorney of the Tichborne family, and the information which he could impart was invaluable. He and the claimant got on together wonderfully well. But if the defendant was at great pains to see the ex-clerk, he was by no means at equally great pains to see the attorney himself. Him, indeed, he preferred sedulously to avoid, and took care to prepare himself very carefully for their meeting, when at last it was inevitable.

Gosford also, his own old and trusty friend, confidant, and counsellor, the trustee and executor under his will, — not the Australian testament, but a will made by Roger before leaving England in 1854, — the custodian of the famous sealed packet, Gosford he was loath rather than desirous to encounter. When that gentleman was at the trouble of coming all the way to Gravesend to see the heir *redivivus*, the defendant actually refused to meet him, and sent him back from a bootless errand. But a few days afterward Gosford made a second expedition, and this time he found his man and also his man's new solicitor, Mr. Holmes. The three came to London together, Gosford upon the road putting many interrogatories to the claimant. But the claimant could not answer them, at least not correctly. Especially he was asked as to the contents of the sealed packet and could offer no suggestion at all concerning it. Gosford thereupon made up his mind that the claimant was an impostor, and told him so very bluntly to his face.

While thus looking around Tichborne Park, carefully avoiding every one whom he might have naturally sought to see, he wrote to his "Dear Cousing Kate" (not Lady Radcliffe, but another Kate, a Mrs. Greenwood) that his "head was so bad" that he couldn't come to see her, a circumstance for which he expressed his regrets and apologies. But he wrote to his mother a different story; viz., that his cousin Katty would have liked to come to see him, but that her husband would not permit her to do so.

Lady Tichborne, his mother, was at Paris. Thither he at last went to see her. But after he had come to the city, the poor lady was obliged to go to call upon him, instead of receiving the

first visit from him. He was lying in his bed as
she was ushered into his apartment, in the presence of two witnesses, one of them a lawyer, the
other a "brewer's clerk," his friend. His account
of the interview was very indistinct. He could
not say who spoke first; or whether his mother
recognized him "at once, or after a time, or what;"
but she did recognize him in time, — indeed, it was
the errand on which she had come, and she was
resolved and predetermined upon the fact of the
identity. They talked a long while: his answers
to her questions were ludicrously wide of accuracy.
He spoke of his grandfather, whom Roger had
never seen; said he was a private in the army,
whereas Roger was an officer; said he had had St.
Vitus's dance, whereas Roger had had rheumatism;
that he was at school at Winchester, whereas Roger
was educated at Stonyhurst, so far as he was at
school at all. But the infatuated mother pardoned
every blunder, and wrote: "He confuses every
thing, as if in a dream; but it will not prevent
me from recognizing him, though his statements
differ from mine!" Poor lady! her part in the
drama is sad and pathetic enough; so constant
was she in the belief that her son was alive, so
faithful to his interests, and all the while obliged
by the circumstances to see in such an unfeeling,
ignorant, degraded wretch, the child for whom
she was doing and braving so much. It was a
most astonishing deception to practise on a mother,
— that must be admitted; yet that she made her

assertions in good faith cannot reasonably be questioned. Her letters give no very high idea of her intellectual capacity.

A great number of photographs of letters were introduced in evidence. Mr. Hawkins called the attention of the jurors to the hope expressed at the beginning by the defendant, that the Dowager had " got some of the letters." At first no resemblance between the handwriting of Roger and of the defendant could be seen; but after 1867 a resemblance began to exist and to increase, as the result doubtless of careful practice. But the defendant and Arthur Orton wrote alike, and made some identical and very peculiar errors in spelling. For example, they both wrote " nothink " for " nothing," " lick " for " like ; " both used the phrase " a-going," and other like points of similarity would be readily noticed.

In connection with the letters may be introduced a few entertaining sentences selected by Mr. Hawkins from the defendant's diary or pocketbook. On one leaf he had written, near the time when he first set up his pretensions to be an English baronet: " Some men has plenty brains and no money; some has plenty money and no brains. Surely the men as has plenty money and no brains are made for the men as has plenty of brains and no money." * These were singularly communistic sentiments to fall from a rich member of the British aristocracy; and it was especially

---

* This was afterward stated to be an exact quotation from a novel by Miss Braddon.

amusing to find Roger Tichborne formally stating that rich and stupid men were the proper victims of poor and clever ones. It was a very melancholy and unpromising doctrine for him, but a very natural and attractive belief for Arthur Orton, in his character as claimant of the Tichborne landed estates and title. Again he wrote: "R. C. Tichborne, Bart., some day, I hope." And yet again he recorded in a moment of indignation the following amusingly artless and inconsistent outburst: "I, Thomas Castro, do certify that them as thinks that is my name don't know nothink about it." The merriment caused by the reading of these extracts was loud and prolonged. On another leaf was written the address of Mary Ann Loder, the old love of Orton, but a person whose humble existence could not reasonably be supposed ever to have come to the knowledge of the heir of Tichborne.

Every one of course remembers the inquiries that were prosecuted through both hemispheres concerning the "Osprey." The custom-house registers and all manner of other records, not in England alone, but in Australia, in North America and in South America, were diligently searched for traces of such a vessel. The story as developed during the first trial, and told by Mr. Hawkins in his opening speech, was as follows: The defendant said he had been picked up at sea by a passing vessel, and by her had been carried to the port of Melbourne in Australia. Eight sailors, he said, had been rescued with him. After some hesitation he suggested that "Osprey" was the name of the craft which picked him up. Investigation showed that an "Osprey" had indeed arrived at Melbourne in July, 1854, about four months after the wreck of the "Bella," and that this would have been a natural time for her to have arrived had she sailed from the neighborhood where the "Bella" must have been lost, direct to Melbourne. But the plausibility of this simple and not intrinsically improbable tale, was dispelled by a series of circumstances. The eight sailors were each entitled to wages: sailors are well aware of their rights in this respect; yet no one of these eight men had ever been heard of by any person in any form. The defendant described the "Osprey" which saved him as being much larger than the real "Osprey" that came to Melbourne, and also as having a very different complement of men. He gave a wrong name for the captain, after at first hesitating as to whether he could remember the name at all. Two other names, also, of men among the crew he finally gave. They turned out not to be the names of any persons on the real "Osprey;" and inquiry showed that all three of these names had been borne by persons on board the "Middleton," the ship which, it will be remembered, carried Arthur Orton to Hobart Town in 1852. There is a custom-house, an emigration office and a Lloyd's agency at Melbourne; but nowhere did there appear any trace of the arrival of any shipwrecked passengers at the specified time. The log of the "Osprey" had been produced and no entry was made in it of the rescue of any person on this voyage, — a most improbable omission had the event really occurred. Altogether such a gross degree of unlikelihood began to attach to this narrative concerning the "Osprey," that in course of time the defendant, never very positive in the matter, was tempted to change his mind concerning her.

Strangely doubtful at first as to the name of the vessel to whose opportune appearance he had owed his life, and in which he had spent nearly four months of voyaging, he now suggested that it was the "Themis." There was a story that a "Themis" had landed a second-class passenger at Melbourne in 1854. This passenger had given to the captain a check for seventeen or eighteen pounds, which had never been paid. The defendant now became quite sure that it was the "Themis" that had saved him. He said he remembered giving the check to the captain, and that he had heard that the check had been presented at his banker's, but that the funds which should have been standing there to his credit had been withdrawn, and though his relatives acknowledged the genuineness of the check, they had refused to pay it, and it had been dishonored. He hastened down to Liverpool, to follow up this new thread, and thence wrote very hopefully: "It is now beyond a doubt it was the 'Themis' picked me up. The owners and agents are doing all they can to find me evidence." He even saw the "Themis," seemed to remember her, went on board of her, and at last actually went so far as to point out the room which he said that he occupied in her. But unfortunately, before the end was reached, the investigation was somewhat over warmly and thoroughly pursued. For the log of the " Themis " was found, and showed no record of the rescue of any shipwrecked mariners; the check had never been heard of at the banker's, nor by any of Roger's family; and to crown the whole the first mate of the " Themis " in 1854 turned up in person, and absolutely shattered the whole story. So the defendant was left very nearly in the singular condition of one saved from drowning, yet without a rescuer. As a *pis aller* he came back to the story of the " Osprey," which with all its weak points, — and it had several, — was yet the best that could be set up.

As early as August, 1850, Roger had avowed his love for his cousin, Miss Kate Doughty, the heroine as she may be called of this novelette. On January 11, 1852, the attachment was acknowledged to the parents, and in February following, they gave to it a kind of qualified and conditional sanction. But, as it would appear, Roger's conduct was far from becoming such as the parents of the young lady desired that it should be; and a due regard for their daughter's welfare impelled them in the succeeding summer to break off the match. Roger was apparently very plainly spoken to by Sir Edward Doughty on this occasion; for he afterwards said to Kate that after her father's words to him it was no longer possible for him to marry her. Yet he seems not to have dismissed all hope of some ultimate favorable turn in the affair. It was in this time of anxiety, of mingled despair and hope, that Roger deposited the sealed packet with his friend and counsellor Gosford; also afterward, having his foreign tour in his mind, he made his will. On the fifth of January, 1853, he wrote to Slaughter: "My private wishes and intentions, as I intend to have them carried out if I live, I have confided to Mr. Gosford, and I request you and Mr. Gosford to act as trustees and executors of my will." January 17 he wrote to Gosford: "I have written my will and left it with Slaughter; and the only thing I have left out is about the church, which I will only build under the circumstances which I have left with you in writing."

When the defendant was questioned in the witness-box as to the contents of this mysterious packet, he manifested extreme reluctance to reply. But being hard pressed upon cross-examination he stated that his unwillingness arose out of "considerations of delicacy for others." The contents of the packet had in real truth never been disclosed to the defendant, and unless indeed he were the genuine Sir Roger he had had no means of discovering, or even distantly surmising, what they might be. At first he understood from Gosford that the document confided to him was still in existence in his hands, but after a time he learned that it had been destroyed. Emboldened by this discovery he ventured to remember more about it, and in 1868 he made the following affidavit in Chancery: "Shortly before leaving England, in March, 1852 [he should have said 1853, which was the year of Roger's departure], I placed in the hands of Gosford the document, with instructions not to open it except on certain events, one of which I know has not happened, and the other I hope has not happened."

In the witness box he stated that the engagement between himself and his cousin was broken off in August of the year 1852; and that the next time that he saw her after this change in their relationship to each other was in November or December of that year. He was then staying at Winchester; but he saw her at Tichborne and there met her and walked with her, and told her that after what her father had said he could not marry her. To the question what were the "certain events" referred to in his affidavit above quoted, he said that the one which he knew had not happened was his own return before his cousin's marriage. But afterward, being asked the same question again, he said, "I don't know, — I suppose it was my death." The other event, that which he hoped had not happened, he strove hard to evade mentioning. But at last in reply to repeated and obstinate inquiries he said: "The confinement of my cousin." The Attorney-General then said "solemnly," while Lady Radcliffe, that was Miss Kate Doughty, sat in full view beneath him in the court-room:

Do you mean to swear, before the judge and jury, that you seduced this lady?

Witness. I most solemnly, to my God, swear it.

Atty.-Genl. When and where did it happen?

Witness. At the mill.

Atty.-Genl. When?

Witness. Not long after I came from Ireland.

Atty.-Genl. When?

Witness. About the month of July or August.

Atty.-Genl. Of what year,—1852?

Witness. It was about the latter end of July or the beginning of August.

Atty.-Genl. Was it before or after the breaking off of the engagement by Sir Edward?

Witness. Before.

Atty.-Genl. You say this took place at the mill. Where is the mill?

Witness. Almost facing the house, in the village of Tichborne.

Atty.-Genl. Were you staying in the house?

Witness. I was.

Atty.-Genl. How long before the engagement was broken off?

Witness. About a week or ten days.

Atty.-Genl. Do you mean to say you left your cousin with child?

Witness. No, I didn't say so.

Atty.-Genl. You left, you know, in March, 1853. You say you seduced her in July or August, 1852, and before the breaking off of the engagement. You say you never saw her but once after that in the village, and you spoke to her about her confinement?

Witness. I didn't say so. She wished to impress it on me.

Atty.-Genl. When and where did she tell you?

Witness. To the best of my belief, when I met her in the village.

Atty.-Genl. Did you make any further inquiry afterwards?

Witness. No.

Does all this, said Mr. Hawkins, sound credible? But there was further proof. Defendant after giving these replies was pressed as to the packet. He said it was dated in November, 1852, was read over by him to Gosford and then intrusted to Gosford's keeping; that it related to his cousin's being *enceinte*. In 1862 he gave to his attorney this version of it:

> In the event of my father being in possession before my return or dying before my return, he (Gosford) was to act for him according to instructions contained in the document. In the first place he was to have Upton to live at and there to manage the whole of the estate. He was to keep the farm in hand and show the greatest kindness to my cousin Kate, and let her have every thing she required. My cousin gave me to understand she was *enceinte* and pressed me very hard to marry her at once. I did not believe such was the case nor have I since heard it was. I always believed it was said to get me to marry her at once. For this my father try and persuade me. It also refer to the village at Prior's Dene. He (Gosford) was to have the cottages repaired and also to improve the estate in general. Was also to make arrangements for Kate to leave England, if that was true. Both Gosford and wife urged me very hard to marry her at once. I do not think Mrs. Gosford knew about Kate.
>
> (Signed)   R. C. D. TICHBORNE.

Being driven at the trial to give his recollection of the writing itself, he wrote as follows:—

CHERITON, Nov. 1852.

If it be true that my Cousin Kate Doughty should prove to be *enceinte,* you are to make all necessary arrangements for going to Scotland, and you are to see that Upton is properly prepared for her until I return or she marries. You are to show great kindness to her and let her have every thing she requires. If she remains single until I come back I will marry her. In the Event of my Cousin's death you are to take charge of the Estate on my behalf, to keep the home farm and to repair the Cottages at Prior's Dean.

(Signed) R. C. TICHBORNE.

Not a word, it will be observed, was said in either of these expositions concerning that church, which Roger had written to Gosford that he had not mentioned in his will, and would " only build under the circumstances which I have left with you in writing." The defendant also cut himself off from the assistance of supposing that there might have been some other instrument given to Gosford, for he expressly swore that there was no other; and Gosford corroborated the testimony.

But the confidence which led the claimant to furnish contents for the sealed packet was misplaced. For though Gosford's copy had indeed been destroyed, yet a duplicate existed; a duplicate which the defendant, not being the real Sir Roger, had never known or heard of or suspected. That duplicate had been written later; indeed it bore date June 22, 1852, but otherwise it was identical with the original. That duplicate had been given to Miss Doughty and had most fortunately been preserved. It would be produced at the present trial. Its language was as follows:

TICHBORNE PARK, June 22, 1852.

I make on this day a promise that if I marry my cousin, Catherine Doughty, this year, before three years are over at the latest to build a church or chapel at Tichborne to the Holy Virgin, in thanksgiving for the protection which she has thrown over us, and in praying God that our wishes may be fulfilled.

(Signed)   R. C. TICHBORNE.

Here was the explanation about the church. The packet and the letter of January 17, 1852, to Gosford, were consistent.

But incredible as the whole of the defendant's story appeared, even when thus told, Mr. Hawkins said that he proposed to furnish actual proof by dates of the impossibility of the seduction. Had it happened early in the year the results must have been known when Roger and his cousin " met and walked together" in November or December. But in addition to such circumstantial and inferential proof the witness himself had placed the occurrence in the latter part of July or beginning of August. It was fortunate that he was thus nailed to the definite point of time; for the whereabouts of Roger could now be adduced to show the story to be impossible. An *alibi* of the supposed seducer could be proved. In the early part of the year Roger was in Ireland with his regiment. In June he came back with it, and still remaining with it, was sent to Canterbury. He then obtained a leave of absence from June 15 to 23 : went to London for a visit of three days ; on June 19 left London and came with Lady Doughty and her daughter Kate to Tichborne ; on June 22 he left Tichborne Park and returned to his regiment at Canterbury. These movements of the real Roger were unknown to this defendant, who had not the knowledge requisite to enable him to fix the visit in June. Rather he had chosen to connect it with his uncle's final disapproval of the match, which did not take place until much later. Moreover his testimony required a visit lasting for a week or ten days, because he said the event occurred by that space of time before the disruption of the engagement, which arose out of a personal interview between his uncle and himself. The visit of two or three days in June, therefore, would not serve his turn in this respect either. During that short period Mr. Hawkins admitted that it was probable enough that the cousins walked and rode together, but it was extremely "improbable that these young people would have been allowed to be alone with each other under the circumstances," *i.e.*, of their *quasi* engagement.

Mrs. and Miss Nangle, aunt and cousin of Roger, were staying at Tichborne Park all this while, and remained there till June, 1853, after Roger had sailed. They would be called as witnesses, and would swear that Roger was never at the Park after June 22, 1852. Lady Doughty had been examined on her dying bed, and then and there she also swore that Roger had not been at Tichborne after June 22. Letters written by Roger himself from Canterbury and elsewhere would be produced and would also disprove the possibility of his having been at Tichborne in July or August.

Lady Radcliffe would be placed upon the stand, and would swear that the whole story was a base and infamous fabrication.

If all this evidence failed to satisfy the jury, "I declare to God," exclaimed Mr. Hawkins, "I do not know what evidence could be required, or by what evidence a lady of honor and character could vindicate her character against a foul aspersion."

A very important portion of the case for the prosecution consisted, said Mr. Hawkins, in a comparison of certain physical peculiarities and marks. Upon the person of Roger Tichborne were certain indelible and ineradicable marks which did not exist upon this defendant; and upon this defendant were congenital marks which were not upon Roger Tichborne, and artificial marks the presence of which upon Roger Tichborne was not satisfactorily accounted for. Upon the arm of Roger Tichborne had been tattooed the emblems of the heart, cross, and anchor, with the initials R. C. T. Many persons had seen these marks before Roger's departure for South America. This defendant not only had no present tattoo marks on his arm; but he swore in the ejectment suit that he never had been subjected to the process. Nevertheless he had a scar which the prosecution expected to show was the result of an effort to erase by cauterizing the tattooing of the initials A. O.

In Roger's childhood he had on his arm an issue, kept open by his mother's directions for several years. This had been by some persons confounded with a seton, but was quite different from a seton and had left a very different mark. On the defendant's arm were the traces of an attempt to form a seton, though there were no marks of an issue. The defendant had evidently heard that Roger had had a seton, and hence this effort to fabricate the apparent remains of one. Roger's ears adhered firmly to his cheeks; the defendant's ears, on the contrary, had unusually pendant lobes. Roger had been bled in the ankles, and the bleeding had left inerasible scars; the defendant had upon his ankles certain scars not of a real bleeding, but clumsily fabricated to simulate such genuine vestiges of the actual operation. The defendant had the brown birth-mark on his side; but Roger had not been thus marked. The defendant still suffered from the "twitching" of the eyebrows which was the remnant of the St. Vitus's dance which Arthur Orton had had in his youth and which had never been fully eliminated from his constitution. This man had a scar on the back of his head which he said was caused by a fall which happened to him in his childhood in Brittany. Roger had indeed had such a fall, which some of the defendant's friends and informants in the family had doubtless mentioned to him, but the contusion had been at the side of the head near the temple and had left no scar. In the course of the former trial it had been suggested that Roger had a peculiar thumb and that this man had it. The suggestion was not made until after the seventieth day of the trial. In fact Roger had no peculiarity of the thumb; and this sudden illumination had come to the mind of the claimant from the examination of a daguerreotype of Roger, in which, either because the plate had been rubbed or from an original defect, the appearance of the thumb was rendered somewhat deformed.

In addition to all this mass of living testimony which I propose to offer, said Mr. Hawkins, in closing his long address, "I shall lay before you also the evidence of the dead. In December last, the late Lady Doughty, with intellect unclouded, closed her eyes in death. She ended her days in peace; and ere she died — in the hour of her death — and with the consciousness that in a few short moments she would enter into the presence of her God, to whom she swore, she recorded her oath that the defendant was not the man he had falsely sworn himself to be."

As a foundation and explanation for the testimony of the government witnesses in this case it was, of course, necessary to produce the evidence given by the defendant in the civil proceedings. The report of this evidence as written out by the short-hand reporters covered several thousand pages. The prosecuting counsel proposed to read a part of it; then to put in their evidence bearing upon that part; then to read more and adduce more evidence, and thus to proceed step by step through all that was material to their case, bringing the defendant's testimony and their own contradicting evidence into as close juxtaposition as possible. Dr. Kenealy, for obvious reasons, strongly opposed this scheme and insisted that the whole mass of the defendant's examination, both in chief and upon cross interrogatories, should be read through continuously at the outset of this trial, and should not be furnished to the jury piecemeal in carefully prepared and pertinent connection. He said that he and his colleague were so far deficient in a minute knowledge of the prior case that this course was essential to them in the conduct of the present one. The point was of the first importance for the government, since to have had it determined against them would have obliged them to rely upon the memories and clear-headedness of the jurors to a perilous and unreasonable extent. After an eager argument, however, the court ruled for the prosecution.

The defendant had testified that he had lived in Paris with his father and mother during his childhood, until he was sent to Stonyhurst in 1845. At first he had stated that he went to school at Winchester, and not at Stonyhurst; but, having been obliged to acknowledge and correct this error, he afterward testified that he never went to a school at all until he went to Stonyhurst; that previously he had only a private tutor, and that he had had only one such, a M. Chatillon, who taught him in Paris until the time of his leaving there; that he never studied Greek or Latin, — indeed he did not know the difference between them; that he studied no chemistry, and in fact supposed it meant the art of mixing drugs; that he had no memory of persons named respectively Lefèvre, Jollival, Cornet, Laforet, and Dupanloup; that he did not remember Gousset the valet, who for years was in personal attendance on Sir James Tichborne; that the Abbé Salis, his mother's confessor, confessed him, or at least, as he preferred to put it on cross-examination, he confessed to the abbé, "if he did to any one" in Paris.

The Abbé Salis, "a venerable-looking ecclesiastic of the old French school," was called as the first witness for the Crown. He was wholly ignorant of English, and had to give his evidence through the medium of an interpreter. He was tutor, but never on any occasion had acted as confessor, to the young Tichborne; was not confessor to his mother, Lady (then Mrs.) Tichborne. The vicar of the Madeleine and Lefèvre were the confessors. Saw the young man in Paris, when he came to bid farewell to his mother, before going to South America. Was always on the most kindly terms with him, and then parted with him in the most friendly manner. The young Tichborne spoke French perfectly; began to translate Latin under the abbé's tuition. Witness was then asked if the defendant was Roger Charles Tichborne, and replied emphatically "*Non!*" A juror asked, "Is there any resemblance to him?" The abbé, laying his hand upon his heart and speaking with Gallic earnestness, much to the amusement of his English auditors, again responded "*Non!*" To Dr. Kenealy the witness then said, that Roger was "slow in mind and disposition," "not lazy, but idle," yet withal "a perfect gentleman." In 1850 or 1851 witness had seen the tattoo marks on Roger's arm, but never mentioned them to Lady Tichborne, because they were so "disagreeable." Lady Tichborne told this witness of her son's return, and hoped he would recognize the wanderer. But the abbé had already been prepossessed against the claimant, by hearing from Chatillon that he was not the real Roger. He had preferred to believe Chatillon rather than Lady Tichborne. "Was not she a truthful, honorable person?" asked Kenealy. "*Elle avait la tête malade*," responded the abbé, which is translated in the columns of the "Times," and doubtless was so rendered also by the interpreter, by the unpleasant phrase, "She had a diseased brain." Being asked to explain his meaning he said that she had "*une idée fixe*," intending thereby to designate her resolute belief in the survival of her son. It was suggested to him that Napoleon also had "*une idée fixe;*" and Kenealy reiterated his aforesaid interrogatory, badgering the bewildered abbé in approved fashion, but to the same question ever receiving the same reply, until Chief Justice Cockburn said it was evident that the witness also had "*une idée fixe*," and the matter had to be dropped.

The abbé remarked that Lady Tichborne was "*très distinguée*," but was bent upon "pursuing a phantom." He further said, that she had even approached him with offers of bribes if he would recognize the claimant as her son. He repeated the words used on this occasion, and certainly they could bear but one sensible interpretation. He did not *see* the persons who confessed to him in the confessional; he was able, however, to recognize them by their voices with accuracy and certainty. This defendant's voice was no more like Roger's than day is like night. Between 1839 and 1845 Roger had as tutors, at different times, the abbé and Messrs. Laforet, Jollival, and Cornet. A letter from Roger to the abbé, written in French from Stonyhurst, and inquiring about Cornet, was put in evidence.

Père Lefèvre was next called, a priest whose very name the defendant professed never to have heard. He was Roger's confessor in Paris for many years, and prepared him for his first communion. Told to Roger very often the story of how his hair had turned white early in his youth by reason of a terrible dream he had had; a remarkable tale, to which Roger always listened with deep interest and wonder, but of which defendant could be brought to remember nothing. Had seen the tattoo marks upon the lad's arm, and had reproached Roger for them, saying that they were fit only for soldiers and sailors and were "not seen in good society." He and Roger were ever on the most intimate and affectionate terms. Defendant was not Roger and did not resemble Roger. Shortly before sailing Roger confessed to witness. The witness was asked on cross-examination, whether Roger did not confess to him the seduction of his cousin, and replied that he did not: "It would have been infamy to disclose it if he had said it in confession; but *he never said it*. If he had said it to me in confession, *I should not have known it;* but I say that *it was never said.*" When he heard of the appearance of Roger, or of one calling himself so, he at once said that if it were indeed Roger he should know it, for Roger "would come at once to throw himself into his arms." But the claimant showed no haste to see this witness and no propensity to rush into his embrace. Defendant's tones were wholly unlike Roger's. Roger had confided to this witness his love for his cousin, which seemed ardent, but "respectful beyond expression;" also his intention, if he should succeed in marrying her, of building a chapel, on which he would spend, he said, 200,000 francs.

The defendant had said in the civil cause that he had been prepared in Paris for his first communion by the aid of a book called the Garden of the Soul. This proved to be a volume much used by Roman Catholics in England, but it had never been heard of by Salis or Lefèvre.

The report of the evidence given by defendant at the previous trial had thus far been read by Mr. Hawkins very "dramatically;" but at this point Dr. Kenealy interfered to check the dangerous effect produced by this oratorical rehearsal and insisted that for the future the reading should be done by the officer of the court. His request, as calling for an undeniable right, was granted.

Chatillon, the Parisian tutor of Roger, was next called. He taught him daily from 1834 till 1840, not, as averred by defendant, till 1845. After him Roger had some half dozen tutors, the name of not one of whom could defendant remember ever to have heard. Roger was at the *séminaire* of M. Dupanloup near Paris for a short time; but this defendant had been unable to tell, when interrogated, what a *séminaire* or a seminary was, even confusing it with a cemetery! and swore he had never been to any school at Paris or elsewhere, prior to going to Stonyhurst. Roger, the witness said, always spoke French, even during his visits to England, and when in the company of his parents, who likewise habitually used that language. When witness saw this defendant in Paris he went to his lodgings with Lady Tichborne. Witness took the precaution to request her not to mention his name, being anxious to see whether defendant would be able to recognize him. But her ladyship at once introduced the witness by name to the defendant. Chatillon saluted him, but saw directly after the first greeting was passed and so soon as he could look the defendant well in the face, that he was not the real Roger. Witness undertook to converse with him, but defendant was totally ignorant of French and had to use an interpreter. Tried to recall to defendant divers incidents, as, for example, a farewell dinner which took place just before Roger's departure for South America; but defendant could at that time remember none of these matters. During the interview defendant sat writing, concealing his features with a handkerchief. Afterward, when Chatillon again sought to call upon defendant and upon the Dowager Lady Tichborne, he was told that they were ill and could not see him. Witness swore positively that he discovered no resemblance in appearance or voice between the real Roger and defendant. Witness had seen the tattoo marks, representing a heart, cross, anchor, and the initials R. C. T. on Roger's arm; had often seen him naked, but had never observed any brown mark on his body.

The fall at Pornic in Brittany was a grave event in Roger's childhood, and well remembered by his tutor. Roger lay insensible for thirteen days after it. But the blow was not upon the back of the head, but close to his temple, and it left no mark visible after his recovery. Defendant had knowledge of the occurrence of such a fall, but he had placed the contusion at the back of his head and undertook to show the scar.

Madame Chatillon was next called. She noticed the tattoo marks, just above Roger's wrist, one day as he was talking to her. He told her he had made them with a pin and gunpowder. There was a heart, cross, anchor, and his initials. But the sketch drawn of them by her husband did not seem to her an accurate representation.

M. D'Aranza, a Spanish gentleman, came next upon the stand. He was an intimate and confidential friend of Roger in Paris, but the defendant had been unable to remember his name or existence.

It was manifest, he said, that Roger's education had been neglected. But he spoke French fluently, and "such as it was, it was the French of a gentleman." He spoke "bad English, but not vulgar. *Vulgar* was not the word. He mixed up French and English together." His English was "imperfect or broken." The habitual language of his conversation was French, which was also customarily used by his parents, especially by his mother. Roger was always gentlemanly in feelings and behavior. Witness was positive that defendant was not Roger.

Gousset, valet of Roger's father for fourteen years in Paris, next testified. His name and existence also had escaped the defendant's memory, though as an old family servant Roger had always manifested a kindly interest in him and had even been to see him and bid him good-by before sailing for South America. Had often seen Roger stripped for the bath and observed no brown mark on his side, but had seen a "cautery" (meaning thereby, as was explained, an issue) on his arm. Witness was asked whether he looked for marks, and replied, "The question is not well put. I did not look for them; he had none. If you see a person's body, you cannot help seeing whether he has marks." Roger "was slim, carried his head erect, and had the air of a gentleman." Witness was positive that defendant was not Roger. He saw him just before his departure for Valparaiso and Roger was then talking French as usual.

These witnesses all testified that there was no

peculiarity of "twitching" or otherwise about Roger's eyebrows, and no peculiarity in his walk, save only M. D'Aranza thought it might have been a very little odd in some respect which he did not explain.

Several more days were now devoted to reading the examination and cross-examination of the defendant as given in the former suit. This record covered eleven hundred printed pages, and the examination of witnesses in this cause was not renewed until the twenty-first day of May.

Then the Abbé Toursel was called. He testified that the defendant was not Roger. He had confessed Roger, but acknowledged that he had seen him only once. Roger then spoke French perfectly. To this witness the poor infatuated mother expressed her conviction that the claimant was her son; but acknowledged that she had grown weary of the life which she led with him at Croydon, of the number of people always at the house, the turmoil and expense there. She had arranged therefore to allow to her son a fixed weekly stipend, leaving him to go his own separate ways and do with it as he would. The unfortunate lady seemed shaken and depressed; she was very worn and thin, mere skin and bones, so that witness looked after her as she left his house, fearing she might fall. Soon afterward death removed her from the strife.

Donna Clara Novas de Hayley, a Spanish lady from Melipilla, gave much interesting testimony. She was wife of an English physician resident there, and for the compensation of one thou-

sand dollars and her expenses, had come across
the ocean to testify in this cause. She knew all
the people of that town, the Castros and all the
rest, very well. She perfectly remembered the
arrival of an English lad there, in 1847 or a little
earlier; apparently about sixteen years old. [Arthur
Orton was then about this age, but Tichborne would
have been at least five years older.] He gave his
name as Arthur Orton, son of George Orton, of
London, butcher to the Queen. He was dressed
as a common sailor and said he had been badly
treated by his captain. He mentioned his sisters,
Mary Anna and Margaret Anne, and a third whose
name had escaped Donna Clara's memory. — [Orton
had three sisters, Mary Anne, Margaret, and Eliza-
beth.] — This young stranger had been taken into
their house by her husband, partly from hospitality,
partly " as a curiosity. For an Englishman was
extremely rare." He lived in her house some
three months. He did nothing but amuse himself,
ride horses and the like. The people there lent
him their horses, and occasionally even lent him
pocket-money. He picked up some knowledge of
Spanish, but spoke a broken jargon. She herself
did not know French, but thought he might occasionally have interpolated a French word. His
hair was light, with a reddish tinge (*rubio*). He
showed her two letters on his arm, about midway
between the wrist and elbow, occupying a space
as large perhaps as a shilling, and which he told
her meant Arthur Orton. She admitted that
another Englishman with a larger mark on his arm

had been at Melipilla some two or three years later, a man twenty-five or thirty years old, who came with an American party. But she did not confound the two. Orton, this witness said, was a Protestant, though once he had told her that he was not a Christian at all. While at Melipilla he had been baptized as a Catholic, a fact which made much stir in the village. " Fixing her eyes with a stern look " upon the defendant she said that he was her old guest, Arthur Orton.

Mrs. Jury from Hobart Town was next called. She was now a widow; her husband had been brother to the husband of one of Orton's sisters. She knew the defendant very well, and he was Arthur Orton, who came over in the ship " Middleton" in 1852. She was perfectly positive about it. She sketched his life at Hobart Town; he was a slaughter-man there at first; then he opened a butcher's stall. She sent him geese to sell for her, and also she lent him money; indeed she had his note of hand promising to pay her husband £14, and duly signed " Arthur Orton." But she said, regarding him " steadfastly and indignantly," he had never paid the money. His attorney's agent had indeed promised that she should get her money and be paid handsomely; but her testimony did not suit; and she had since seen neither the agent nor the money. She identified several letters written by him. She had also seen the tattooed initials, " A. O.," on the arm, when she met defendant one day in the street; " and he knows it too ! " she added, looking him full in the face. Being asked if she had the slightest doubt as to defendant's identity, she said: "He is Arthur Orton; the man I paid my money to. The only difference is that his hair is a little darker. He has the twitching of the eyes which he had in Hobart Town." She described him as being not quite so stout in Hobart Town; but large-framed; with rather small hands and feet; a habit of twitching his eyebrows, one more than the other; an inability to look a person straight in the face; and as being of a rather lazy, round-shouldered, and generally slouching style. At the close of her evidence, before leaving the box, she paused to bestow what the reporters noted as "a look of intense bitterness" upon her delinquent debtor, the defendant. This witness expected £500. She did not think the government would expect the mother of ten children, seven of whom were unprovided for, to take such a journey without compensation.

Mr. Hopwood from Victoria, Australia, was asked, "Have you seen Arthur Orton in court?" Looking at defendant he replied: "Yes, I see him now; that is he." Witness said that defendant was precisely like Orton except in being rather stouter. Witness knew him first as Orton, at Hobart Town. Afterward meeting him inland and addressing him as Arthur, he was silenced by a gesture from defendant. They then adjourned to a public-house to take a drink together, and defendant said he had changed his name to Castro on account of a horse-scrape. This witness was to have £250, and assented to the suggestion of Dr.

Kenealy that he was being shabbily treated by the government in not getting more.

Miller, an attorney, had known the defendant by the name of Castro in Australia. This witness had lived for some years at Albury, where the defendant had said that he had left Orton, but witness had never heard of such a person there.

Gibbes, the Australian attorney, was next called. He said that Orton at some time between July and September, 1865, had applied to him to be put through insolvency, bearing then the name of Castro, but asked whether he would be obliged to disclose certain property to which he was entitled in the south of England. Witness told him that he would; that the penalty for a concealment in the event of discovery would be very heavy. This apparently deterred defendant from proceeding further in the business. This witness had at one time, when the pretension was first in course of preparation in Australia, been under the honest impression that defendant was the genuine Roger Tichborne. He saw Cubitt's advertisement in the "Sydney Morning Herald," and for a while believed that he himself had perhaps "spotted" the missing man; but he felt no absolute certainty. The defendant had shown to this witness the famous pipe with the initials R. C. T.; but upon interrogation had acknowledged that he had not preserved it ever since the shipwreck, but had cut the letters a year or fifteen months before. It was this pipe, in connection with the advertisement, which first aroused Gibbes's suspicions and caused him to communicate with Cubitt. Defendant had told witness that he had been able to receive but an imperfect education on account of his being afflicted with Saint Vitus's dance; that a Christian brother had gone about with him and had taught him from time to time what little he could. Defendant further told this witness that he had not written to his mother since April 11, 1854, and felt embarrassed at reopening the correspondence. Witness suggested that he himself would draught a letter for him. But defendant preferred to write for himself, saying that his mother would recognize his style and his handwriting, which had not changed. The reason why the foregoing date was changed in the letter (*ante*, p. 19) from April 11 to April 22, this witness could not remember, though he was sure that defendant did at the time give some explanation for it.

From this time defendant began to borrow money in small sums of two or three pounds each from this witness. One of his applications was signed R. C. Tichborne, and the first syllable — *Tich* — was on one line, and *borne* was on the next lower line. His wife being delivered of an infant at this interesting juncture in his fortunes, he wrote: "I am more like a manic than a B. of B. K. to have a child born in such a hovel." He was certainly a rather illiterate and ignorant " B. of B. K."

This same witness, Gibbes, wrote the will in Australia. It was written, as he said, only in order to have executors appointed, because defendant wanted to borrow money, and witness advised him that no one would lend him money unless some provision in the way of executors should be made to provide for the contingency of his death. But there was no idea that this would ever be really used as a last testament. The testator did not contemplate an immediate or sudden decease and was not undertaking to provide for it.

This witness had received a letter from the Dowager Lady Tichborne, in which she said that her son had been educated at Stonyhurst and had been in the 6th regiment of Carabineers. Pushing his investigation as to identity witness then went to Sydney, found the defendant at that place, took him before a respectable solicitor there and questioned him. Defendant then said he was born in Dorsetshire, and that shortly after her confinement his mother went to Cherbourg. That he had two sisters born in Paris. He distinctly denied that he was ever at Stonyhurst; said he was in the 66th regiment of Light Dragoons; that the uniform was blue and the arms were a sword and carbine; that he was a private; that he ran away and joined the dragoons; that he was forthwith after the lapse of only thirteen days bought off by his father, and that he was thereafter kept under careful *surveillance* till he went abroad; that the cause of his joining the army was a card case at Brighton, in which he had been swindled out of several hundred pounds. Afterward, being taxed with the glaring discrepancies between many of his statements and the accounts given in his mother's letter, he exclaimed:

"I never was an officer! and by God I've a damned mind never to go near her when I go home."

In the will the defendant had given his mother's name as Harriet Frances. When it was suggested to him that his mother's name really was Henriette Félicité he only said: "I've a notion that she was called Lady Harriet." Mr. Hawkins remarked that she was not called "Lady" at all till long after Roger left home. But Henriette Félicité seems to have proved quite too much for the butcher's son from Wapping; he could not get the name right in spite of the French education which he had enjoyed in his character as Roger Tichborne, — not even after he had heard it. So in an affidavit made a little later he gave her yet another alias, an approximation to accuracy, — "Harriet Felicia."

Defendant had thrown out hints and mysterious statements to this witness as to his being entitled to property in England and that his family had a title, and that his name was assumed; and all this had taken place, as Gibbes averred, before witness heard of Cubitt's advertisement and of the missing Tichborne heir. Then witness by way of testing defendant and for his own information spoke a few words to defendant in French, and was answered by him in the same language. Witness then said: "Shall I call you by your real name?" and defendant, apparently much annoyed, cried out, "Oh, for God's sake, don't!"

Divers small incidents which led witness to believe in defendant's identity with the lost heir were : his recognizing a street in Paris from a photograph ; his being visibly affected on hearing of his younger brother Alfred's death ; his recognition of his mother's handwriting ; his gentleman-like behavior in many respects, — for example, said the witness, the easy manner in which he opened the door for my wife, bowed and sat down again, — in all which he had the air of gentlemanly breeding.

Defendant told witness that the reason he was not married by the Catholic ceremonial at first was because he was not on good terms with the church. This, however, turned out to be not for any thing he had already done, but because he meant to cut off the Tichborne dole, which he said was three shillings in the pound of the income. In fact, the dole was only a few loaves of bread.

To Mr. Justice Lush the witness acknowledged that defendant might conceivably have seen the name on the back of the Parisian photograph.

This witness was to be paid £600 for his trouble, — not for his testimony. Indeed, as the Chief Justice remarked, there was very much of what he had said that was quite as useful to the defence as it was to the prosecution, which had called him.

Captain Oates was next called. He knew the Captain of the " Bella," and saw him a great deal at Rio in 1854. The witness remembered a young English gentleman, slim and sunburned, with darkbrown hair, who applied to be taken to New York on the " Bella." This person had, as he said, come across the country from Valparaiso to Buenos Ayres. He was not then in funds to pay his passage money, but said he had rich friends, and the captain finally consented to take him, in the expectation that that matter would be made all right in time. There were no other passengers. The young man was "in trouble," and though he was able to come on board the ship openly enough, it was necessary to smuggle him out of the port. This was done by hiding him in the "lazarette." The inspecting officer was duly "feed," and did not find the concealed passenger. The young Englishman was perfectly sober when he came on board, and supped that evening with this witness and the captain of the "Bella." The defendant, it should be noted, had given none of these incidents in his account of his departure from Rio; and, on the contrary, he had professed to remember nothing distinctly about it; he accounted for this deficiency and inaccuracy of his memory, because, as he said, he was put on board in a state of drunkenness. The account of the discovery of water in the hold, and of the gradual settling down and sinking of the ship in fair weather, giving time for the crew to take to the boats, as given by the defendant, was also stated by this witness to be in many respects impossible. The theory of the prosecution was that the "Bella" foundered in a sudden and violent gale.

Mary Ann Loder, the *quondam* inamorata of Arthur Orton, was called, and, with a "faint smile," admitted that defendant was the person who used to "keep company" with her under that name; the same in voice and figure, save only that he was now a little stouter. She had no doubt: if she had the slightest, defendant should have the benefit of it. She identified the similitude between the photographs purporting to come from Stephens, and to be likenesses of the wife and children of Orton, and photographs now presented to her, and which were likenesses of the defendant's wife and children. She also testified to the twitching of the eyebrows of her lover; but she could not be brought by any urgency to admit that her old admirer was a " raw-boned " man. She said his hair was light, and being shown a lock which was cut from the head of the defendant in Chili, she said it was like that of Orton.

Robert Chew, lighterman, from Wapping, knew Orton well, and identified him with defendant by face, figure, and voice. This witness had held his peace until defendant told the story of the seduction of Miss Doughty, and then witness volunteered his information in order " to vindicate a lady's honor." " Then you were indignant?" queried Dr. Kenealy. " I were," replied the honest lighterman, and everybody laughed loudly.

Mr. Hawkes, from Hobart Town, knew the butcher, Arthur Orton, there. To the question, whether defendant was the man he so knew, he replied: " He is not the man, but he is the individual," which somewhat enigmatical statement he explained by saying that defendant " is so stout; he is like a bullock to what he was when I knew him."

But it is impossible to continue to give even the briefest note of the testimony of each individual witness; such a course would produce a book which not the most patient reader could be trusted to peruse. What has been recited may serve as a specimen of the nature of the testimony and of the manner in which the witnesses were examined. For the future, a more condensed form of narrative must be adopted.

A great number of witnesses, chiefly from Wapping, testified to their belief that defendant was their old acquaintance, Arthur Orton; some of them being more and some less positive. It is needless to reproduce their evidence categorically; but it should be noted that whereas it had been made a point by the Claimant that Arthur Orton was pock-marked, and had his ears pierced for ear-rings, each and all of these Wapping witnesses said that he was not pock-marked, or at least not noticeably so, not so much so that they had ever observed the marks. Some, however, said that he had had the small-pox, but had escaped substantially unscarred by it. Also they all agreed that they had never seen him wear ear-rings, and had never seen holes for rings in his ears.

In the description of the person of Arthur Orton given by himself and filed at the shipping office, that individual was found to have stated that he had no bodily marks, meaning, of course, none that were noticeable; whence Mr. Hawkins inferred that Orton was not marked with the small-pox, and that he then had no scar on his face. Of the scar we shall hear more hereafter, when witnesses for the defence will be found testifying to its presence on Arthur Orton's countenance. One of these above-mentioned witnesses from Wapping was a "scripture reader." He had knelt down that morning and prayed God to give him grace to tell the truth: he knelt because he was afraid of slipping, as indeed he always was. He had made the trial a subject of daily prayer from its beginning. He owned that he "had a weakness for making all things in his life a matter of prayer for God's directing grace."

There was testimony also from several of these witnesses that Arthur Orton had been bitten in the arm by a Shetland pony, and that the wound had left a scar; that his brother dealt in Shetland ponies, and that Arthur took a span of them with him in the "Middleton" to Hobart Town. This coincided with the testimony of other Australian witnesses for the Crown, who had said that the defendant had had a pair of Shetland ponies with him at Hobart Town.

Proof was next offered sustaining the allegations of Mr. Hawkins in his opening speech concerning the names of the crew given by defendant, and the material difference between the size of the only English vessel which in 1854 was called the "Osprey," and the size ascribed by defendant to the vessel which rescued him. The "Bella" was of five hundred tons burden; defendant said he was saved by a vessel larger than the "Bella." But this English "Osprey" was only sixty-six tons. This "Osprey" was a sloop, and the vessel described by the defendant had three masts. The records showed no other English "Osprey" than the one thus described. But, as the Chief Justice remarked, this left the whole case as to an American "Osprey" untouched.

Arthur Hodson, late Colonial Secretary of Queensland, made the passage with defendant, who appeared ignorant and fond of low company. Defendant frequently told this witness that he was saved by the "Osprey." Witness admitted that at Panama the defendant spoke a *patois* which was intelligible to the people of that country.

Mrs. Fairhead, the landlady of the public-house at Wapping to which defendant went immediately after his return to England, testified to the interrogatories which he put to her. He asked after the members of the Orton family, calling some of them by name. He knew of his mother's death; but had not heard of his father's, and seemed quite affected by the news. He also inquired about some of the neighbors, and when told that one John Warwick, of whom he asked, was dead, he said, "Poor John." He showed witness a likeness of Arthur Orton's wife and children, which was identified by witness with likenesses of defendant's wife and children. She interrogated him quite earnestly as to whether he was not an Orton himself, being much struck by his resemblance to the family and telling him so; but he resolutely denied it.

On the morning of Tuesday, May 27, the Chief Justice said he had received a letter asking if it would be contempt of Court to send in subscriptions for the assistance of the defendant in meeting his expenses; in reply, he would say that mere subscriptions could not be contempt so long as no effort was made to prejudge the case. Thereupon the defendant arose and asked if it would be contempt of Court for him to appear at the theatres and read the answers returned from the Home Department to certain applications which he had made for financial aid from the Treasury in conducting his defence, — applications which his fast friend Mr. Whalley had ventured to bring up in Parliament. The Court said that such a proceeding would not be proper, and though urgently importuned by the defendant refused to say more. That which was " not proper " was not necessarily contempt. So the defendant after this appeared frequently at the theatres, especially at the east end of London, and at other halls and public places, and there read the reply of Mr. Bruce, the Home Secretary, to his requests for pecuniary assistance in securing and paying his witnesses and otherwise. Twice his proceedings of this kind were near bringing the trial to a very abrupt and unsatisfactory termination; for twice platforms gave way beneath him, and the bulky Claimant, with many of his adherents, was precipitated several feet among the *débris;* but he emerged unhurt, not being destined thus to escape from the prosecution of the Crown. Later in the season he began to show himself at pigeon-shootings, and to make addresses to the crowds who gathered at these merry-makings. But at the same time some of his supporters were also delivering very objectionable speeches, letters were vexing the patience of the Court, and ill-advised newspaper articles were bringing editors into trouble upon charges of contempt. The endurance of the judges was by degrees exhausted, and finally the Chief Justice said that a public agitation was being stirred up, which was very subversive of the ends of justice. The unusual liberality of the court in allowing the defendant his full and free personal liberty during the trial had been grossly and outrageously abused. The Court could no longer place confidence in the defendant, and now gave him fair warning that, if from this moment he should attend any other public gatherings, the liberty allowed him to go at large on bail would be withdrawn, and he would be committed to gaol. The Court was resolved to draw the line " tight and close," and to allow no other public appearance so long as the trial should last.

The sentiments of the mass of the people were often and strongly manifested in favor of the defendant. To their eyes the contest was that of vulgarity, insolence, and ignorance against wealth, culture, and aristocracy. Naturally, they took the side of the party whose traits bore the nearest similitude to their own. Every afternoon at half-past four o'clock, when the Court adjourned, the ample space of Palace Yard, outside Westminster Hall, was thronged with a dense, riotous rabble, who threw up their caps and cheered the defendant as he was driven away in his brougham. A large force of policemen was detailed to keep order; but even a body of one hundred and fifty of these guardians were unable to hold the cordon unbroken, and at times the tumultuous and offensive throng overcame all restraint, filled up the exit from the Hall, and hustled and crowded the dignified judges and barristers, the unfortunate jurors and witnesses, till extrication became a serious matter. Towards the close of the trial, Mr. Hawkins was one day set upon with the most violent animosity, and narrowly escaped with unbroken bones, or indeed even with his life.

Nor were these outrages of the mob the only annoyances to which the nerves of those concerned in this extraordinary trial were exposed. Anonymous and threatening letters were sent, apparently more especially to those who were supposed to have a leaning hostile to the defendant. Yet not a few also were written in the opposite interest. For example Mr. Gosford, while in the witness-box, received such a communication, beginning, "Reflect in time." Later, one of the jurors complained that he had been notified that his days were numbered; and that such notifications had been received in the interest both of the Crown and of the defendant; so that whichever way the case went he was to be immolated. Mr. Justice Mellor remarked that the juror did not stand alone in this danger; and the Chief Justice heroically hoped that every one connected with the case would fearlessly discharge his duty.

Some epistles, however, of a more amusing character were occasionally received. Thus one was sent to the Chief Justice, in which he was gravely urged to have the defendant mesmerized, and then questioned while in that condition! Having regard to the old adage, *in vino veritas*, it might have been as effectual, and doubtless would have been more agreeable to the propensities of the individual, to have had him reduced to an advanced stage of intoxication. The suggestion was not acted upon.

Early in June, Mr. Hawkins began to introduce a new series of witnesses, persons who had known Roger Tichborne, and who stated their belief that defendant was not he. Many persons who had known him at Stonyhurst were called. Some of these gentlemen, schoolmates of Roger, were subjected to a peculiar cross-examination by Dr. Kenealy. Thus one of them was asked to define a scalene triangle; to give the title of the second book of the Iliad; and to state the contents of the sixth book of the Æneid. The witness protested that he did not come into the box to stand an examination in Latin and Greek. Kenealy said he only wished to show that his client retained as much of the learning acquired by him at Stonyhurst as was retained by his fellow-pupils at that institution. But the Chief Justice said that "nothing approaching the questions he was asking" had been put to the defendant, and put a stop to such interrogatories.

With a view in some measure to discrediting the seduction story, the prosecution sought to show that Roger's training had been such as to leave him singularly pure-minded and unsophisticated in such matters. Accordingly the Rev. Christopher Fitzsimon, chaplain at Stonyhurst during Roger's term there, was summoned. As a specimen of the style of training which the youths received on this exemplary foundation, he referred to the Christmas plays in which the boys there were wont to act. In these, female characters were never allowed to appear: all such were changed into male characters, or else were ruthlessly eradicated altogether. Often enough, indeed, this singular process ruined the drama. How a love plot could be carried out the witness was unable to explain; he could not tell how Romeo and Juliet could be played without a Juliet. But he clung to his statement. Mr. Hawkins then came to his aid, and said that he himself had a number of the school playbills, from which it appeared that " Box and Cox " had been acted without a Mrs. Bouncer; " Hamlet " without an Ophelia; " Macbeth " without a Lady Macbeth; and the " Merchant of Venice " without a Portia.

Some military witnesses were called, who knew Roger, and said defendant was not he. Most of the officers of Roger's old regiment appeared on behalf of the Crown. Lord St. Lawrance, in conversing with defendant, had recalled to his memory a walk from Dublin to Howth, describing the distance as two miles. Defendant readily said he remembered the circumstance, whereas, said his Lordship, the walk in fact never took place, and the estimate of distance was ridiculously wrong. Dr.

Kenealy said this was "a trap." "You may call it a trap," said the Chief Justice, "but when you suspect a man of falsehood you have a right to test him."

Kenealy. It is wrong at any time to suggest a lie.

Chief Justice. This is an insulting and offensive observation which the witness does not deserve.

Mr. H. Danby Seymour, an old acquaintance of Roger, said that in his first interview with defendant, he said, "If you are Roger Tichborne you will know this gentleman." "My Uncle Nangle, I believe," replied defendant. Whereas the "gentleman" was an ex-servant of Sir James Tichborne, Roger's father, and was "about half the age" of Mr. Nangle, who had passed his allotted period of three-score years and ten.

Viscount de Brimont said there was no resemblance between Roger and defendant. The Dowager Lady Tichborne had said to him in Paris that "if he liked to please her," he would see the Claimant and "admit him to be her son." The viscount declined, and remonstrated with her. She said, "Oh, very well; we can get some one else who will."

R. B. Mansfield, barrister, connected with the Tichbornes by marriage, used to know Roger. He said, "There is only one person in the world more confident than I am that this man is not Roger Tichborne, and there he is;" and he pointed at defendant.

Mrs. Greenwood said she had been disappointed

to find it so, but she must say defendant was not Roger Tichborne.

Mr. Gosford, friend, confidant, executor, trustee, and the custodian of the sealed packet, was called. He gave a long account of the condition of the family property and the legal arrangements concerning the estates. It would require too much space to repeat and explain these complicated matters, and it must suffice to say that the facts thus narrated gave rise to strong inferences that defendant was not Sir Roger, because of the ignorance he had displayed of some important facts which Roger must have known, and in truth did know, before his departure for South America, as was shown by the provisions of his will.

Respecting the packet, Mr. Gosford said: I recollect having a long conversation with him [Roger] in my room at Tichborne, — I think on the 1st of January, 1852, — upon the subject of his attachment for his cousin. He knew there would be no recognition of it by Lady Doughty, Sir Edward, and his father, and he determined to give expression to his feelings in his own way. He appeared very low and dispirited. He jumped up, and saying, "I'll tell you what I'll do," he went to the desk, wrote on a piece of paper, showed it to me, and said, "If I marry my cousin, that's what I'll do." Every syllable of it has been in my memory ever since. I told him that such vows should not be lightly made, and that he had better think it over. He however said that was his intention, folded over the paper, put it in an envelope, and sealed it with wax, using his own seal. He then wrote on the outside: " Memorandum. Private and confidential," handed it to me, and asked me to keep it. I put it in my desk, thinking no harm would come of it, and kept it for years, but ultimately destroyed it. Roger never gave me any other document. The writing was this: " If I marry my cousin within two [or three] years "— I can't recollect which — " I promise to build a church at Tichborne to the Blessed Virgin." Lower down he wrote: " I also intend to build a house at Tichborne." He signed it Roger Charles Tichborne, Tichborne Park.

Witness also gave the contents of Roger's will, which he made before sailing for South America, and of which this defendant had no recollection.

Dr. Kenealy tried to elicit from this witness that certain references, in a letter from Bishop Brown to Lady Doughty, referred to an illicit relationship existing between Roger and a woman. But Mr. Gosford indignantly repudiated the insinuation; and said the passage related to Roger's propensity for drinking.

In the cross-examination it appeared that this witness had received a check for eight pounds from a member of the Tichborne family. Kenealy, as though he had struck an important trail, began to inquire into this transaction. Mr. Gosford, protesting against being obliged to give the names of other persons in his reply, simply stated that he had relieved the distress of an unfortunate " person of the ne'er-do-weel order," and that a wealthy relative had subsequently thought proper to refund him the money. This, with more of the like kind from Dr. Kenealy, finally provoked the Chief Justice and Justice Mellor to rebuke the counsel for "raking up people's affairs in connection with a check, which evidently had nothing to do with the case;" and a juror chimed in with a request that the time of the jury might be considered. Mr. Gosford, however, though thus unkindly tormented, succeeded in accomplishing a feat quite unique in the course of this trial: he actually extorted from Dr. Kenealy an apology for an insolent comment uttered by that gentleman.

John Etheridge, an old man, a resident in the neighborhood of Tichborne, who remembered Roger well, met defendant near the park in 1866. Defendant referred to the rumors of Roger's return, and then said, "Do you think I am he?" Witness replied, with more of vigor than of compliment in his language, "No, I'm damned if you are. If you are, you are turned from a race-horse to a wagon-horse." Yet the defendant had had the audacity to swear that Etheridge had recognized him.

On Tuesday, June 24, Lady Radcliffe, that was Miss Kate Doughty, was put upon the stand. She gave a long and circumstantial account of the love affair between her cousin Roger and herself, and of the opposition it encountered from their parents. Her answers were frank, natural, and went direct to the point. So far as can be judged from the printed report of her evidence, she must have appeared very well indeed.

The Chief Justice then interposed to read a letter, produced at the last trial, written by Roger to "My dearest Kate," and which gave an affecting account of his feelings at their farewell interview. Other writings of Roger were also read, in which he avowed an ardent attachment for his "own dearest Kate," and promised to devote the three years which he proposed to spend in foreign parts to trying to become all she wished. She was, he said, the first person he had ever loved in the world.

Lady Radcliffe said that, on June 22, 1852, at one o'clock in the afternoon, Roger gave her a letter, saying, "This is a promise I have made; and I have given a similar one to Gosford." They read it over together. Two hours later, at three o'clock that afternoon, Roger left Tichborne, and she had never seen him since. The contents of the paper have already been set forth in Mr. Hawkins's opening: it was a promise to build a chapel or church if he should marry his cousin.

Mr. Hawkins. Was there any familiarity between you and Roger other than that you have told us of to-day?

Lady Radcliffe (emphatically). No, never — never!

Mr. Hawkins. Is the defendant's statement at the last trial, that Roger seduced his cousin, perfectly false?

Lady Radcliffe. Utterly false — utterly false! Roger would never have thought of such a thing.

The Claimant's narration of Roger's meeting with his cousin alone one day in Tichborne village, in November, 1852, dismounting from his horse and talking with her "about her condition," was repeated, and the witness was asked, "Is there one syllable of truth in these details?"

Lady Radcliffe (in firm audible tones). Certainly not! not one single word! And God knows I am speaking the truth.

Dr. Kenealy asked, on cross-examination, whether the witness had not, on more than one occasion, been seen alone in her cousin's company, at various spots which he named, near the Park. She replied that she had never walked alone with Roger, except in her father's grounds: she "should never have dreamed of doing such a thing!" She was next asked if Dr. Lipscombe did not prescribe for her between August 19 and September 6, 1853. She replied that he did, and that she took the medicine.

Mr. Hawkins resumed the direct examination:—

It is not suggested that any act of impropriety ever took place between you and Roger. But I ask you, as a matter of fact, was there ever any such act?

Lady Radcliffe. Never! never! never! in the whole course of my life, I solemnly protest.

Mr. Hawkins. Or had you, before you were cross-examined this morning, ever the least suggestion that any questions would be put to you with reference to Dr. Lipscombe's treatment?

Lady Radcliffe. Never. Dr. Lipscombe was the family doctor, and he attended me with the full knowledge of my mother.

Sir Percival Radcliffe, Mrs. Nangle and her daughter (Roger's aunt and cousin), and a large number of other witnesses, mostly persons of rank and distinction, were now examined. They had all known Roger well, and all testified that defendant was not he. Some of them bore witness to the existence of the tattoo marks on Roger's arm.

Defendant had testified that while quartered with his regiment at Canterbury, he had paid his attentions to a Miss Mary Hales, resident there. Miss Hales was called and said that, so far from having received the addresses of Roger Tichborne, she did not even know him.

A gamekeeper on the Tichborne estates, having testified that defendant was not Roger Tichborne, was asked by Dr. Kenealy whether he was to be paid any thing for his evidence. He replied that he was not. The doctor then read a letter in which this witness stated that the solicitor for the family " will pay me what is due." The witness said this referred to some arrears of wages. The Chief Justice strongly denounced such "unwarrantable imputations" from the counsel. Kenealy retorted that he should discharge his duty fearlessly towards his client, and would not be put down by his Lordship. Cockburn said he would not tolerate such conduct as that of which Kenealy was guilty, and finally peremptorily ordered the doctor to proceed with his examination.

Mr. Hawkins then called the brother-in-law of Orton, the physician of the Orton family, and numerous other acquaintances of Arthur, who all testified that in their several opinions the defendant was Arthur Orton. With this, the counsel for the prosecution said that they rested their case.

The case for the prosecution being closed, Dr. Kenealy, on the twenty-second day of July, arose to open the case for the defendant. He obtained leave to remove his wig on account of the excessive heat; and forthwith plunged into an harangue which was in many respects so extraordinary as to show that this precaution for keeping his head cool had been neither superfluous nor altogether effectual. As he appears in this cause, he is indeed a most singular person. He will remind people upon this side of the water in many ways of the notorious John Graham, of the New York bar; though the doctor is a man of much greater intellectual calibre, more extensive professional knowledge and much more manliness than can be attributed to the American advocate. Dr. Kenealy possesses an unrivalled audacity and almost an unrivalled insolence in his manners towards the bench. The acerbity of the temper of the Lord Chief Justice Cockburn is well known on both sides of the Atlantic. But it was reserved for Dr. Kenealy in this trial to bring it forth in its most forcible exhibitions. Nothing so spirited was elicited from his Lordship, even when he sat as an arbitrator at Geneva, as were some of his sallies in this case. Though it must be admitted that he was generally in the right, yet he maintained the right with an energy little short of judicial ferocity. But he met a perfectly fearless opponent. Many were the battles-royal between these two redoubted champions; nor could the judge ever succeed in securing the best of the conflicts, save by falling back upon his offi-

Dr. E. V. KENEALY, Q.C.
(Leading Counsel for the Defence.)

cial prerogatives. When he ordered, and intimated that in case of disobedience the learned counsel might find himself incontinently transferred from the court-room to be shut up in a cell, there was nothing left to Kenealy except submission: valor was useless, and silence was a necessity. The doctor's position was rendered the more embarrassing because he was enveloped in an unmistakably hostile atmosphere; in nearly every instance the Chief Justice was backed by his comrades, Justices Lush and Mellor, and sometimes even the barristers present seem to have shown by their manner or other indubitable signs that they were of the same mind. But the hostility was well merited. Seldom can the method of conducting a cause have been more pertinaciously offensive or more intentionally subversive of the real ends of justice, even in the city of New York, than was the course deliberately and systematically pursued by Kenealy.

There was much elaboration and no small display of real ability in the way in which he "got up" his side of the case. Yet it was not the professional auditory alone that he arrayed against himself by his want of tact in some particulars. He browbeat witnesses, and threw out so lavishly his insinuations of falsehood, fraud and corruption, that the jurors ere long became as much disgusted as the bench and the bar. Moreover, he was too diffusive; he dwelt upon his points too long; he wandered too much into collateral and illustrative matter, and wearied his hearers, who begrudged the long time which this trial obliged them to take from the prosecution of their regular avocations and business. Often they spurred him on, and expressed their impatience; he always promised that he would take the hint, and would hasten as much as possible; but he never seemed to his auditors really to do so.

It is needless to delay the narrative here for the purpose of giving any thorough abstract of his opening address, which consumed twenty-one days in the delivery. To set forth its contents, even by the briefest intimations, would only involve much tiresome repetition, without compensating information. The story of the cause has been already sufficiently developed to render the testimony of his witnesses intelligible; and his closing speech, which was his great effort and was indeed a most interesting composition, will deserve all the space which we can allot to his oratory. The basis upon which he founded his defence, however, deserves to be stated. It shows the daring and originality of the man. It may be regarded as the only course which was open to him; nevertheless, few men would have entered upon it with such bold, uncompromising, confident vigor as he displayed. The ignorance, the degraded and vicious career, and the singular and undeniable lapses of memory, or, to speak plainly, the proven falsehoods on the part of his client, could not be gainsaid or disproved; they were facts inexpugnable by evidence or denial, and as facts they must be met and accounted for in some manner. He boldly resolved to sacrifice the intellect and morals, the native disposition, and the acquired habits of Roger Tichborne, and of his own client, one or both, to this emergency. Nor did he make any imperfect work in this respect. Far from it; he mercilessly slaughtered the good name and reputation which thus stood in his way. He said that Roger was by nature low, depraved, and vicious. At the time of his going on board the "Bella," he "had fallen far beneath every attribute of honor and decency and independence;" he said to himself, "I am an outcast and a vagabond, and I will lead the life of an outcast and a vagabond;" and what he thought himself to be, that in very truth he was. "He fled from that society of which he felt, and rightly felt, that he was unworthy, and to which he knew himself to be a disgrace." He landed in Australia "like an Arab on the face of the earth, — like a second Cain." Thus depicting the unfortunate man whom he claimed for his client in the most revolting colors, the doctor said that it was a gross and absurd humbug for the Crown to instil an opposite theory, and to seek to represent Roger as having been a model of chastity and purity, a lad who could never conceivably have harbored an impure thought towards his cousin, and whose name should be handed down to future ages "enshrined in crystal." The real Roger was a student of obscene French literature, and even had the indecency to seek to make his aunt Lady Doughty the companion of his studies. It was this awful self-consciousness, the sense of his own extreme and hopeless degradation, that made Roger determine not to make known his escape from death, and not to return to take his place and assert his heirship. His younger brother, Alfred, he thought, would more worthily fill the position and discharge its duties. It was only because Alfred had died untimely that he altered his resolution, and came home to claim and take his own.

The most dark and abominable practices were hinted at by the learned doctor, in mysterious language, as having been in vogue to corrupt the morals and destroy the minds of the youths at Stonyhurst; and though the Chief Justice interrupted him to say that no manner of foundation had been laid for such "fearful and appalling accusations," he yet insisted upon reiterating them.

As for his client's narrative, he acknowledged that it was in many parts "absurd" and "ridiculous;" though the word false he carefully refrained from uttering. Never quite of average ability, said the doctor, the accidents which he has suffered cannot fail to have affected his head. Having due regard to his physical condition, and to what he has passed through, " I do not think he should be bound down to every absurd thing he has said or written. *He must be tried on great and broad principles.*" His mind has been " sapped by dissipation and by numerous falls and tumbles;" and though it may be going too far to say that he is under delusions, yet his statements are not to be relied upon. As instances of these "absurdities" on the part of the defendant, Dr. Kenealy mentioned the famous account of the shipwreck, which, he said, was too "ridiculous" ever to have been given by a sailor, as Arthur Orton was. Being pressed, however, by Chief Justice Cockburn and Mr. Justice Lush to say whether the defendant's account of the shipwreck was to be abandoned as incorrect, the learned counsel would only repeat that it was absurd and ridiculous, and that his client was not responsible for his statements.

The same explanation was given of the defendant's averments made in Australia, that he was never at school at Stonyhurst, and was never an officer in the army, but that he had been a private in the Sixty-sixth Blues. All this showed a temporary aberration of common sense, and "folly could no farther go." A juryman hereupon asked: "Are you trying to induce us to find a verdict which would have the effect of sending the defendant to Broadmoor?" [a lunatic asylum], to which the doctor replied: "No, sir; but, as I said to Mr. Justice Lush when he asked whether I called these things 'delusions,' I say they are *absurdities*."

The will made by his client at Wagga-Wagga was admitted by the doctor to contain much that was unfounded in fact, and much " pure and perfect nonsense ; " but he explained that it was only designed to be used as a pretext for borrowing money, and such ruses were of common occurrence among the young members of the higher classes in their transactions with money-lenders. The Chief Justice interfered in behalf of the youthful aristocracy of England, protesting against so sweeping an imputation against them, which amounted substantially to charging them with swindling or obtaining money under false pretences. The introduction into the will of the name of John Jarvis, of Bridport, a friend of the Ortons, arose from the fact that the defendant had associated much with Arthur Orton, and that, having the weaker mind of the two, and hearing Orton talk much of his past life and acquaintances, defendant got his own mind gradually but thoroughly saturated with these matters and things, and poured them out in his characteristic reckless way when dictating his will. Altogether, the will belonged to the class of "absurdities" to which no attention should be paid. The real issue was not whether the defendant in that will uttered a parcel of ridiculous stories and fables, but whether or not he was Roger Tichborne.

The doctor enumerated various other acts of his client "bordering upon insanity," such as his visit to Wapping immediately after his arrival, made for the purpose of inquiring about the Ortons, and his sending to Orton's sister the photographs of his own wife and children as the likenesses of the wife and children of Arthur. This Wapping exploit the counsel afterwards spoke of as "maniacal;" and it certainly deserved the epithet. The defendant was a man of a very "impressionable mind," and it was in fact the "powerful influence of Arthur Orton over his mind which so imbued him with every thing connected with that person that he was led to do all these silly things, such as no clever impostor would ever have dreamed of." Another statement of his client's, such as could have been expected to fall from "no sane man," was, that he had "danced the *can-can* in 1847 before a lot of ladies and gentlemen in the library at Burton Constable." The Chief Justice asked if he meant that this assertion of his client's was to be taken as *untrue;* but again he evaded the unwelcome phrase and said only that such things were "too absurd to require to be seriously considered." False statements made by the defendant, if arising from no other motive than to avoid the difficulties of examination, were alleged by the learned counsel not to constitute perjuries punishable by law. But the Court interposed and, "as the Court of Queen's Bench, sitting here *in banco,*" ruled that an answer on oath made from any indirect motive, to avoid giving a direct answer, if known to the answerer to be false, is undoubtedly perjury.

Nor was it contusions, drunkenness, debauchery, and general vileness of habits, which alone in the opinion of his counsel had corroded the morals and enfeebled the intellect of the defendant. His obesity, said Dr. Kenealy, with consummate gravity, was strongly against him. "Dulness and fatness always go together." This announcement, so solemnly put forth, was encountered with equal solemnity and some degree of feeling. The Chief Justice, though certainly his own "withers were unwrung," for he is a spare man, said the proposition was "new and startling," that it was a mere popular prejudice that as a man waxes in flesh he wanes in intelligence. Dr. Kenealy appealed to the records of obesity as sustaining his assertion.

The foreman of the jury suggested that there were two or three fat men in the panel; but the doctor politely averred his inability to see them. The judges too, he said, were all thin. The Chief Justice said it was attributable to their being worked so hard, and Mr. Justice Lush said this trial was likely to make them thin enough. " You will grow the more intellectual," replied Kenealy. But the weighty discussion was cut short by the entrance of a barrister of really vast dimensions, who appeared painfully forcing his way among the crowd of his learned brethren; every one laughed at him loud and long, and not until all had been satiated with merriment did Dr. Kenealy continue his address.

The marriage in Australia under the assumed name of Castro was additional proof that the defendant was Tichborne rather than Orton. For Orton had no reason to take an *alias*; but Tichborne had. This heir to a titled name and to great estates " had entered into a menial employment, and now had before him the vista of a free independent untrammelled existence, like a wild animal in sylvan shades;" of course he wished to conceal his true name. This fluent rhetoric was unkindly interrupted by the Chief Justice, who continued to torment the poor doctor more mercilessly than the gadfly pursued Ino, and who now recalled to his memory that his own client had himself said that Orton had in fact changed his name; and Mr. Hawkins added that the cause assigned for the taking an *alias* was that Orton had done something not in conformity with the law. Again the doctor flung down the threadbare sacrifice of the defendant's veracity and acknowledged that he should be sorry indeed to have all that his client had said taken "for gospel."

Speaking of the famous cross-examination of the Claimant conducted by Sir John Duke Coleridge in the ejectment cause, Dr. Kenealy said that his client was at that time suffering from mental alienation which had been caused by his deep drinking. But the Chief Justice said that he had been struck over and over again by the intellectual capacity exhibited by the defendant while under cross-examination; and that in his opinion the defendant had then beaten Sir John Coleridge. Dr. Kenealy said that Sir John had indeed said so, but that that eminent advocate had surrendered his laurels too readily. Though if the learned gentleman was just now, when it suited his purpose, inclined to be thus civil and complimentary to Sir John Coleridge he was by no means always in the same amiable humor towards others. The language of compliment fell seldom from his lips. One day he spoke of Chatillon as a "valet."

Chief Justice. Sir, that is not a proper observation.

Kenealy. It is a proper observation. I have a duty to perform.

Justice Mellor. Your duty is to be performed undoubtedly; but still under the obligations which a gentleman knows how to observe.

Kenealy. My Lord, I understand my duty, and will not be taught it by your Lordship.

Chief Justice. And I will not allow you to address language like that to a member of the bench.

At another time Dr. Kenealy said of the tattoo marks that they had not been known or thought of at first; that evidently Sir John Coleridge had not been instructed about them when he cross-examined the defendant.

Mr. Hawkins (interrupting). Dr. Lipscombe, one of the plaintiff's witnesses at the last trial, said that he once saw tattoo marks on the plaintiff's arm, and that [the then] plaintiff had told him they were made by a school-fellow. It is *false* to say that Sir John Coleridge was not instructed as to the tattoo marks, for I know that he was.

Dr. Kenealy bade the jury pay no attention to that disgraceful statement.

Chief Justice (to Dr. Kenealy). I cannot allow such language.

Kenealy. Mr. Hawkins had no right to make such a statement to the jury. He ought to withdraw the expression.

Chief Justice. You have yourself used quite as strong language. Let the matter drop.

Kenealy. If *you* look with indulgence on language of that kind, *I* cannot do so — I reiterate.

It is noteworthy that in neither of these fracas, nor indeed in the majority of the many similar ones which were of frequent occurrence, was there any apology or any kind of submission or acknowledgment of error on the part of Dr. Kenealy towards the judges. The battles were usually drawn. The doctor was as stubborn as the Chief Justice, more audacious and not less insolent. Moreover, he handled the facts and the evidence in the case as if they had been potter's clay to be moulded to his fancy.

This last passing of the "lie indirect" rankled in the memory of the parties longer than such encounters are wont to linger in the professional recollection. Several days afterward, when Dr. Kenealy had begun to examine his witnesses, he became involved in one of his numerous altercations with Mr. Hawkins. Both gentlemen waxed somewhat warm. The Chief Justice interposed, and, of course, the lash of his rebuke fell upon the devoted shoulders of the defendant's counsel, who surely had need to be thick-skinned as well as learned in the law.

Chief Justice (to Kenealy). Don't show such temper! I don't know what has happened to you this morning. You seem desirous of offending somebody.

Kenealy. I hope I have not offended your Lordship.

Chief Justice. But there is a tone of asperity in your manner.

Kenealy. When Mr. Hawkins called me a liar in open Court, *he* was not reproved.

Hawkins. I never called you a liar.

Kenealy. You said I stated what was false; and there was no interference on the part of the Court.

Chief Justice. Because we thought it was six of one and half a dozen of the other.

At one time the Chief Justice said that Dr. Kenealy had treated him during the trial with marked disrespect, and that gentleman had the hardihood to reply that he (Kenealy) had shown "*great forbearance*" *towards his Lordship!*

So different is an English court-room in fact from what we in this country are wont, fondly and admiringly, to picture it to ourselves. But such scenes are better than those exhibited in New York, in so far as they are, at least, fair and honest fights.

Speaking to the story of the seduction of Miss Kate Doughty, the learned counsel complained of its introduction as one of the three main issues in the case, inasmuch as it tended to cause the decision to be influenced by feeling, passion, and prejudice, rather than by calm and sober reasoning and judgment. But the Court gave it as their unanimous opinion that the seduction and the sealed packet constituted a cardinal point, and that if it had not been included in the indictment the Crown would have been open to serious and just complaint. Dr. Kenealy spoke of it as a most lamentable affair, of which he thought with sorrow by night and by day. The story had been "forced" from his reluctant client in the witness-box by Sir John Coleridge. But since the issue was made by the prosecuting counsel, Dr. Kenealy would meet it, and asserted his intention of maintaining its truth.

During this long speech of the worthy and facile doctor, his auditors were not always able to control their impatience. The jury were often provoked into expostulation at his usurpation of their time, and even the better-trained members of the bench could not always restrain the expression of their similar feelings. Mr. Justice Mellor one day told the counsel that "Life was not long enough for such a trial," and on another occasion, in picturesque metaphor, he begged the gentleman to "use a shovel instead of a teaspoon." The doctor, undoubtedly, needed a good deal of time for the double task of explaining how he designed to meet the elaborate case made out by his opponents, and of setting forth his own even more lengthy narrative; but he could have done this more briefly had he taken the pains to compress, and it was obviously bad policy to harass the tempers of those who had the fate of his cause at their disposal.

When, at length, Dr. Kenealy sat down at the close of his address, and it was found that he had really finished it and that the strong hours had at last conquered even him, he was greeted with rounds of applause; whether in recognition of the excellence of his achievement or in gratitude that he had brought it to an end, does not fully appear.

Collateral to the trial, yet perhaps not an uninteresting illustration of the enterprising spirit of the age, is an advertisement which just at this time found its way into the "London Times" (we may be excused for inserting it), as follows:—

"The Claimant's house, his butcher's shop, now standing in Wagga-Wagga, New South Wales, for sale. A splendid investment for speculators. The house is made of logs, has a brick chimney and a bark roof. On the door still remain pencilled accounts of sales of meat, written by the Claimant himself. The whole structure can be easily taken down; the door, chimneys, and sheets of bark (roof) packed in cases, and by the aid of plans and photographs erected anywhere. The logs will be numbered and also the sheets of bark, and every thing done to render its re-erection an easy matter. This remarkable specimen of an Australian bush house, rendered particularly interesting through the most remarkable trial of modern times, will be sent some four hundred miles by bullock wagons, and put on board a ship bound direct to London, for the sum of £2,400. Affidavits will also accompany it to prove its authenticity. The time occupied by transit will occupy nearly five months. When the above-named sum is paid to the London branch of the Union Bank of Australia, in my name, immediate steps will be taken to forward the house, and instructions will be sent by the bank to the Melbourne branch.— G. B. ALLEN, *Melbourne, Victoria.*"

Dr. Kenealy began his evidence for the defence by marshalling a perfect host of witnesses from Wapping, who overflowed the court-room and Westminster Hall, that most spacious of anterooms, in abundance like the locusts of Egypt. They were the old acquaintances of Arthur Orton, and constituted a horde much less distinguished, if more numerous, than the gentlemen and ladies who had appeared as the friends of the lost heir of Tichborne Park. Taken in the mass, their testimony must be acknowledged to present a somewhat motley aspect; yet, though many weak spots were developed in it, altogether it was by no means devoid of force and value. By sheer virtue of its great quantity, it commanded attention and respect, if it fell short of bringing absolute conviction to the minds of the hearers. To present this evidence in detail, would be to set before the reader a task almost as fatiguing to his patience as Homer's "Catalogue of the Ships." It must be treated generally.

The witnesses were all introduced for the purpose of swearing that the defendant was not, in their opinion, the Arthur Orton whom, in days long past, they had seen and known, more or less intimately, at Wapping. This assertion they all gallantly made, pouring in interminable succession for many days through the witness-box. They were, of course, for the most part, ignorant persons, whose beliefs and judgments, individually considered, were not very impressive or convincing. Beyond this, too, they were far from agreeing with each other in all particulars, even in all essential particulars. Yet a few facts were established by them with some approach towards unanimity. Thus those who could say any thing accurately of the hands and feet of Arthur Orton united in asserting that they were very large and coarse. The hands and feet of the defendant, as Dr. Kenealy contended, were unusually small for a man of his size. The witness of especial importance to this point was a shoemaker. He said he had made boots for Arthur and for his elder brother George, from the time that Arthur was five to when he was fourteen years of age. Arthur had exceedingly large feet; and indeed the reason why this witness was obliged to make boots for him was because he had none ready-made which were large enough to fit him. By good fortune he still had by him the identical last which he had used, and upon the toe of which he had nailed pieces of leather, not to increase the length, but to fill out and give more room over the top. The statements of this witness appeared strong, not to say robust, on behalf of the defendant; but they were somewhat toned down by a cross-examination. He was then obliged to admit that the difference in size between the defendant's boot and the boot made for Arthur was less than an inch; indeed this difference was finally reduced to half an inch: and two witnesses who had made boots for the defendant said his foot was a good middle-sized foot, but unusually large in the heel measure. The length was $11\frac{1}{4}$ to $11\frac{3}{4}$ inches. Witness further admitted that defendant's boot was thin, and nicely made, whereas the boot of the butcher-boy was coarse and heavy, and was necessarily made much too large for the foot. He said he made boots for Arthur and for George; that George was the oldest, and Arthur was the next to him; whereas the baptismal registers, being put in evidence, showed that George was eleven years older than Arthur, and that there were seven children intervening between them. Later in the day he brought the last into Court. It was handed up to the Chief Justice, who remarked on the freshness of the leathern scraps, and the brightness of the brass nails. He reminded the witness that, by his story, these should be twenty-five or thirty years old. But the shoemaker stuck to his last, and stoutly averred that the leather would still look fresh, and, provided it were not greasy, that the nails also would be bright, even after the lapse of that period. Afterward in argument Mr. Hawkins said it was proved that some of this leather was fresh.

To one witness the defendant owed money. Another witness was reminded by the Chief Justice of a certain lawsuit which had occurred during the preceding summer, and in which this witness as plaintiff had presented an uncommonly poor appearance, and been nonsuited, under circumstances equally ignominious and discreditable. Another witness stated that he had cauterized a wound in Arthur Orton's arm, caused by the bite of a pony; and that he performed the operation so clumsily that it left an indelible scar about the size of a shilling. No scar which could fit this description was found upon the defendant. The wife and family of this witness were at present residents in the workhouse; not because he had abandoned them, as he persisted; for he had been all the while living in the very next street; but because it was a sort of whim or fancy with his wife. Witness supposed that she was not satisfied with his house, and so left it for a larger one. Another witness said he had bathed with Arthur, and had seen no brown mark on his body; but witness's recollection was, that Arthur was then a mere lad, whereas it was shown that he must have been twenty-three years old.

The witnesses for the Crown had sworn that Arthur Orton did not wear ear-rings; and the medical testimony was to the effect that the defendant's ears had never been pierced. On the other hand, a large proportion of the witnesses for the defence were quite positive in asserting that Arthur Orton did wear wire ear-rings; though there were some few of a contrary opinion. But the testimony of many of these witnesses was weakened by showing that not improbably they had confused their recollections of Arthur Orton with their recollections of his brother Edmund. Edmund, it was clearly proved, had worn such ear-rings as these witnesses described. In support of this theory of a confusion, it was elicited from several witnesses that there was "a strong family likeness" among the brothers. Numerous different opinions were expressed as to their respective ages, showing the indistinctness and uncertainty of the reminiscences; and that what was thought honestly enough to be the recollection of one of the family might in fact be the recollection of another. Some said that Arthur was quite visibly pock-marked, which others denied. Some said that he had a scar on his face, and some said that he had not. One witness, striking out an original theory of his own, said that the defendant was not Arthur Orton because he was "not big enough." Another had a story that he once came into George Orton's butcher's shop at Wapping, and fell down suddenly ill with the cholera; that Arthur was present, holding a knife in his hand, and was so startled that he let it slip, and it cut him across the palm of his hand. At least Arthur afterward showed to this witness a scar across his palm, and accounted for it in this manner. Defendant had no such scar.

While all these witnesses, amid so numerous discrepancies and contradictions in the minutiæ of their recollections, and in the reasons for their opinions, still united in expressing the same pivotal belief that the defendant was not Arthur Orton, many were yet induced to say that the defendant did resemble George Orton, the father. Some said that such a resemblance existed about the upper part of the face; some that they traced a likeness in the lower part, about the neck. One, though asserting that he was almost positive that the defendant was not Arthur, nevertheless acknowledged that he had "the eyebrows of the old gentleman." One or two others went so far even as to acknowledge that there was a resemblance between Arthur Orton himself and the defendant in some features. It was suggested by Mr. Hawkins that these witnesses might have been confused and deceived by having their old acquaintance, whom they had been wont to see in his butcher's frock, suddenly presented to them, after so long an interval, clad in fine clothes, and in the company of gentlemen. Following up this idea, some of them were brought to admit, in cross-examination, that at first they "fancied it was Orton," or that they were not at once satisfied that it was not he. The memory of one was tested by showing him a photograph of

Arthur, taken in the Wapping days, which he failed to recognize.

A "pharmaceutical and analytical chemist," whom untoward fate obliged to live in the obscurity of a garret at St. George's-in-the-East, said he dressed a cut on Arthur Orton's cheek, caused by a fall from a pony; that this defendant did not resemble Arthur in the least; that Arthur was "a big, burly man," whereas defendant was "a stout gentleman." The difference was marked and substantial in the opinion of the chemist.

Referring to all this class of testimony in his closing argument, Mr. Hawkins said that between them the witnesses had managed to make a perfect Arthur Orton out of the features of the defendant; one acknowledging a likeness between the two in one feature, another tracing a similitude in another feature, and so on through the entire physiognomy and even figure. Nor, as he well said, could such attempts at accurate reminiscence and description be safely trusted, even if made shortly after seeing a familiar face, as any one might learn by trying the experiment.

Some Tichborne witnesses, called for the defendant, had seen Roger and his cousin, Miss Kate Doughty, walking, unattended, in each other's company about the neighborhood of the place. A laborer at the Park had seen them thus in the "by-walks" there; and, on the day of Roger's departure, he saw them near the park wall, standing alone together "a-kissin' and cryin' and rubbin' one another's eyes with a white hankychuff."

Another had seen them in the appropriate propinquity of the "Lovers' Seat," and others had seen them at a spot romantically called the "Grotto." A photograph of this grotto was put in evidence, which gave the idea of a secluded spot. But the judges said they had seen it, and it lay exposed to full view, enclosed between a public footway and a towing-path. Kenealy said the sun could not lie. But the judges said that the likeness did no credit to the photographer's skill, and gave an entirely erroneous impression of the spot. One witness, at least, was sure she had seen Roger at the Park only a week or fortnight before he went away to South America; thus contradicting Lady Doughty's dying deposition and the evidence of Lady Radcliffe, of Mrs. Nangle and of Miss Nangle. But this testimony was badly mangled, in good time, by cross-examination and evidence in rebuttal; by which it was made to appear that some of the occasions referred to must be set back in the years of early boyhood and girlhood, and that others were either wholly imaginary or else very inaccurately remembered; for, at the times very positively named for them, Roger was elsewhere.

Miss Eliza Froude remembered Roger Tichborne with especial clearness, from the fact of his having offered to wash two favorite cats which she "idolized." She should know him among a thousand, and was sure defendant was he. But she seems to have been an eccentric old lady, for she obstinately refused to look at a photograph of the veritable Roger, saying that she had never been willing to accept a photograph in her life save one of a pet dog! Her peculiar aversion was respected, and the photograph was withdrawn from before her unwilling eyes.

Some Australian witnesses gave evidence, which if believed must have proved a part at least of the defendant's case: they had seen and known in Australia a man named Orton, and another man named Tom Castro. Castro and Orton were different individuals: there could be no doubt about that, for they had been seen together frequently, so that it was impossible to account for and explain away this evidence by saying that one and the same man had gone by the different names at different places or times. Castro and Orton had associated together; they had kept low company and been bushrangers — which is Australian for highwaymen — together. This defendant was certainly not Orton, and as certainly was believed by these persons to be Castro. Orton, as they remembered him, had broad feet, was pock-marked, and had a scar on the cheek. One of these witnesses described himself as "a highly respectable sly grogsman and butcher," who supplied meat and drink to the bushrangers, but himself never got mixed up in any dishonest scrapes. Mr. Hawkins suggested that he did not undertake to prove that no person save this defendant had ever borne the name of Orton in Australia, nor could the jury safely make such an assumption.

Several persons from Tichborne testified that the defendant was, in their opinion, the genuine

Roger. A charwoman at the Park "proved him in her own mind to be Sir Roger," because Sir Roger had a gruff voice and spoke like a Hampshire man. A directly opposite cause persuaded the wife of the farm bailiff of the same identity: she knew the defendant was Sir Roger because he had the "same quiet soft voice," which had been an attribute of the young heir.

Several of the Tichborne witnesses swore that Roger was not tattooed upon the arm. One had seen his arms bared when he was helping to make a cairn, and saw no tattoo marks upon him; another had seen him with his shirt-sleeves turned up, grubbing up an oak stump. Another had seen him with his arms bare while shooting. A barmaid had seen him washing his hands, with his shirt-sleeves rolled up, after he had been thrown from a dog-cart. All these and many more had never seen any marks on either arm. Some of the servants and soldiers in Roger's old regiment told also when and how they had sometimes happened to see his arms bare, and said they had noticed no tattooing. One had fenced with him, another had sparred with him, and so on through an enormous list.

Bogle, a negro, and an old family servant at the Park, went out to Australia, met the defendant at Sydney, recognized him, and was recognized by him and had ever since lived with him, accompanying him in his voyage home, and being since supported by him. His evidence was all that Kenealy could desire. He knew defendant, he said, by his likeness to the Tichborne family. He had often seen Roger's bare arm, and had noticed no tattoo marks upon it. He had seen Roger and Miss Doughty go out in each other's company unattended, and return in the same manner. He thought Lady Tichborne's mind to be quite sound and well-ordered. He had given the defendant no information, and had not in any manner " posted him up " as to family matters and incidents. A thorough cross-examination failed to shake his consistency. It was part of the argument of Mr. Hawkins that this Bogle, who had adhered firmly to the defendant from the beginning, had been sedulously coaching him and helping him in every way, as he was so well able to do, if he chose.

An old friend of Roger was convinced of his identity with defendant, because defendant had remembered that on a certain occasion they had smoked two death's-head pipes together,—a circumstance which he was morally confident he had never mentioned to any one. The fact that defendant remembered such minute and trivial matters as this, while he wholly forgot many of the really grand and important events, was made by Mr. Hawkins an argument to support his theory of coaching. Whatever he had learned from the greatest to the smallest matters he recited accurately. Of all other matters he was ignorant. But the defence urged that such insignificant scraps of recollection were the very surest and safest tests of genuineness that could possibly be furnished. All this was like the famous interview:— Have you a strawberry-mark on your left arm? Yes. Then you are my long lost brother!

Only the proofs of identity were much simpler than a birth-mark. A person would be summoned to visit defendant and see if he could identify him. The visitor, said Mr. Hawkins, would then say, Do you remember giving me a pipe of 'baccy one day? The defendant of course replied, Yes; and the interrogator exclaimed, Then you are the man! and forthwith came upon the stand to testify to this conclusive rencounter and to assert his own perfect conviction of the identity.

So another witness would be told to walk down Pall Mall in the forenoon about a certain hour, at which time defendant's daily habits usually led him to walk through that thoroughfare, and to see whether he could see the defendant; but he was forewarned that the defendant had changed in some respects very much, especially in becoming an extremely bulky man. So at the appointed hour the predestined witness would go into Pall Mall and forthwith would encounter an extremely fat and well-dressed man. A recognition inevitably followed.

There had been much testimony offered by the prosecution concerning the color of Roger's hair, which was supposed to have been much darker than that of the defendant, and a more pure brown, with less of the reddish tinge. The bulk of the testimony would go to establish that Orton's hair was quite light, and that Roger's hair was quite dark; but naturally there was much discrepancy in this respect. One of the witnesses examined upon this subject, a woman, remarked that she had noticed that during the trial of the civil cause the claimant's hair grew gradually but steadily a darker brown day by day. Dr. Kenealy accordingly called the hair-dresser who had attended with great frequency, often as much as once a day, pending the ejectment suit, upon the defendant, and who stated that the defendant's hair had not changed color while it was under his charge. He brought a bottle of the only hair-wash which he had been wont to use upon defendant's head, and proposed to test it by application to the hair of Mr. Hawkins, if that gentleman had any, otherwise upon his learned wig. It was an odd circumstance that Cubitt in advertising the personal traits of the missing heir in Australia in 1865 had by a blunder described him as having "light brown hair." One of the marks of identity then noted on behalf of the claimant was that he also had light brown hair. The truth, as was abundantly shown afterward, was that Roger had dark brown hair, and now it was said that any one could see that this defendant had also dark brown hair; that the color was natural, and not affected by any artificial process; and that this was a pointed difference between him and Orton, who had light brown hair.

Miss Braine, who had been governess to Miss Kate Doughty in 1850, and in that employment had become well acquainted with Roger, testified that when she first saw defendant she did not think that he was Roger; but that continuing to look at him she had come to fancy that she traced a resemblance to the family face in his features.

In the course of conversations with him he had appeared to remember incidents which had occurred at Tichborne at times when he and she had both been there; and she had become convinced that he was indeed the person he claimed to be. She recognized Roger's "dimpled knuckles" in defendant's fat hands; but, strange to say, her minute observation had never led her to notice the peculiar or deformed thumb. She asserted that the defendant's manners were those of a "perfect gentleman." She had been living in the house with him, appearing in the character of his friend, if not of a direct dependant on his hospitality, since his return to England. Mr. Hawkins, cross-examining her, asked if she still entertained the same good opinion of defendant after hearing him allege that he had seduced her former pupil. She replied that had he been in possession of his title and estates she should have discontinued her friendship for him after such a confession, but since he was oppressed and persecuted she still preserved her intimacy with him, though certainly she had been deeply grieved at the tale. British ideas of the perfect gentleman were somewhat peculiarly developed during this trial, for if nothing else was established it was certainly very clearly shown that Roger Tichborne was intoxicated with much frequency. An officer testifying for the defendant, said that Roger used to get into a stupid, soaked state every night, so that one could hardly say whether he was drunk or not. Some evidence also went to show that he was ignorant to an extraordinary degree, even of the rules of grammar.

The Carabineers came up literally in platoons to swear that defendant was their old officer, Roger Tichborne. Sometimes the counsel for the Crown declined to be at the trouble of examining these witnesses. At other times a few questions were put to them with a view to showing that they had not been given a fair opportunity of forming unprejudiced and impartial opinions upon the point; for that they had been in nearly all cases carefully prepossessed, and their judgment biassed by being told beforehand that Sir Roger was come home, and that they were to be taken to see him. The British private soldier is seldom a man of very nice observation or keen intellectual power, and the testimony of these bands of military swearers seems to have gone for little in the general estimation. The officers, to whose perception greater weight was attached, appeared, generally, to be upon the side of the Crown. At this trial only two, Colonel Norbury and Captain Cunliffe, testified in behalf of the defendant.

During the days devoted to the examination of these witnesses, the foreman of the jury applied to the Chief Justice for orders to have lunch served to the jury at the expense of the treasury. This would apparently cause the expense to be included as a part of the costs of the suit; but Dr. Kenealy, far from offering any objection, expressed a politic hope that the desired repasts might be furnished "on the most magnificent and splendid scale." So it was arranged that the jury should thereafter be lunched at the public charge.

The regimental tailor was called, and said that he took his ledger with him when he first went to see defendant, and by its aid he propounded various interrogatories concerning clothes furnished by him to Lieutenant Tichborne. Defendant said it was a severe test of his memory, but did not shirk it, and answered with such accuracy that witness was convinced he was the person he assumed to be.

A "professional pedestrian" testified to the smallness of Roger's feet. A butcher from the Australian gold diggings directly afterward, testified to the uncommon largeness of Arthur Orton's feet and hands. He had met Orton at the gold-diggings, and thought him a man of "villainous appearance," much like a ticket-of-leave man, with a rough vulgar voice, and greatly addicted to the use of oaths. Witness had good reason to remember the size of Orton's hands, for they had once been used in his own castigation. Indeed the big-fisted Orton had knocked this witness down, and witness was quite sure that the "pleasant gentleman" who appeared as the defendant in this cause was not the person who had used him so ill.

This last witness said that Orton had wires in his ears and a scar on his cheek. The next witness knew Orton well, and remembered neither ear-rings nor a scar. The next witness did remember the ear-rings, and did not remember the scar; and so the testimony for the defendant went on. It was a perfect *pot-pourri* of discordances. Legions of witnesses were called; it would fill a large volume to give the briefest categorical abstract of their evidence. They left Arthur Orton's personal appearance in the most dubious condition possible. A dozen different men might have been constructed out of the features and peculiarities which were furnished for this single individual. But all the witnesses were agreed on the one point, that their memory of Arthur Orton differed in essential particulars from the form, features, voice, manners, and other characteristics of the man before them. This was really the important point; for two persons may describe the same physiognomy very differently, and yet both will doubtless recognize it with equal accuracy when it is before them. A very large number of witnesses had only just seen the defendant on the day before, or perhaps on the very day on which they gave their testimony, and consequently it was obvious that they had had only very slight opportunity for forming a deliberate, careful, and impartial opinion, or for comparing him with their memory of Orton. For it could not be pretended, if the defendant really were Sir Roger, that he had not so far changed that it was impossible to recognize him instantly. Even his predetermined mother could hardly achieve that feat.

One Brown, styling himself "Captain," but at present the "proprietor of a pudding-shop," took the stand with the very best will toward the defendant, but whether he did his *protégé* more good or himself more harm may be regarded as a fair question. Before the case was concluded, his name had become a sort of by-word, which Dr. Kenealy could not mention without exciting ridicule and laughter, and laying himself open to a series of embarrassing queries.* The dates in his testimony should be noticed as of special importance. In 1853 and 1854 he was, as he said, a shipping clerk at Rio. In April of the latter year he was introduced to Mr. Tichborne by Captain Oates (one of the witnesses for the Crown, it will be remembered), and Captain Birkett in command of the "Bella." He and Mr. Tichborne played billiards and drank together, and twice when his friend drank too much he put the poor gentleman to bed in his own room; on each occasion he saw Mr. Tichborne take a bath the next morning, and noticed a brown mark on his left hip, and a mark about four inches above his wrist on the left arm; but saw no tattoo marks. Captain Oates and other captains and Roger were seen frequently by this witness at Rio playing billiards together, and also pretty often being very drunk indeed in each other's company. Especially, witness confirmed the defendant's story of his having come on board the "Bella," the day she set sail, quite drunk, — so drunk that, as defendant said, he had little or no memory of what occurred. Witness went on board the vessel that morning to collect a bill for goods supplied to her captain by his employer. He defied the whole world to say he was not speaking the truth when he said that he saw Captains Birkett,

* At the time of this printing, he stands committed for examination on a charge of perjury in this case.

Oates, and Hoskins and Mr. Tichborne, all come on board together, "all being pretty well drunk." This witness also testified that he saw an American bark (a three-masted craft), hailing from New Bedford, lying at Rio in 1853. He went on board her; knew the captain, Lawrence, and the mate, Louis (the Luie who is to be heard of later); she was named the "Osprey;" lay in port there for a long while; but the date of her sailing he could not state. While playing billiards with Mr. Tichborne, he had noticed a malformation or peculiar formation of the thumb of his right hand, causing him to hold his cue in an odd fashion.

This was a pretty good body of evidence to come from one man, and Mr. Hawkins cross-examined him severely. He admitted that, in 1868, he had gone off to sea, and had left his family in a state of destitution; that he had been in England in 1866–1868, and was then well aware of the claims presented by this defendant; that he well knew that his old comrade of the bar and the billiard-table at Rio had been committed to Newgate for perjury; that all this while he had carefully kept the secret of his own knowledge in the premises, because he wished not to be mixed up in the case; that the motive which finally induced him to "unbosom himself" when all other incentives had failed was hearing the testimony given by Captain Oates for the prosecution, which was all untrue, and which he forthwith resolved to contradict. He was confronted with statements made by him to the Local Marine Board of London for the purpose of obtaining a certificate of competency to act as Master Ordinary in the foreign trade. He had at that time given a list of the vessels he had sailed in, with the dates; he had said that, from December 15, 1853, to January 1, 1858, he had been a mate on board the "Equity" of Boston (England?) He sought to explain this painful discrepancy by saying that the date 1853 should have been 1854, and the mistake could have been rectified by the original certificate, had he not unfortunately lost it. But he admitted that a great part of the statement then made by him to the Board of Trade was false, and given only to meet their requisitions. He was asked to look at defendant's thumb. By an oversight probably on the part of the defendant, that person extended his *left* hand, and witness readily saw and recognized the malformation which he had noted upon the *right* thumb of Tichborne. When his attention was called to the circumstance, he was in no wise abashed; saying only that he had indeed thought it was the right thumb; his memory must have been in error.

Two or three witnesses were called to testify to the appearance of an "Osprey" in the port of Melbourne, or in Hobson's Bay hard by, in the summer of 1854. One of them liberally testified to seeing *two* "Ospreys" there at that time; one bark-rigged, the other a small vessel. The defendant had the option between them. A corporal in the Royal Engineers was on board the "Comet," steamer, in Hobson's Bay, when, on July 23 or 24, 1854, a young man and several sailors were transferred to it from a vessel called the " Osprey." [The defendant had said nothing of being put on board such a steamer.]

On Tuesday, October 14, the one hundred and fifteenth day of the case, the famous Jean Luie was called. In the cosmogony of the defence this person was intended to assume the part of Atlas. It was an unfortunate design, as will be seen. He was a Dane, and by his own report of himself had lately come from America to Belgium, on board the steamship " Circassian," in pursuit of a runaway wife. This errant damsel, in addition to abandoning her lawful spouse for another victim of her charms, had unfortunately burned all papers of her proper husband, which might otherwise have been of inestimable service in corroborating his very strange and important testimony. Until July 7, 1873, he had never mentioned to any person whomsoever the story which he now related. But though this silence had been kept for a period of nineteen years, his reminiscences emerged from this long tunnel of time in a singularly fresh and complete condition. In February, 1854, the American vessel, " Osprey," sailed from Staten Island, this witness being on board in the capacity of steward. In April following, being then some four or five hundred miles off the coast of Brazil, the " Osprey " picked up a boat, purporting to come from the wrecked vessel " Bella," containing this defendant and five sailors. The defendant was then delirious and physically helpless. Witness took charge of him during the remainder of the voyage; frequently washed him, and saw upon his body an "olive" mark in the place where this defendant had a "brown" mark. The defendant at that time gave his name as "Rogers." He wore a rosary with a small silver cross. "Rogers" was never quite right in his head while on board the "Osprey," and witness used to intoxicate him with brandy in order to keep him quiet. His sole occupations were picking oakum and whittling a stick. When this witness came to London, he hunted up defendant with much difficulty; but when he found him, he recognized him as the rescued "Rogers," though certainly much changed in body since that event.

When the "Osprey" arrived at Melbourne, it was in the height of the gold fever, and the suggestion of Dr. Kenealy, that this accounted for the non-appearance of the surviving sailors from the "Bella," was amply borne out by the evidence of this witness. Forthwith, upon making port, he said, the mate and all the sailors deserted; the captain also ran away, having first, as witness believed, sold the vessel to be cut up. Witness himself, with two sailors from the "Bella" and two from the "Osprey," took the "Bella's" boat, and made off for the diggings at Ballarat; some ten months afterwards he had parted from the "Bella" men, and had never seen them since. [It will be observed that this does not agree with the evidence of the corporal from the steamer "Comet," *supra* p. 113]. Witness had the "Garden of the Soul" on board, and it was much read by Mr. "Rogers." This witness had given to Mr. Whalley, the member of Parliament who so warmly befriended the Claimant, the names of the owners of the "Osprey," of the owners of the cargo, of the mate and others on board her, and of the stevedore who loaded her at New York. It was to follow up the information thus imparted that Mr. Whalley made his expedition to the United States. But the result of that expedition had been carefully kept from the witness, so that he was even ignorant whether or not Mr. Whalley had succeeded in bringing over any witnesses. This witness had been with the "Osprey" at Rio, and saw and knew Captain Brown. But it was remarked that he called himself steward, while Brown had called him mate; and that he said the "Osprey" belonged at New York, and Brown had said that she belonged in New Bedford.

During the examination of this witness Mr. Hawkins objected with much indignation that, though the defence had known, as appeared by this testimony, ever since July 7, that the "Osprey" hailed from New York, contrary to what had been averred by "Captain" Brown, nevertheless they had not corrected the information previously given, that she was a New Bedford vessel; but had put the Crown to the useless trouble and expense of sending out to bring the captain and mate, with the log for 1854, of a New Bedford "Osprey." The witness was examined with great care as to his movements and occupations from 1854 to the present time. He was compelled to give a complete sketch of his life during this period, with such data as might be necessary for investigations concerning him and his antecedents. It was noted that he said that he had fallen in with one Jones at the Ballarat diggings; that Jones had there seen the two men from the " Bella," and knew the story of the shipwreck; that this Jones had been previously called by the defence, but that he had not been asked as to his meeting with Luie or the rescued sailors, or in any way examined with a view to corroborating Luie's story in the particulars in which, if the story were true, he should have been able to confirm it.

Medical evidence was adduced given by Sir William Fergussón, that the mark on defendant's right ankle was not in a proper place for bleeding, though his fatness made it difficult to discover his veins, and a clumsy practitioner might have made an incision at this spot. The mark on his side was two and a half or three inches long, and about half as much in width; it was brown, but of so light a shade that it required to be looked at for some time before you could be sure of the tint. The peculiarity of the defendant's thumb might have been caused by a severe blow, a contusion, or a bruise, arresting the development of the nail; if thus caused, the accident must have occurred long since, — ten or twenty years ago. He did not agree with a medical witness called for the Crown, who had said that the same condition might be produced by artificial means, and who even claimed to have brought about the same appearance upon his own thumb by such a voluntary process. Another medical man said he had discovered the scars of bleeding on defendant's ankles. But he had never practised surgery, and otherwise he appeared badly on the stand.

Mr. Whalley narrated as much as was called for concerning his doings in America. He denied that he had communicated information procured by him from witnesses there or elsewhere to defendant, and said that he had interested himself so actively in behalf of the Claimant because he believed that the opposition was the result of "a Popish and Jesuitical conspiracy to deprive him of his rights."

On Monday, October 27, being the one hundred and twenty-fourth day of the trial, Dr. Kenealy announced that his evidence was all in.

Mr. Hawkins thereupon proceeded to call several witnesses in rebuttal. They added no new facts, and simply contradicted divers of the witnesses who had been called for the defence. Thus the story of the barmaid about seeing Roger's arm bared when he was washing after having been thrown from a dog-cart, was contradicted by the gentleman who, as she said, was then with Roger. He said that he had never known Roger Tichborne, and that he had never been thrown out of a dog-cart. Colonel Bickerstaff was present and saw Roger bled upon both ankles, at Canterbury. His recollection was perfect, that one puncture was made on each ankle. Captain Oates denied the whole story of the drunkenness at Rio; denied that he had ever played billiards there with Roger; denied that he had ever seen "Captain" Brown there; denied that he was acquainted with a captain in whose company Brown said he had often seen him there; and generally set himself in full and direct opposition to Brown in every respect that he was able to do so. A medical man said that there was nothing of the character of an issue mark in the scar upon the defendant's arm. Sundry other contradictions of a like kind were made, the most important of which have been already mentioned in narrating the testimony for the defence. Then a prolonged adjournment became necessary to await the arrival of witnesses from the United States, summoned to contradict the statements of Jean Luie about the "Osprey," and to prove him to have testified falsely in his account of himself, and to be altogether a witness not entitled to credit.

At last, on November 27, the American testimony was begun. Mr. Purcell, an English barrister, had been sent over to conduct the investigation at New York and elsewhere. He had searched the records of the custom-houses, the files of the newspapers and the pilots' books at New York city, also at the neighboring ports of Newark and Perth Amboy, and he had found no trace of the arrival or clearance of any "Osprey" in 1853 or 1854. The stevedore named by Luie was dead, but the successor to his business was brought over by Mr. Purcell and appeared in person, testifying that the firm loaded no "Osprey" in 1853 or 1854. Another witness, from a New York custom-house barge, whose duties were in the harbor, showed that it was impossible for the "Osprey" to have been lying at anchor off Staten Island, and to have loaded there at the time named by Luie. Purcell had been unable to find the name of Luie on crew lists at times when he ought to have been able to find it had Luie's statements been true. He could find no evidence of the existence of any person of the name of Luie in New York for some years past. Other witnesses testified that they had made careful search, and had been able to find no trace of Luie or of persons named by him, either in New York or Chicago, though they had pursued the investigation carefully in accordance with the statements which he had given in his evidence for the express purpose of directing them. Streets named by him did not exist. Strong circumstantial evidence was adduced to show that Luie's account of his whereabouts within a short time past, since his arrival in Europe, were false. It was shown that he was not a passenger in the "Circassian" upon the trip when, as he said, she had brought him from New York to Europe. In short, nearly every averment that he had made which was in its nature capable of contradiction, was proved with greater or less certainty to be untrue.

An "Osprey" appeared upon the custom-house records of New Bedford as leaving there June 4, 1851, and returning Oct. 1, 1854. She was a bark; but her master's name was M'Comber, not Laurence nor Lewis nor Owen; her log was produced, and in April, 1854, she was found to have been anchored in Table Bay, Cape of Good Hope. Indeed she was never near the coast of Rio after 1851. No Luie was on board her.

A steamship "Osprey" was recorded at New Orleans; but the rescuing ship was a sailing vessel. Another "Osprey" also appeared to have been at New Orleans in 1853; but she was a British vessel and hailed from Liverpool; her master's name was Willeston, and she was smaller than the ship described by the defendant.

Something led to the suggestion that the "Osprey" had been changed to the "Helvetia;" but this did not help matters much. For though an "Helvetia" was found, Marsh master, yet none of her crew lists showed the name of Luie.

Altogether there was by this time, when Mr. Hawkins ceased to produce his rebutting testimony, so exceedingly little left of Luie's character or evidence that the fragments seemed scarcely worthy of being gathered up by the defendant's counsel. But the miserable fellow was destined yet to be the "teterrima causa belli," and to stir up a fracas between counsel and judges which certainly did the utmost possible mischief, not only to the Dane himself and to the defendant, but also to other persons prominently connected with the cause. It happened thus: When Mr. Hawkins rested, Dr. Kenealy applied to be allowed to produce surrebutting evidence; but after consideration the judges refused to grant the application. Thereupon the Court was adjourned. But in a few minutes Luie was requested to remain, and it was announced that the judges were about to return. They did so, and Mr. Hawkins at once handed to them a letter which he said he had just received;

he knew nothing more of the subject mentioned therein than what the letter itself disclosed, and it only said that two gentlemen wished to identify Luie. But no such gentlemen seized this opportunity to stand forward, and the Court again retired. When they next came together after adjournment Dr. Kenealy read a notice addressed to him by Mr. Hawkins stating the intention of that gentleman to produce two witnesses who would show Luie's account of himself since his arrival in London to be untrue. The doctor thereupon moved for an attachment, and proceeded with much asperity to describe the conduct of the counsel for the Crown on the last preceding day of the trial as unprecedented, shameful, and scandalous; and as constituting a contempt of Court of the worst kind; inasmuch as it was an attempt, deliberately and advisedly undertaken, to prejudice the minds of the jury against Luie, to damage his character and to corrupt and poison the current of justice. The Court thereupon called the solicitor who had made the affidavit, on the strength of which they had returned after adjournment, and examined him. Meantime Mr. Whalley rose and began to address the Court. He was rebuked by the Chief Justice for rising to speak not wearing his barrister's robes, and replied that he spoke not as a barrister, but as "one of the public." In this capacity, he was informed, he had no business to speak at all, and was sternly bidden to sit down and hold his peace.

Mr. Hawkins, being thus pushed to the wall, called the two witnesses who had not appeared according to promise at the last sitting. They were clerks of a firm of insurance brokers. They said they knew Luie; he had called at their office, professing to be Captain Sorenson of the ship "Girda," then lying at Hayle in Cornwall; and he had tried in this character to borrow twenty pounds. But inquiry showed that there was no "Girda" at Hayle, and the loan had been refused. One of the clerks dogged him to a low coffee-house in Whitechapel. He was threatened with prosecution for trying to extort money by false pretences, and promised to reimburse the expense which the firm had been put to in inquiring about his ship, &c., provided they would let him off. All this was quite inconsistent with Luie's own testimony of his whereabouts and employment during the same period.

Luie then promptly took the stand, swore that every thing these witnesses had deposed to was false; that he had never seen either of them before; and that he had had no dealings with the firm from which they came. Wheels within wheels! Here arose another case of questionable identity! But the matter was not further gone into at this stage in the main case; Luie was ordered to enter into recognizances in the sum of three hundred pounds, with two sureties in the sum of one hundred and fifty pounds each, to appear when called upon, and in default of such bail was committed. But we have by no means done with this individual yet; more is to be heard of him soon.

On Tuesday, the second day of December, being

the one hundred and thirty-second working day of the trial, Doctor Kenealy began his closing speech to the jury. The principles upon which this address was constructed were in part excellent, in part faulty. The defendant's case could not have been more ably put; every theory, suggestion, or explanation, which could aid him, was advanced with plausibility as well as with ingenuity. What may be described as the positive or affirmative part of the learned doctor's argument was forcible, temperate, and to an astonishing degree approached towards being convincing. He handled his own witnesses and his own theory of the case as he had presented it with consummate tact. It was not his fault if overwhelming evidence established so many contradictions and absurdities in his client's story that he could not smooth them all away. He showed unquestionably great cleverness in attempting to do so. But it was surprising to see how unevenly he put forth his exertions; for when he undertook the task of assailing the case, and refuting the testimony presented by the Crown, his skill and discretion seemed totally to desert him. In these portions of his speech he seemed to be without any other resource save simply vituperation, and the wholesale insinuation of falsehood, corruption, and perjury. By this course he weakened himself exceedingly. He aroused a reactionary sense of indignation in his hearers by his lavish accusations of fraud and dishonesty launched against persons who had in their appearance given no cause for any such suspicions. Especially unbecoming did such conduct seem in view of the fact that more than one of his own witnesses had been far from enduring satisfactorily the tests of cross-examination and comparison. Luie and Captain Brown were notorious instances of this; but there were other less important and less flagrant examples.

Besides this he had a series of disputes with the bench, which not only exasperated the judges, but inevitably conveyed to the jury the notion that the counsel was straining many points with the unreasonable zeal of a man who feels his case to be desperate. He did not succeed in conveying to the jurors the belief that he himself was being overridden and brow-beaten by a partial and prejudiced bench; an impression which might have availed him something had he only been able to establish it. But the panel continually manifested their bias against the barrister, and their conviction that in the numerous clashings he was the sinning and offending party. Beyond this the speech was too diffuse; the jurors were wearied; their memories were overtaxed; their credulity was openly practised upon as if they had been dullards, so that it was impossible for them not sometimes to be offended; their tempers were vexed at what seemed to them a needless prolongation of their unwelcome confinement. Altogether, by one blunder and another in his conduct, the doctor lost their good-will, and was at last left with nothing to rely upon save their strict and rigid sense of justice. Sheer force of logic and preponderance of argument, unaided by a friendly instinct or an occult sympathy, could alone, after he had closed his argument, be expected to secure for him a favorable verdict.

Influenced by what unwonted feeling of modesty, timidity, or self-distrust, it is impossible to say, Dr. Kenealy opened his harangue with manner so quiet and in tones so low that it was difficult to hear him, and the Chief Justice requested him to speak more audibly. He appealed with much appearance of fervor to the Supreme Being, invoking Him that He would be pleased in this great drama to cause the jury to be guided by wisdom, impartiality, and justice. For himself, if undue zeal had occasionally impelled him beyond the strict limits of moderation, he ventured to hope that the jurors, bearing in mind the enormous difficulties under which he had labored in the conduct of the case, would charitably grant him their indulgence.

Gold and power, as he hoped to make it clear to the apprehension of his hearers, had been freely used in this cause for the purpose of supporting the "most monstrous falsehood that had ever been concocted in this country." The singular and unprecedented spectacle had been witnessed of a cabinet minister in the witness-box. But that minister [Mr. Childers], summoned only to prove something about the gold fever in Australia in 1854, had, if not wilfully, yet recklessly and rashly sworn to what had since been shown to be untrue. The prosecution might justly be characterized as "the worst, the wickedest, the blackest, and the most profligate prosecution" which had been instituted in this country since the old days of the Stuarts. Nor, indeed, was it possible to say when or where the series of prosecutions growing out of this one would be likely to stop. There was poor Jean Luie, who, for the testimony he had given, was only too likely to be put upon his trial for perjury, without being given any proper opportunity for defending himself. And if the defendant should be convicted, divers of his witnesses, such men as Mr. Whalley and other most excellent gentlemen, could not possibly escape the charge of wilful and deliberate falsification.

Appealing to a fine old British prejudice the doctor made an energetic assault upon the Catholic priesthood. That odious body it was that really instigated this unrelenting prosecution. They were the great and unseen power, hidden behind the legal machinery, and guiding and maintaining all its elaborate movements. Their design was, after securing the conviction of the defendant and so getting him out of their way, to shape the infant heir of the Tichborne estates — soon to be worth fifty thousand pounds per annum — to their own purposes. They would thus become virtual owners of this snug property. A valuable prize, truly, and worth an arduous struggle! A juror interrupted to ask if the defendant was not also a Roman Catholic. Yes, replied the counsel; but I fear he is a very bad one. An American hardly appreciates the force of an appeal of this kind. Catholicism is not regarded here as it is in England. The name of Jesuits excites no popular apprehension. But Mr. Whalley himself gave as his reason for befriending the Claimant that he regarded him as the marked victim of the priests.

As for his client his conduct and appearance argued the genuineness of his pretensions. He had led a bad life; he had degraded himself in many ways; he had forgotten much of his early education and culture; indeed, he had very little of either to start with: but he was not the low, illiterate, and vulgar brute that the butcher-born Arthur Orton was, that bush-ranger, horse-thief, and suspected murderer of "Ballarat Harry." On the contrary the defendant, though he might be but a ruin, was yet the ruin of a gentleman. His air and bearing showed it. He could not walk down Westminster Hall without manifesting his breeding. His smile was of "remarkable grace and sweetness,"—at this bold assertion an irreverent burst of laughter escaped from some of his hearers; but the doctor, with much gravity, said that he spoke in all seriousness. The features of the defendant might have been observed, too, to have worn during the trial a certain expression of pensiveness and melancholy, which had been a trait of the young Roger.

Throughout the whole long and trying affair he had manifested the courage, the spirit, and the openness of an honorable and innocent man. It should be remembered that he had not been impelled by a guilty conscience to run away from the prosecution, though he might easily have done so:

he had had ample opportunity in his unrestrained freedom. But he had fearlessly stayed to face his traducers, to let them do their worst, and to abide the consequences; to fight the fight out to the end, to encounter the terrible chances of defeat. The thought of escaping or evading his bail had never been entertained by him for a moment. And indeed it is worthy to be remembered, that in this contest the defendant had little to gain and every thing to lose. A verdict in his favor could simply give him his liberty, nothing more. It could hardly even be said fully to restore his character; for since, in a criminal trial, the jury are bound to give the defendant the benefit of a reasonable doubt, an acquittal is perfectly consistent with a mere preponderance of evidence against the accused. An acquittal in this cause would not have meant that the jury found that the defendant was Roger Tichborne, but only that they found that the Crown had not proved, so conclusively as to remove any reasonable doubt from their minds, that he was *not* Roger Tichborne. If the defendant is really an impostor he is certainly a courageous one; for it would be absurd to say that it is moral principle, or gentlemanly honor, or even loyalty to those who have stood by him with their countenance and their money, or indeed any other motive whatever save sheer pluck and dogged persistence, that has induced him to await the verdict of the jury in this cause. Dr. Kenealy called attention also to the frank and liberal manner in which he has exposed himself to general inspection. He has not been jealous of being seen. On the contrary, he has ranged throughout the kingdom, showing himself everywhere, seeking public gatherings, courting notice and observation. He has feared no detection, but has conducted himself in every respect as one who anticipated corroboration rather than the contrary, from being seen on any chance occasion by an old acquaintance.

The cause had been conducted by the prosecution, as the doctor continued to argue, upon a theory utterly abhorrent to the English law, and indeed to every sound notion of justice. For the crime had been taken for granted; the evidence for the defence had been treated as if it were evidence of the crime. Mr. Hawkins had distinctly requested the jury to assume the guilt of the accused. " This has never been the law of England," said the doctor, " and in my opinion it is the law of hell."

Chief Justice Cockburn. Really, Dr. Kenealy, we must interpose. This is not an expression to use in a Court of Justice. *It is taking a great deal upon yourself to say what the law there is!* Such language is most improper and indecorous.

Dr. Kenealy stood by his words.

Chief Justice. I say such language is not proper, and it shall not be used. It is needless, and must shock some ears if it does not shock yours.

Kenealy expressed the hope that his ears were as fastidious in such matters as those of any other person.

Returning to his argument, and refraining from the use of the offensive word, he said the conduct of the case by the prosecution had been a disgrace to any earthly tribunal, and fit only for *the tribunal to which he had referred.*

A most unjust burden had been thrown upon the defendant. His memory, undermined as it was, had been tested by the memories of two hundred witnesses. They came armed with diaries, journals, letters, memoranda; and if any of them could remember any thing which the defendant could not, or if any of them stated any thing in any slight particular differently from his statement, then this discrepancy or forgetfulness of his was assumed as proof of his falsehood. If he remembered any thing correctly, upon the other hand, it was said that he had been informed and " coached " by Bogle, the old servant, or by the governess, Miss Braine, or by Carter, or by Mr. Onslow, or by Mr. Whalley, or by other of his friends or witnesses. He was impaled on such a dilemma that the things which he forgot and the things which he remembered were equally made to militate against him. Evidence, which was rightly evidence in his favor, was distorted into evidence of his guilt, in gross contravention of the rules of justice and the established doctrine and practice of the law. Yet, indeed, if the defendant had been " coached " by these people, he would have avoided many an error into which he had fallen. The very glaring imperfections of his memory were themselves the best proofs of its genuineness, and that he had relied upon himself in utter neglect of such aid as he might have had from others. Certainly it was a tolerably extensive conspiracy that was thus suggested by the prosecution: it involved the complicity of a good many corrupt plotters, liars, and perjurers besides the Claimant. Yet it was not so far-reaching as the plot which the defence in its turn charged against the Crown. Indeed in whichever way this trial might result a good many reputations for truth and honor were at stake. Further, it was obvious that the defendant had not sought to obtain any information concerning the life of Roger in Paris, or while quartered with his regiment in Ireland. Just such " coaching " as this would have been considered by an impostor to be essential. But Roger, relying on himself, had not made such an effort.

If the defendant's story of his life of vice and dissipation were true, the jury must be prepared for any act of folly and absurdity on his part. Thus must they account for the sudden, unprovoked, and complete cessation of his correspondence with his family and friends at home. This, which the Chief Justice regarded as one of the most formidable difficulties of the defendant's case, was treated as the result of a weakened brain and disordered fancy. As well, said Dr. Kenealy, might it have been argued that Joseph was not Joseph, because he sent no communication out of Egypt to his father.

Speaking of Luie, the doctor said that he had not introduced into his opening any mention of

him or of the facts to be proved by him, but had
held him back so long and then had put him on the
stand so suddenly, and so much to the surprise of
every one not for the sake of springing any trap
upon his opponents, but because the witness had
dropped upon the defence like a man from the
clouds. They had never heard of him, never
sought for him, never received any intimation of
the existence of such a man, until he had unex-
pectedly presented himself to them in the middle
of the summer. Then the counsel had not thought
it proper to summon him to tell his story until they
had had time to investigate its truth. Hence they
had withheld him while Mr. Whalley was hastily
despatched to the United States to make an investigation and to seek corroboration of Luie's tale.
The doctor was now far from giving up his witness
in spite of the discredit which had been cast upon
unessential parts of that witness's narrative. He
was not terrified by the threats and rumors which
he had heard uttered concerning him; he did not
abandon him nor an important word in all that he
had said! Whatever the government might set up
concerning his general morality, whatever they
might prove about him in the way of specific sins
which he had committed, even should they show
him to be a murderer, the doctor would yet ask
the jury to believe that what he said about the
"Osprey" and the defendant in 1854 was true.
He had come forward voluntarily, at the instigation of no person connected with defendant's case,
simply to tell what he knew in the matter. The

unfortunate man himself meanwhile was lying incarcerated in Holloway jail, soon to create an independent sensation of his own, agreeable neither to himself nor to his learned champion and vindicator. If he burned even now in the fingers of the counsel who yet with Spartan heroism endured the uneasiness with a hardy unflinching air, he was soon to become such an intolerably hot coal as to be dropped incontinently with unfeigned misery.

It has been said that Dr. Kenealy blundered badly in the violent character of the assaults which he suffered himself to make upon the witnesses and managers of the prosecution. To show that the charge was not groundless, sundry passages occurring on the third day of his speech may be mentioned. Having already accused one or two of the Crown witnesses of having spoken falsely, which was as much as to say, of perjury, he dared to assail poor Mr. Gosford in extravagant terms. Gosford was utterly unworthy of credit, he said; he was a man proved out of his own mouth, upon cross-examination, to have been guilty of a felony. The Court interrupted and said this statement was unwarranted by any thing which had appeared at the trial. Dr. Kenealy said it was felony for an employee to appropriate his master's money and be unable to pay it back. Justice Mellor said that there was not a particle of evidence on which to ground this charge of felony.

Dr. Kenealy. *I* call it felony.

Chief Justice. You may call it felony; but it is not.

The only foundation for this accusation seems to

have been that Gosford, in his capacity as solicitor
and agent for certain gentlemen of property, had
led them into partially speculative investments
which had resulted in loss. In this sense only was
he unable to return the funds of his principals.
But the losers themselves had never blamed him
in the least. Kenealy then referred to the large
sums of money which had been paid to some of the
witnesses called by the Crown, as had been elicited
in his cross-examination. Mrs. Hayley was to have
one thousand dollars; Mr. Gibbes was to have six
hundred pounds. Of such great hire had the chief
laborers been thought worthy! He asked what
sums persons, who paid such bounties to bring
their own witnesses, would not, *e converso*, unquestionably be willing to pay to persons who might be
witnesses for the defence, in order to keep them out
of the way. Whereupon the Chief Justice said:
" This is really beyond all limits of propriety and
decency, — charging persons with these things
without a tittle of evidence, making accusations
by wholesale against every one! You suppose
everybody to be mixed up in some hideous system of corruption and iniquity. . . . There is
not the slightest foundation for such black imputations." Surely all this was very clumsy blunder-
ing on the part of the doctor.

To preserve something like continuity in this
brief abstract of the proceedings, it is necessary
here to interrupt the sketch of Dr. Kenealy's argument in order to dispose finally of the Luie episode.
On Friday, December 5, he was brought into Court,

and a sort of trial within a trial was had. The problem in the less as in the greater proceedings was one of identity. But the question was much more summarily disposed of without the intervention of a jury or the delay of a defence. Eight officials from Chatham Convict Prison identified Luie as one Lungren, received into that place in 1868, under sentence of seven years penal servitude, and liberated on a ticket-of-leave, March 25, 1873. Others identified him with Lungren, a Swede, who was sentenced in 1862 at Bristol to three years of penal servitude for the theft of a bill of exchange for £242; and again he appeared to have been sentenced at Cardiff in 1867, for obtaining £20 under false pretences. He was identified as a clerk in the employ of merchants at Bristol, from 1859 to 1861; when he was sent to gaol in a civil suit, and afterward to prison on a criminal charge. A great many witnesses testified to his having extorted or tried to extort money by falsely pretending to be a sea-captain in the manner already narrated.

A policeman from Bristol said the man Luie or Lungren had a wife and child living there, though not under the name of Lungren; the woman had taken the name of another man, Hawkins. [Much laughter at the expense of the counsel for the Crown.]

Mr. Hawkins. What was her maiden name?
Witness. Miss Sarah Cockburn.

[Renewed laughter; this time at the expense of the Chief Justice.]

But the witness explained that the name was spelled differently, — Colborne; both *Cockburn* and *Colborne* being in England pronounced *Coburn*. Whereupon the Chief Justice triumphed over Mr. Hawkins. But that gentleman promptly retaliated that his namesake in Bristol also spelled his name differently — with a *g* — Hawkings. So everybody laughed merrily at this tiny pleasantry, as if all the crimes and the arguments, and the great weariness of the interminable case, were not resting upon their overweighted spirits. Then the wife with the amusing *alias* was called, and identified Luie as her husband, whom she had not seen since 1865. "Did you recognize him at once?" said the Chief Justice. "Rayther, sir," responded the damsel, with a suddenness and emphasis which again set the auditory into roars of laughter.

But this Luie investigation was far from being marked throughout with such good feeling and jollity. Dr. Kenealy gallantly stood by his witness in this hour of his trouble, and cross-examined the hostile witnesses with all his usual keenness, not to say offensiveness of manner, and with more than his usual prolixity. The task must have severely taxed his temper, for he could not extract much that was satisfactory from them. Especially must it have been provoking to be unable to break down the testimony of some who testified that Luie or Lungren had been at Hull, in the employ of a firm there, from the spring of 1854 till the middle of 1855; thus covering just the very time when Dr. Kenealy wanted this same person to be sailing from near Rio to Melbourne, in the "Osprey," washing Mr. Tichborne, and giving him brandy to keep him stupidly drunk and quiet. So the fuel of his wrath was well prepared to blaze up, and it was not long before the match was applied, and a grand conflagration ensued. Dr. Kenealy was cross-examining a witness, reiterating questions which seemed to be idle and unimportant, and harassing him apparently to no good purpose. The Chief Justice expostulated upon so needless a waste of time. But Dr. Kenealy said the question was for the jury; he must convince them. Then Justices Lush and Mellor, and many of the jurors, thus indirectly appealed to, intimated that they fully agreed with his Lordship. The discussion began to wax warm, and Kenealy finally so far forgot himself as to say to the Chief Justice: —

Your Lordship is perpetually insulting me from the bench; I don't know why.

Chief Justice. Don't, sir, use that language to me; for I will not bear it.

Dr. Kenealy. I consider that what you have said, my Lord, taking all things into account on this and other occasions, justifies the use of my language.

Justice Lush. I think we should put an end to such a waste of time. . . .

It is obvious that much time is unnecessarily and uselessly occupied with these questions.

Justice Mellor. I am of the same opinion. I must say that I regretted to hear you say what you have just said to the Lord Chief Justice. It is the first time I have ever heard that a judge was not at liberty to interpose an observation when questions are reiterated so uselessly. The judges have a duty to perform, and are bound to discharge it.

The Lord Chief Justice. . . . It is the duty of the judges to interpose and protect the public against the waste of the public time, and it is not consistent with decency for counsel to tell a judge that he insults him when he makes such an observation.

Mr. Kenealy. My Lord, I must exercise my own discretion.

The Lord Chief Justice. But, sir, it is not discreet nor decent to make such an observation to a judge.

Mr. Kenealy. My Lord, you have addressed me in similar terms, and my opinion is not altered.

The Lord Chief Justice. Seventeen years I have sat upon the bench, and I have never had an unpleasant word with counsel.

[The reporters say that this remark was received with a murmur of assent from the barristers sitting in the courtroom.]

Mr. Kenealy. My Lord, I have done all I could to avoid it.

Mr. Justice Lush. I cannot help adding that when I first heard your expression I was very much astonished that any gentleman of the bar should have so conducted himself. But I think the offence is aggravated when it is committed by a queen's counsel, who owes a special duty of proper respect to the Court.

Mr. Kenealy. Your Lordship has more than once reminded me of that.

Mr. Justice Lush. I think it is an aggravation of the offence when it is committed by a person in that position.

Mr. Kenealy. I have borne what no other counsel has had to bear.

The Lord Chief Justice. Because, sir, you have brought it upon yourself by your own conduct.

Mr. Justice Mellor. If this kind of conduct should be repeated in any other trials the administration of justice would be seriously impeded. . . . The good relations between the bench and the bar cannot continue to subsist if a judge is to be treated in the way in which you have treated not only the Lord Chief Justice, but every other member of the Court.

Mr. Kenealy. I have been treated as no other counsel has ever been treated in Westminster Hall.

The Lord Chief Justice. Because, sir, you have brought it on yourself. Counsel cannot be allowed to violate all the ordinary rules of the administration of justice, and outrage all the rules of propriety without calling down upon himself the censure of the bench. The judges are bound by the duty they owe to the administration of justice to censure conduct of that description.

Mr. Kenealy. I would not complain, had the censure been conveyed in different terms, but your Lordship has used to me the most bitterly offensive language that could have been selected.

The judges gave to this assertion an indignant contradiction.

Mr. Kenealy declared that he could not alter his opinion.

The Lord Chief Justice said he was sorry for it, and desired him to proceed.

Mr. Kenealy, however, sat down without pursuing his cross-examination any further.

But all this miserable discord and wrangling did no manner of good to the defendant. The fight was one in which there was no chance for him to win a victory. In addition to being in the wrong, the odds against Dr. Kenealy were altogether too great. He could hardly have prevailed had he been in the right. Every man's hand had been against him, and he had been obliged to use his hand against every man: — against the crown counsel, against the fierce old Chief Justice and the two associate judges, against the jurors, against the witnesses; nay, even against the barristers who sat idly by and listened, and though taking no part in the proceedings yet managed occasionally to make their sentiments perceptible in an indefinite but unmistakable manner. No wonder that he did not prevail. The end of the matter was, that the Chief Justice said that neither he nor his comrades on the bench felt the slightest hesitation as to the course which they should pursue. The Solicitor for the Treasury should be bound over to prosecute Luie for perjury. Luie himself was committed for contempt of court, in that he had been guilty of perjury before it. A few days later he was brought up at Bow Street, and sent to Pentonville to undergo the remainder of his sentence. Such was, for the time, the untoward end of the most important witness introduced by the defence.

But a grave question was opened by this matter, being no less than whether or not the defendant and his counsel had been aware of the nature of the evidence which they had offered. Nor if this were so could the honor of Mr. Whalley, radical agitator, reformer, and member of Parliament, easily escape uncontaminated by grave suspicions. It had been a matter of strong inference from parts of

Luie's testimony that he expected to be corroborated by persons who would come forward in the characters of pilot and sailors from the "Osprey." The Chief Justice himself had remarked upon this. Of course neither the pilot nor anybody else from that phantom ship ever put in an appearance. His Lordship said, that if indeed Luie had been induced to testify by the false promise held out to him that other persons, assuming to be shipmates of his were really at hand ready to confirm his tale, then a most scandalous and wicked scheme had been hatched by some person, to the Court unknown. Proceedings against him for perjury were soon after begun, when Luie made some most startling assertions upon this point. He said that he had been deliberately assured by the friends and supporters of the defendant that the pilot and others from the "Osprey" had been found, and would confirm his narrative; that there was a well-formed conspiracy in this matter, by the stipulations of which, if the defendant should ever acquire the Tichborne estates, he was pledged to divide them with those who had been most zealous and useful in his behalf. Among these Mr. Whalley rose pre-eminent, and was to have the lion's share of the noble spoil.

This witness also said that he himself, in addition to being deceived by these men, had also been most sedulously schooled by them in his part. They had trained him in his testimony with extreme and anxious care, and it was because he had learned his lesson with indifferent aptitude, so that they had not dared to trust him earlier, that he had not been put sooner upon the stand. The excuse that he had been withheld in order to give Mr. Whalley time to go to the United States, and establish his veracity and trustworthiness, was all a falsehood.

Luie had turned out to be such a thorough-paced criminal that nothing was worthy to be believed merely because he said it. His assertions against Mr. Whalley and the real or supposed confederates of that individual were no more intrinsically worthy of belief than were his assertions in favor of the defendant. Yet they received from circumstances some degree of confirmation which his testimony in the Tichborne case wholly lacked; for it was noted that though Mr. Whalley had professedly gone to America in search of confirmatory evidence to sustain this witness, and though Dr. Kenealy said he would not put the witness on the stand or even mention his existence till Mr. Whalley had returned and reported, yet not one tittle of confirmatory evidence secured by Mr. Whalley had ever been produced. Had he then not obtained any? Had he on the contrary become satisfied that the witness was a liar and an impostor? It seemed incredible that he should not have reached this conclusion if he had really thoroughly sought to follow up such clews as the witness said had been furnished to him.

The unfortunate member had already been in well-merited trouble in this matter. He had written a letter to the "Times," after Luie's testimony had been in some measure impeached, but before it had been utterly discredited in which he had said: "I consider that I am called upon to state that nothing that has occurred in relation to this man affects my belief that his evidence as to the 'Osprey' is substantially true." Imprudent words! After all the countless processes for contempt of court which had been issued in this case, here was one more obvious and flagrant than any which had gone before. The sin of prejudging and criticising in a cause on trial could not have been more openly or deliberately committed. Mr. Whalley was summoned and appeared, attended by counsel. He could not, however, restrain his impetuosity, and tried to obtain leave to speak in the matter himself. This was not allowed, nor probably could it have benefited him much to do so. His offence was too clear, and he could no more escape the talons of the Chief Justice than he could have shunned fate itself. He was fined two hundred and fifty pounds, and ordered to be committed to gaol until payment. He was hot and contumacious that morning, and cried out, disregarding the expostulations of his counsel, that he would never pay. So he went to Holloway Prison and spent the night there. Probably he did not like his quarters. The next day the fine was paid, and he regained his liberty.

When the Luie trial was in progress, Mr. Whalley made a desperate effort to clear himself of any complicity in the production of the fraudulent testimony. His reputation certainly stood very much in need of purgation. We will not pretend to pass upon the success of his efforts. He is evidently an impetuous person, who must plunge into hot water by an irresistible law of his nature like that which induces the lightning to seek the same fluid. His story was, that he had offered to give to the Solicitor for the Treasury all the information at his disposal concerning Luie, and that that gentleman had refused to become the recipient of the proffered intelligence. He insisted also upon thrusting before the reluctant observation of the Court the papers which he had in relation to this matter; he declared that they were all that he had; that they covered Luie's instructions furnished to him for his guidance in the American investigation, and the results of his tour in that quest. Even if he was innocent, his gross imprudence and folly were punished scarcely beyond his just deserts in the suspicion which still rested upon him. For the tribunal was not sitting to convict or acquit the good name of Mr. Whalley; no official approbation could properly be elicited which should send him forth again before the world in possession of an untarnished, unquestioned, or unquestionable fair fame.

Much natural curiosity was felt, after the publication of these transactions which at first had been in part kept in some measure private, to see how Dr. Kenealy would comport himself in so embarrassing a quandary. It was a severe trial for him, but he showed neither nervousness or despair. He approached it deliberately and in due course, and reached it only after arguing for a day or two upon the testimony concerning the "Osprey," seeking to show from what the witnesses had said that there was an "Osprey"—indeed that there were two "Ospreys"—at Melbourne in 1854; that one of them was a large three-masted vessel, as described by his client, and that the story of his having been saved by such a craft was not only possible, but in every respect probable. Coming then at last to "the Luie episode," he met it in the only sensible way in which he could meet it; for, after all the surmises as to his probable conduct, there was really only one course which he could adopt. He acknowledged that he had been deceived; he gave up his witness; he frankly said that he could not do otherwise, nor did he wish to try to do otherwise. But he did seek most earnestly to clear the defence of any connection with the abominable fraud. He declared solemnly that he himself had believed Luie to be an honest witness until the recent testimony had clearly proved the contrary, for some medical testimony which had been produced he acknowledged to be conclusive against the veracity of the man; his identity with Lungran must be considered to be established; the extraordinary skill and daring of the wretched fellow had imposed upon the counsel as it had upon others. Still the fraud was all of Luie's own private and independent concoction. He it was who, alone and unaided, had conceived it and had carried it out totally without the instigation or privity of any person connected with the defence, at least so far as the doctor knew. Indeed, no true and intelligent friend of the defendant would have borne any part in such melancholy folly. It was even more likely to have been a keen subterfuge of the other side to throw a burden of shame and discredit upon the defence. For the witness had done, the doctor feared, a material and irreparable injury to his client in exciting against him a suspicion which, though wholly unjust, it might be impossible to remove from some minds.

But it is not so easy to wash one's hands of pitch. Dr. Kenealy's own fingers might be as clean as he declared them to be, but the vestiges of defilement were not so readily to be removed from the Claimant. To him the fraud seemed to stick fast. Some one asked the doctor how he accounted for the fact that, if Luie was an impostor, he had been so readily recognized and remembered by the defendant. Luie had said that when he first came into the presence of the defendant, that person had known him and had greeted him in Spanish, saying, "Como esta Luie?" This was, therefore, a hard question, but the doctor had ready not one answering suggestion only, but two, whereof the doubters might take their choice. In the first place the defendant, while on board the "Osprey," never fairly recovered his clear intelligence, and he might easily be deceived, or fall into involuntary error concerning circumstances which then occurred. Moreover, Luie might resemble the man who really had taken charge of his client on the "Osprey," and whom his client had thought bore the similar name of Louis. Next, the jury should remember that the only proof they had of the recognition was Luie's own statement of the fact. But Luie's statements were now admitted to be worthless; wherefore he should request the jury to disregard the allegation of recognition as very probably being as false as were the other statements coming from the same source. If the first proposition was weak, the second was altogether ludicrous; for it was certain that the defendant had seen Luie and had not repudiated him. The doctor was also obliged by the Court to call to mind that Luie's affidavit had been sworn to in the presence of the defendant; also that his statement had been taken so long ago as July 7, and must have been carefully considered by those chiefly concerned therewith in the long intervening period. A juror suggested that the meeting between the defendant and Luie had taken place in the presence of Mr. Whalley. If there had then been no recognition, what was to become of the remnants of that poor gentleman's good name? Altogether this matter left a very bad odor behind it. Nor is it surprising that, after an altercation with the judges, in which they said that his conduct in respect of Mr. Whalley's testimony had been very peculiar, poor Dr. Kenealy was fairly hounded beyond his patience. In his despair he declared that he was "prepared for any amount of gullibility and folly in a man whose mind was constituted like that of the defendant." Nor was he surprised that one of his farmer friends had named a donkey "Tichborne." Really the name was not inappropriate. At this announcement the defendant seemed to think that his counsel had at last carried things rather too far; he spoke to the doctor and appeared to expostulate indignantly; but the doctor would condescend no further for the purpose of smoothing the matter over than to say that, after all, other men apparently of stronger minds had been known to do things equally foolish, and to illustrate his statement by copious historical allusions.

But even yet Luie could no more be exorcised than could the ghost of Banquo. He was more omnivorous of victims than ever was an idol of the cannibals. He confronted the miserable Kenealy at every turn, and at every turn he exacted a fresh sacrifice. A merciless juror was so unkind as to remember that "Captain" Brown, who had so circumstantially narrated the story of Roger and the three captains, all arriving together, so gloriously drunk, on board the "Bella" at Rio, who had also sworn that an "Osprey" had been lying in that port, *et permulta alia*, had recognized Luie as the mate of that vessel. Luie also had recognized the "captain." This unkind juror with the untoward memory now asked the doctor how he reconciled these statements with the veracity of Brown. The doctor suggested that Brown was mistaken in the identity of his man; but being further hard pressed by the Chief Justice, he sought a temporary release from his difficulties, by saying that he would consider the evidence of Captain Brown at another time. The prompt explosion of Luie's false narrative he regarded as, upon the whole, reassuring. It had not been able to stand any examination at all. It had been shattered to fragments almost as soon as it was set up. This showed the inevitable fate of false testimony in this cause. But the remainder of the points in the case for the defendant had been before the public for years, and none of them had been thus impeached and destroyed. By a fair inference and comparison, then, all these other averments must be regarded as corroborated. If they had not been true they would in many months and years have assuredly met the destruction which overtook Luie's story in a few short weeks. Ingenious if not convincing!

It is impossible not to be a little surprised after all these developments, to find a favorite motto of Dr. Kenealy to be *falsus in uno falsus in omnibus*. He even had the hardihood to introduce this common proverb as a doctrine of the law. The Chief Justice, however, declined to recognize it as entitled to such an honor. But whenever the learned counsel could raise a suspicion of possible inaccuracy, no matter how slight, on the part of a witness for the Crown, he forthwith fell back upon this grand and fundamental principle of the law of falsehood, if not of the common law, and demanded that the erring deponent should be regarded as altogether unworthy of credit. "Does the rule apply to Captain Brown?" irreverently queried a juror one day. Kenealy parried the innuendo, but did not abandon his pet dogma.

In treating of the mental weakness of the defendant, upon which, as has been seen, he had so freely dilated in his opening address, Dr. Kenealy ransacked history for instances of persons whose minds had worked unevenly, showing strength on some occasions and extreme weakness on others. Persons who had led wild and irregular lives were apt to impair their intellectual powers. The sorrows and misfortunes of Roger's early career had made him so far eccentric that he was not to be judged by ordinary rules. Mr. Justice Lush interrupted to point out that this was not an argument to prove that this defendant was Roger, but that resting on the assumption that he was Roger, the learned counsel was seeking only to explain and account for the extraordinary character of much of his testimony. Dr. Kenealy admitted this, and said that he could make no argument save upon the basis that his client was Roger; that the crime charged against him was, substantially, that he was not Roger, though he had sworn that he was; that by the rules of law he was entitled to the presumption of innocence until he should be proved to be guilty. Mr. Justice Lush appeared to think that there should be no presumption in either way. But the Chief Justice, for once, inclined to take Dr. Kenealy's view. He added, however, that there was certainly a distinction between eccentricity and mendacity; nor could he see that to say that a man was eccentric was to furnish a sufficient excuse and explanation for his giving false answers under oath as to the most simple matters of fact, such, for example, as the place of his birth, education, &c.

Where the genuine Arthur Orton was, Dr. Kenealy did not pretend to know. He suggested that, not improbably, he was dead, and that Charles Orton's knowledge of this fact was the reason why that person had not been put upon the stand by the prosecution. Neither had the prosecution ventured to call Arthur Orton's sisters, fearing that the lack of any family resemblance between them and the defendant would be remarked by the jury. "But why did you not call them yourself?" cried a juror; and the Lord Chief Justice also expressed his own surprise that the counsel for the defence had neglected this step. Dr. Kenealy, in the absence of a sound explanation, fell back upon his abundant armory of dark insinuations. "Oh, gentlemen!" he exclaimed, "am I to shut my eyes to the fact that any amount of gold is ready in this case, whenever witnesses are wanting?" Mr. Justice Lush rebuked him for casting such imputations. "After the experience of the last ten days," he said, "I listen to such aspersions with astonishment. We know nothing to justify such charges against the public prosecutors, but we do know what kind of witnesses have been brought here on the part of the defendant." But Dr. Kenealy was not to be driven from his position; and later in his argument he said that he had not called those witnesses because he believed that the prosecution had been in communication with them, and had elicited from them information which had been used by

Sir John Coleridge in cross-examination at the civil trial.

The truth was, with regard to these persons, that both counsel seem to have been equally afraid of them. Charles Orton had been upon both sides of the question since the first case had been instituted. He had first made an affidavit that the Claimant was not his brother; he had then asserted that he had changed his mind, that he had been under a mistake when he gave his affidavit, and that this defendant was his brother. Neither barrister cared to encounter with such a two-edged knife as this.* As for the sisters, at the trial of the civil suit they had been present in the court-room, and had been asked to stand up and allow the Claimant to look at them. They had done so, and he had then sworn that he saw them for the first time. At that time, certainly, they were understood very plainly to be upon the side of the plaintiff in that cause, the defendant in this. This furnished reason enough why Mr. Hawkins should not now have called them; but it does not seem to have been satisfactorily explained why Dr. Kenealy refrained from doing so, unless they also had changed their minds. It was tantalizing that neither side caused to become known the opinions of relatives who stood almost as near to Orton as Lady Tichborne did to Roger. Some curious disagreements between persons who should have known so well of the subjects of which they

* As this goes to press, a telegram from London brings the news that Charles Orton has formally declared the defendant to be his brother.

were respectively speaking might have been produced.

The size of the defendant had already served Dr. Kenealy as a foundation for charging him with mental dulness. He now put it to another use. It often happened that men who, like Roger, — as the doctor sketched that unfortunate gentleman, — had given way to mighty passions, and had indulged in the wildest excesses, and in the extremities of folly, developed to an enormous size. In proof and illustration of this assertion, the jury might contrast the statue of Charles Fox, which they could see in Bloomsbury Square, with the figure of his client; and history told the same of Mirabeau, Danton, Daniel O'Connell. The Chief Justice again made the cause of the fat man his own, and adduced instances of very lean men who had led lives of sin and dissipation.

Speaking to the personal appearance of his client, Dr. Kenealy dwelt upon his " aristocratic " hands and feet, so unlike the broad splay feet and huge, ungainly hands which were attributed to Orton. Fifty-one witnesses had said that Orton's hands were large and clumsy; defendant's were singularly small, and his fingers were delicate and tapering. Seventy-eight persons had described his feet by the most various and uncomplimentary epithets. One witness was made by the written testimony to say that Orton had " a Norman hand." Dr. Kenealy said this signified a large hand, whereas defendant's were *plump*, but not large. But neither judges nor jurors had ever heard of a Norman hand, and the meaning of the phrase was questioned. Dr. Kenealy tried to explain by telling the old story of William the Conqueror falling, when landing in England, and grasping a handful of earth; which, he said, showed that William had a long, large, sinewy hand, whence the expression " Norman hand." Great was the merriment which this original sally of the learned counsel called forth. But, as usual, he was quite in earnest. Nineteen out of twenty-seven of his witnesses had stated that Arthur Orton's ears were pierced for rings, whereas the defendant's were not. His client had not dyed his hair: the jury saw its natural color, — it was of a rich, dark-brown shade, such as Sir Roger's had been described. Of sixty-six witnesses called by the defence to testify concerning the color of Orton's hair,

35	said	it	was	remarkably light.
4	„	„	„	fair.
6	„	„	„	flaxen.
6	„	„	„	sandy.
1	„	„	„	ginger colored.
1	„	„	„	amber.
3	„	„	„	auburn.
1	„	„	„	white.
1	„	„	„	light yellow.
26	„	„	„	light brown.

Of all these descriptions, not one could be forced to apply to the defendant's dark locks. Ninety-six witnesses had said that Orton was a " big large man," which defendant was not. He was a " stout fleshy man;" but that was widely different. Others had said that Orton was a man of large build, with big limbs, large-boned, burly, hulking, broad-set, &c., &c. Defendant was describable by none of these adjectives. He was a small-boned man, though now overladen with superfluous flesh. Many had said that Orton was coarse and vulgar in features, stupid and sullen in expression. The doctor appealed to his auditors to say that the defendant was far from being correctly described by these terms. On the contrary, his expression was almost painfully pensive and melancholy, such as Roger Tichborne's had been described to be. He was, moreover, particularly neat in his dress and precise in all his habits. The Crown witnesses had given such vague descriptions of Roger, as might easily be fitted to a very great number of people. Nay, for the matter of that, these descriptions, for the most part, really did tally with the appearance of the defendant, if reasonable allowance were made for the changes naturally produced by lapse of time and increase of size. What the prosecution called the " nervous twitching " of the defendant's eyebrows was really nothing else than the habit of raising the eyebrow which Roger had when he became animated in conversation. As for the tattoo marks, only some eighteen witnesses had sworn to their existence; whereas the defendant had produced not less than thirty-five, all of whom had given excellent reasons for knowing the truth in the matter, and all of whom had denied the presence of any such marks. If there ever had been any such appearance, it must have been produced by some expedient of temporary effect, such as painting or the like, of which all traces had quickly been removed.

Coming finally to the matter of the seduction of Lady Radcliffe, Dr. Kenealy expressed his deep regret that it had been introduced into the case at all. It did not belong there; it had nothing to do with the main issue, which was simply the identity of the defendant. It had been dragged in by the prosecution, because the rest of their case was so weak that they wanted to sustain it by the general feeling of sympathy which could be safely anticipated on behalf of the traduced lady. It was a tonic administered to a feeble cause. It was true that the Chief Justice had called it a crucial test, and had said that the prosecution would have been blameworthy had they omitted to present it; but the doctor differed from his Lordship, and ventured to declare it to be wholly extraneous. For after all if the jury should find that the defendant was Arthur Orton, then Lady Radcliffe's fair fame would be as completely vindicated as it was possible that it should be. But if they should find that he was Roger Tichborne, it was not likely that they would disbelieve this portion of his story. For himself, he confessed that, to his mind, the evidence on this point appeared so far conflicting that it would justify the jury in coming to no conclusion concerning it. If they believed the defendant to be Roger Tichborne, they might content themselves with acquitting him, holding their peace with regard to this subordinate and collateral matter, and not deciding it to be proved either way. This result would best agree with his own private feelings. But though admitting that he occupied this position in the matter, so far as his personal sentiments were concerned, yet the necessities of his case compelled him to sustain his client's veracity.

On the subject of her own seduction, he did not regard Lady Radcliffe as a credible witness. He had not, for this reason, chosen himself to examine her directly upon the point; but the answers which she had given to Mr. Hawkins were not entitled to belief. Not only was she fighting for her reputation before the world, for her fair fame as a chaste lady, without reproach; but, to a certain extent, she might be said to be fighting also for the not remote prospect of twenty-five thousand pounds sterling per annum. For if this defendant's claim were thrown out as bad, there was only the one small life of an infant heir between herself and the vast Tichborne estates. The first question put to the Claimant by Lady Radcliffe at their meeting, after his return to England and the publication of his pretensions, had been: " When did we last meet?" This, said the doctor, is corroboration of the tale of seduction; by this query she sought to " disarm " the defendant, and to prevail upon him not to disclose her shame! But at this point the judges interposed, to express their adherence to a contrary inference. The question was the most natural one which could have occurred to the lady, seeking to test the defendant's genuineness by trying his memory; and was also a question such as it was scarcely conceivable that a woman, guilty as she was said to have been, should have voluntarily put, especially in the presence of her own husband. Moreover, the defendant would naturally have sought to answer in such a manner as to show her his recollection of the occasion, without at the same time uttering any thing to compromise her.

To show the difficulties which the worthy counsel had to contend with in this portion of his case some idea of the extraordinary nature of the evidence of the defendant should be given. His cross-examination by Sir John Duke Coleridge had drawn forth such a series of inconsistencies, inaccuracies, and admissions of forgetfulness that from them all it was difficult to construct any plausible or even intelligible account. A few interrogatories and replies may be interesting as showing better than the mere language of description can do his manner of answering and of stating facts in this matter:—

Sir John Coleridge. How did you discover that your attentions to Miss Doughty were not acceptable to Sir Edward?

Plaintiff.* It is simply impossible for me to answer the question.

Coleridge. You cannot give me the slightest notion?

Plaintiff. No, I cannot.

* These questions and answers, it will be remembered, took place in the ejectment suit in which the Claimant appeared as plaintiff, and Sir John Duke Coleridge was of counsel for the defence.

Coleridge. When did you last go there?

Plaintiff. A few days before I went away.

Coleridge. When did you last see Miss Doughty before you left England? [He left in February, 1853.]

Plaintiff. Not for some weeks.

Coleridge. Were your attentions ordinary attentions? or were you paying your addresses to her?

Plaintiff. Well — ordinary attentions, I suppose. . . . What might have been known privately to ourselves was not known outwardly to the world.

Coleridge. Now do you mean the jury to understand that you were at that time paying her attentions with the motive of inducing her to become your wife?

Plaintiff. Yes.

Coleridge. Now, sir, tell me what it was which led you to discover that the attentions which you were paying to her for the purpose of inducing her to become your wife, were displeasing to the person you meant to make your father-in-law, according to your own account?

Plaintiff. I do not know that I can do that.

Coleridge. Had you any explanation with her before you parted from her, when you discovered your attentions were displeasing to her father?

Plaintiff. I do not remember.

Coleridge. That you swear?

Plaintiff. That I swear.

Coleridge. Did you break off your connection with her? Did you cease to pay her your addresses?

Plaintiff. No, I think it was the other way.

Coleridge. The other way! She ceased to pay attention to you! — Do you mean that she broke it off?

Plaintiff. I believe it was so.

Coleridge. You mean that she broke it off?

Plaintiff. Yes.

Coleridge. Did you write to her?
Plaintiff. I cannot say; I believe I did.
Coleridge. What passed between you and Sir Edward?
Plaintiff. I do not remember what passed.
Coleridge. Did it produce much impression on you?
Plaintiff. Well, really I cannot say. I do not remember how I felt at the time.
Coleridge. Did it produce any impression on you?
Plaintiff. I think not.
Coleridge. You think not! — The matter did not go very deeply into you?
Plaintiff. Really I cannot answer such a question as that.
Coleridge. Surely you can tell me whether you cared much about it at the time? Did it grieve you much for a time?
Plaintiff. Well, I dare say I felt it at the time.
Coleridge. Did it produce much impression upon you?
Plaintiff. I do not remember what it did at that time.

Coming then to the matter of the seduction, a part of the testimony of the Claimant given in the civil suit has been already stated (*ante*, pp. 37–39). He was further asked, —

Coleridge. When did she tell you she was with child?
Plaintiff. It was in November, or before November, I think.
Coleridge. Where?
Plaintiff. At Tichborne. I met her in the village.
Coleridge. Was it the last time you saw her? — the last time you were at Tichborne?
Plaintiff. It was one of the days I was hunting there.
Coleridge. Were you ever at Tichborne after that?
Plaintiff. I believe I was there.

Coleridge. You did not see Miss Doughty?
Plaintiff. I do not think so.
Coleridge. You could hardly forget that, surely?
Plaintiff. I tell you, I don't think I did — to the best of my belief.
Coleridge. Did you go to Tichborne a few days before you went away?
Plaintiff. I believe I did.
Coleridge. In November or December?
Plaintiff. About that time.

. . . .

Coleridge. About what time was it that you first saw your cousin after the engagement was broken off?
Plaintiff. About the latter end of November or December, I think.
Coleridge. Where?
Plaintiff. At Tichborne.
Coleridge. What passed?
Plaintiff. Really, I do not recollect — all these many years — what passed.

Being hard pushed as to his memory of this conversation he finally said: —

It was merely a conversation about my uncle. . . . As regarded what my uncle and aunt had said to me.
Coleridge. What said she?
Plaintiff. I cannot remember what she said at the time.

. . . .

Coleridge. Do you really mean to tell the jury that this is all you can recollect of your first interview with your cousin after your engagement was broken off?
Plaintiff. No! But what I should like to explain to both judge and jury is, that there are matters which I am

very reluctant to state in any public Court. If I do so it will be because I am compelled to do so by the Solicitor-General. Be pleased to understand, as I have already told you, that there are two parties to this.

The plaintiff was further urged to recollect more of this conversation, but reiterated his inability to do so. He was then asked when he next saw his cousin after this and before his departure. He replied that he did not see her again. He was reminded that he had been speaking of the first time he saw her after the engagement was broken. He said he was aware of that. He was then induced to say that he did not see her but once from the breaking of the engagement to his departure. Being pressed as to whether he did not see her again, he replied, —

"I think not," and "I am pretty sure."
Coleridge. But surely you cannot have forgotten whether you went to wish her good-by?
Plaintiff. Well, I do not think I did.

He could not remember whether he ever wrote to his uncle Sir Edward or his aunt Lady Doughty, after the breaking of the engagement. Finally, however, he concluded that he did not write to his uncle, but did to his aunt; and then further made up his mind that he did not write to his aunt between the breaking and his departure. Yet in fact Roger's correspondence with his aunt was frequent and confidential.

Such are fair examples of the manner in which the Claimant answered the cross-interrogatories of

Sir John Coleridge concerning the relations existing between himself and his cousin. They show his astonishing lapses of memory; but they do not show, or very imperfectly show, his numerous contradictions as to dates, places, and interviews. These inaccuracies were scattered throughout the examination at such intervals that they cannot be brought together in this shape.

Dr. Kenealy, having read these answers to the jury, proceeded to comment upon them in his customary vein. They were not true; they were evasive, confused, fencing answers. But then the Claimant was not a truthful man; Roger Tichborne was a very bad and corrupted man and might well have replied in precisely this manner. How absurd were many of his failures, or rather his refusals, to remember! He *must* have remembered; but he would not acknowledge that he did. He was generously reluctant to tell the story of his cousin's shame! But, interposed the Chief Justice, the first questions had reference not to the alleged seduction, but only to the breaking of the engagement; surely they might have been truly answered without compromising Miss Doughty's reputation. Ay, indeed, continued Dr. Kenealy, those questions might have been honestly replied to; but the plaintiff knew what was coming; he knew what they were leading to, and he entered upon his course of reluctance and refusal at once. He would not tell the truth if he could help it. Hence he had so often set the date of the event wrong. He had put it in April, in July or August; in the autumn; from some of his statements calculations would surely throw it into June. He had said that Sir Edward broke off the engagement about the first of July, and again had said that this event occurred perhaps a week or ten days earlier. This would make it about June 22. The prosecution had themselves shown that he was at Tichborne, on leave of absence, in that part of June.

Dr. Kenealy next came to the question put to the Claimant as to whether he had made no inquiries as to the condition of his cousin before he left the country and to his extraordinary reply, — that he had made " no direct inquiries, but had no doubt that he must have spoken of it to Gosford." " Gentlemen," cried the barrister, " let' us hope for the honor of human nature that he would not have been so entirely infamous as to leave the country without making inquiries about the matter."

Lord Chief Justice. It has always struck me that he was in this dilemma: that either he did make inquiries about it, or he did not. If he did not, then heavy infamy would attach to him, as you have said. If he did, and if he was told, as he would be, that there was not the slightest appearance of any thing of the kind, — then why did he not ask to have that packet given up to him? — and why did he leave it in Gosford's hands with the chance of its turning up at any time to destroy the reputation of his cousin.

Dr. Kenealy. My Lord, that is a difficult question for me to answer! — And I cannot answer it. I cannot answer for the thousand things this man has done and said.

The counsel then proceeded to discuss the evidence of the witnesses who had testified to having seen the cousins alone together. This testimony had not stood the test of investigation very well. Some of them had sworn that they had seen the cousins walking alone together at times when it was shown by Roger's letters, and otherwise beyond a doubt, that he was elsewhere: others had spoken of times when Roger and his cousin were little more than children. Yet as a general rule these witnesses had been very positive and accurate as to the time to which they testified; and had, in some instances, even given reasons to support and account for their recollection.

It was not necessary, the doctor said, to suggest that there was any deliberate and designed seduction. Indeed it may not have been a *seduction* at all; all he said was, that his client thought it was a seduction. This from a man whose delicacy had been shocked at the mere introduction of such a subject into the case! It may have been a casual impulse of passion between two young persons engaged to be married. It was not necessary to fix the time and place. A witness had seen them go into the grotto alone together.

Chief Justice (interrupting). The defendant swore it was at Cheriton Mill.

Dr. Kenealy. That meant the grotto.

Chief Justice. The grotto!

Dr. Kenealy. Certainly.

Chief Justice. I have seen the place.

Dr. Kenealy. And so have I.

Chief Justice. Having seen it, I ask you whether you think the act could possibly have happened there.

Dr. Kenealy. I did not see it in 1852.

Chief Justice. But you have seen it in 1873?

Dr. Kenealy. We have seen it only in the winter, not in the summer.

Chief Justice. But we can judge what it would be in the summer.

Dr. Kenealy. The trees were perhaps thicker in 1852.

Chief Justice. They would probably be thicker now than they were then. When I saw the place, I must say, I was never more astonished in my life, after having seen the photograph which was exhibited to us.

Mr. Justice Lush. I also have seen it, and I never supposed a photograph would have so disguised a place. There is a public footway alongside the path called the grotto, which is higher than the grotto, so as to overlook it.

[The grotto seems to have been nothing else than a path, about a hundred feet long, shadowed by trees, having this public way upon one side and a public towing-path upon the other.]

Lord Chief Justice. I must add that it reflects the greatest discredit on the man who *concocted* that photograph.

[The much maligned picture had been taken by the direction of Mr. Guildford Onslow, M. P., a gentleman who had bet six hundred pounds on the Claimant's identity with Roger Tichborne, soon after the story of his reappearance had become known, and who had since figured as one of the most prominent and least respected among his supporters. As the Chief Justice said, it represented the grotto to be a regular *spelunca* or cave, a most retired and private spot; which, as has been seen, was most incorrect.]

Dr. Kenealy despairingly exclaimed that he did not care where or when it happened.

A Juror. Supposing it happened, how would it be known?

Chief Justice. Supposing that it happened in the grotto, it would have been very well known.

Dr. Kenealy. I repeat that I fix it neither in time nor place.

Chief Justice. Then what is to become of Lady Radcliffe if her accuser is to be fixed to neither time nor place.

Dr. Kenealy. She swore she never walked or rode with Roger outside the Park. But I have called witnesses who have seen her do so, and who destroy her testimony as to that.

Chief Justice. Do you suggest then that because a young lady walks with her cousin a little outside of her father's park, therefore we are to suppose any truth in the story of her seduction?

Dr. Kenealy. Surely that question cannot be put to me seriously?

Chief Justice. Why, your argument is this: "Your client, you say, is to be bound to no circumstances of time or place. Then you are asked how Lady Radcliffe can make out a defence unless her accuser is fixed to time and place; and you answer that she has sworn that she never walked alone with her cousin, and that you have proved that she did."

Dr. Kenealy. It does not follow because she did that, that seduction occurred. But I say that if it be true that she walked out alone with Roger, then she is not the witness of truth, and she is not to be believed when she denies the seduction.

Chief Justice. He swore it was at Cheriton Mills.

Dr. Kenealy. If Lady Radcliffe is not a credible witness, then there is only oath against oath. " False in one, false in all."

Chief Justice. If a single departure from truth destroys the credibility of a witness, how are we to accept the statements of a man, to whom you yourself, his counsel, impute utter recklessness as to truth?

Dr. Kenealy. No doubt there was a great deal of untruthfulness. But I say the greater part of his evidence is true. As to this matter, if neither he nor Lady Radcliffe is worthy of credit, then nothing is proved, and a verdict cannot be found against him. I am satisfied if there is a doubt; it saves the defendant. But no servant from Tichborne was called to prove that the cousins were never together, or that no suspicious circumstances occurred.

Chief Justice. There was no need to do so, when you never suggested that any thing occurred in the house.

Dr. Kenealy. I don't know where it was.

Chief Justice. Well, but there sits your client beneath you who must know. He must know where it was. He has sworn that it was at the mill at Cheriton. If it was not there, but elsewhere, then when Lady Radcliffe was in the box there sat the man who could have instructed you as to the proper time and place to ask her about.

Dr. Kenealy. Quite true, yet there is the man who never told me one word as to the most important part of his conversation with Gibbes.

Chief Justice. But if you intended to suggest that Cheriton Mill was not the place, then you should have asked him for the necessary instructions about it.

Dr. Kenealy. I do not feel myself at liberty to tell your Lordships publicly what I might say privately as to what I know.

This retreat of the tortured counsel into the

mystery of professional secrecy reminds one of the manner in which the defeated heroes in the Homeric tales were so often saved from imminent and utter destruction, by being suddenly enveloped by some friendly deity in an impalpable cloud. Only, since no god or goddess intervened in his case, Doctor Kenealy had to create his own nimbus.

In conclusion, Dr. Kenealy said that many things had occurred in the case which he would "give his heart's blood" to be able for ever to forget, — things which had cast a slur upon persons whose character and fame ought to be dear to the country. He did not specify more accurately to what things or to what persons he referred. Perhaps it was to Mr. Childers, the cabinet minister, who had testified for the prosecution, and whose evidence had been declared by the learned counsel to be either a falsehood, or a mistake which under the circumstances could have been scarcely more creditable. Perhaps he might have in his mind Mr. Chichester Fortescue, who had recently given to Captain Oates a government appointment. But Mr. Fortescue had written to the Chief Justice to say that, at the time of this act on his part, he had been ignorant that Captain Oates was a witness for the Crown; and he, therefore, had been fully exculpated. Possibly Dr. Kenealy might be covertly assaulting his own friends Messrs. Whalley and Guildford Onslow. They amply deserved the thrust, though not perhaps from his hands; only it might have been questioned whether

England had any reason for holding their reputations to be exceptionally dear, in spite of the fact that they had succeeded in becoming members of the House of Commons. The respectability and intelligence of that body had but feebly impregnated either of them.

Thousands and thousands of persons had come to opposing conclusions concerning this cause. But the doctor rested firm in the belief that there was but one conclusion to which the jurors could possibly come after hearing the whole overwhelming mass of his evidence; in all which he had the audacity to say that there had been but one weak point, — the unfortunate Luie. 'Was there a man in the country who believed this defendant to be Arthur Orton? The universal conviction of the people of England was the other way!

Chief Justice. Really you ought not to say that. We have nothing to do with the belief of people out of doors.

Dr. Kenealy. I hope we have.

Chief Justice. Certainly not for the purpose of influencing the judges or jury.

Dr. Kenealy. Not for that object certainly. But I hope I may be allowed to express my own belief as to the all but universal conviction of the people of England. The prosecution had staked their case upon this man being Arthur Orton. He had proved that he was not; and if not Orton, who could he be but Tichborne. A few " miserable hangers-on of the government" might still call him Orton, but no one else did so.

All the witnesses, some fifty or sixty in number, who had sworn for the government, as to the defendant's identity with Orton and to the fact that there was no bark-rigged "Osprey" at Hobson's Bay or at Melbourne in 1854, had been shown to be testifying falsely or to be in error. Beyond this a conclave of relations and a few Carabineers had sworn that his client was not Tichborne. But the defendant had held his own among gentlemen and men of honor, as their peer and comrade, for seven long years, — a longer period than any lie could live! Two or three hundred people had sworn in his behalf on the question of identity. They could not all be perjured; no impostor could gather such a host. But was it possible that two or three hundred persons could all be mistaken as to the identity of this one man? Such numbers must force belief. They could not all have been deluded or deceived by the defendant. He was not clever enough to achieve such a feat.

As for that solitary scandalous witness, the discarded corner-stone, the incarcerated Luie, he had deceived the defendant as he had deceived thousands. The defendant was in such a condition when he was rescued that he remembered nothing accurately, and the minute narrative of this impostor, tallying in so many respects with what the defendant did happen to be able to recall, had completely deluded him.

Lady Radcliffe the defendant had proved to be his cousin. Yet what a cousin was she, who had left him to lie in gaol! She had had a sweet revenge, no doubt. But was she a woman for whom a spurious sympathy should be invoked and aroused?

There was his mother, Lady Tichborne: she had died, and in her death her son's case had met with an irreparable loss. Three other most important witnesses had also unkindly fled beyond the reach of earthly subpœnas, leaving only their memories to be vilified by the counsel for the prosecution. One of these was the Tichborne family attorney, Hopkins; two others, Garter and McCann, were old military servants of Roger. They were a great loss, but the loss of the Dowager was more hopelessly irreparable. That mother could never have been mistaken in her son; her conviction that the defendant was her son was well known and had been proved to the jury. Her maternal instinct furnished them with a trustworthy, an unerring guide. They must not for a moment cease to bear this impressive fact in mind. In the name of that dead mother, as well as in the name of justice, he demanded an acquittal for *Roger Tichborne*.

He sat down, and the reporter says that there was "some applause at the back of the court."

The closing speech of Mr. Hawkins was, as a forensic argument, extremely able. More temperate in tone, more condensed in style, than that of Dr. Kenealy, it set his case plainly before his auditors in clear narrative form, and dealt with the case of his opponents with a minute and critical accuracy which appeared to be very destructive. But inasmuch as it would convey to the reader no material facts or reflections which have not been already suggested, or which will not be contained in the charge of the Chief Justice, not even an abstract of it need be given. Repetition would be an unpardonable sin in the story of so long a cause.

On January 29, 1874, being the one hundred and sixty-ninth day of the trial, Lord Chief Justice Cockburn began his charge to the jury. The case had been a painful one, he said, not only by reason of the many issues involved, but also by reason of the course which had been pursued in the conduct of the defence. It bore hardly upon a judge to be compelled, as had occurred in this trial, constantly to overrule and interrupt the counsel upon one side of the cause, because a judge so situated cannot but be conscious that by-standers may conceive him to have some bias or prejudice against that party in the litigation. But, when point after point is badly taken either through ignorance of the law or, as would appear to have been the fact in this case, through a desire to produce an effect upon the outside world and to lead the public to suppose that the judge had treated counsel unfairly, still the magistrate has no alternative. He must do his duty and administer the law.

An additional and unwonted annoyance had been imposed in these proceedings by the necessity which the Court had been frequently under of interfering with the address of the learned counsel to the jury, in order to correct misstatements and misrepresentations. When witnesses are misrepresented, evidence misstated, facts perverted, — and all this not for the purpose of proper argument, but in order to lay a foundation for foul imputations and unjust charges against parties and witnesses, — when one unceasing torrent of invective and foul slander is sent forth to blacken the character of men whose reputations have been heretofore without reproach, then it is impossible for judges to remain silent. Nor can they, especially in a case of this nature, await their closing charge to the jury to set such matters right, for long ere that time injury equally irreparable and unjust may have been perpetrated. Therefore it was that the judges in this cause had felt it to be their duty to interpose and check the torrent of unlimited and undisguised abuse in which the learned counsel for the defendant had seen fit to indulge.

As a rule, if in the fervor of argument a counsel overstepped due bounds, — and for the honor of the bar of England it should be said that even this was of rare occurrence, — a word, nay a hint, from a judge was always sufficient to recall the gentleman within proper and legitimate limits. But not so had the remonstrances which had come from the bench in this cause been taken. On the contrary, they had been met with contumely and disrespect, with insult, with covert allusions to Scroggs and Jeffreys — judges of infamous repute, — as if indeed in days when such a spirit as theirs animated the administration of justice, the learned counsel would not have been quickly laid by the heels and put aside. It was intimated that we were interfering with the liberties and privileges of the bar. But for himself and his colleagues, the Chief Justice indignantly repudiated the charge, expressing the utmost regard for those liberties and privileges. The interference had been only to check the license of unscrupulous abuse, to correct misstatement and misrepresentation, and to restrain slander. The right to use such weapons under cover of argument had never before been claimed by the bar as among its liberties and privileges.

Here the living and the dead had been equally aspersed. Never in the history of jurisprudence had there been a cause in which imputation and invective had been so freely used. Every person, from the highest to the lowest, concerned in a prosecution instituted by her Majesty's Government, and conducted on behalf of the Crown, had been charged with being engaged in a foul conspiracy; with having corrupted witnesses and having induced the commission of perjury by those who, even if their evidence was erroneous, could be fairly accused of nothing worse than mistake. One man has been called a villain, against whom there is no more reason for bringing such a charge than there is for bringing it against any of us. The authorities of Stonyhurst are accused upon no kind of ground at all, of designedly corrupting the minds of their students, and covert hints are given at abominations only half revealed, but from which one recoils shuddering. Yet there is no more foundation for these imputations than if they had been brought against the authorities of Eton or Westminster or any other of the great schools of England.

The dead have been served in the same way. Lady Doughty has been charged with hypocrisy, on the allegation that in spite of the fact that she had learned that Roger Tichborne had taken her daughter's honor, she had nevertheless shown him to the door with bland smiles and honeyed words. Captain Birkett, who perished with his ship, the "Bella," is now averred to have scuttled her for the sake of insurance, having first taken measures which he thought would secure his own safe escape from the sinking vessel. Who could conceive it possible that such vile and slanderous assertions could be uttered in a court of justice? Long ago the Chief Justice himself had illustrated the distinction between that which is allowed and that which is forbidden in advocacy — between the *fas* and the *nefas* of advocacy — by the comparison of the sword of the warrior and the dagger of the assassin. The counsel for the defence had had the singular audacity to refer to this and to liken the conduct of the prosecution to the murderer's dagger. It seemed, said his Lordship, as though the learned counsel paraded that sentiment merely for the purpose of mockery, so utterly and entirely did he disregard it. The liberty of the bar, until this time, continued the Chief Justice, I had thought incapable of being abused; but I have now seen and heard it abused. I think the proper correction for it is censure from the bench, — censure which I believe will meet, as certainly it deserves to meet, with the universal concurrence of the bar of England.

With these words the venerable judge brought to a close the longest, severest, and best merited rebuke ever administered from the bench to a member of the bar. Powerful and scathing as it was, it was also dignified and deliberate. It was free from exaggeration and unmarked by any thing like personal resentment. The gladiatorial element, which is strong in his Lordship's nature, was kept in strict repression, and all the really imposing force of intellect and character which belong to him, appeared at their best. Dr. Kenealy had deserved every word of the stern chastisement which he received; it was properly delivered at this time and in this manner, — indeed it could not have been delivered in any other way. It was not mingled with the summing up of the case, but was made strictly personal towards the counsel, so that no prejudice against the defendant or his cause could be excited by it in the mind of an intelligent juror, save indeed such suspicion and prejudice as always is aroused against a case which seems to require to be conducted in so singular and reprehensible a manner. If, however, any such feeling as that existed it was the fault of Dr. Kenealy, not of the Chief Justice. When he closed this portion of his remarks, there was, says the reporter, " suppressed applause ; " the barristers who thronged the court-room appeared fully to sustain his Lordship.

Coming, then, to the consideration of the case itself, the Chief Justice laid down the broad fundamental principles which it behoved the jury to bear in mind. The first question was, Is the defendant Roger Tichborne? If he is not Roger Tichborne, then the second question is, Is he Arthur Orton?

It does not follow that because he is not Tichborne therefore he is Orton. A third substantial and independent issue is, Whether or not he committed perjury in swearing that he seduced Miss Kate Doughty. Though he may be Roger Tichborne, he may yet have sworn falsely in this matter. For being hard pushed as to the contents of the sealed packet, having really forgotten them, and thinking that it had been destroyed and that true knowledge of its contents was unobtainable, it is conceivable that he may have falsely concocted this tale of seduction.

The defendant's counsel had boldly challenged the verdict of the jury, not merely for the purpose of acquitting his client, but for the purpose of ensuring to him the restoration of his estates. "If you, by your verdict, should acquit him," said Dr. Kenealy, " such restoration must follow as a necessary consequence. The people of England will rise with unanimous fervor, and they will find the means to enable him immediately to recover the estates of which he has been dispossessed." But, said the Chief Justice, the verdict in this case brings after it no such consequence. In the civil case the presumption was very properly against the man who came and sought to oust those who had long held undisputed possession. But in this criminal cause the position of the defendant is very different. He is charged with attempting to gain possession of what is not his own by fraud and perjury; and now the burden of proof is shifted. It is for the prosecution to prove the perjury, which they charge, beyond all reasonable doubt. The question, therefore, is not so much whether the defendant is Roger Tichborne as it is whether the Crown have proved that he is not that person.

The question is one of identity, — a question of the most difficult kind to prove. The Chief Justice then proceeded to set forth and to illustrate by some pertinent allusions the extreme doubt and uncertainty attendant upon issues of this sort. In ordinary cases, as he abundantly showed, evidence of identity is calculated to mislead and embarrass. How much more so, then, in a case like this, a case of double the usual complications to start with, — for the identity of two persons was concerned instead of only one, — and growing steadily more labyrinthine in its developments. Four separate bodies of witnesses appeared, and neither of the four was inconsiderable in point of numbers. There were first the persons who knew Roger Tichborne, and who were divided into two sets, — those who swore that defendant was Roger, and those who swore that he was not Roger. Then there were the witnesses who knew Arthur Orton, and they likewise were divided into the body of those who swore that the defendant was Orton, and the body of those who swore that the defendant was not Orton.

Fortunately it is not necessary to decide the case by deciding to adopt arbitrarily the opinion of any one of these four adverse bodies. For besides the expressions of opinions, there is a mass of facts in the case which may serve to guide the jury to a right conclusion. The life of Roger Tichborne has been portrayed in a manner which it is hard to think can mislead. This will have to be compared with the knowledge and recollections of the defendant. But beyond this, the jury had that to which his Lordship begged to direct their most vigilant and anxious attention. They had before them the conduct of the defendant; most of it admitted, and thus removed beyond the region of doubt. This must be examined, with the view to seeing how far it might seem to be compatible or reconcilable with his being Roger Tichborne. " The facts of Roger Tichborne's life, and the facts which enable us to judge of his character and conduct, his views and intentions, upon the one hand, and upon the other hand the conduct of the defendant when he comes forward and asserts himself to be Roger Tichborne, are, to my mind, that upon which you will have eventually to base your decision, and determine for yourselves the great issue involved in this inquiry."

The first thing, then, is to familiarize ourselves with the life of the real Roger Tichborne during the period of his known existence, so far as we can, and to consider the various circumstances of that life, — personal, intellectual, moral, social; all that we have to make the sum and substance of the individual man. Fortunately the means for doing this are great.

One man may closely resemble another man physically, otherwise imposture of the kind here charged would be impossible; "*but no two men were ever alike within.*" The defendant, it must reasonably be supposed, resembles in some respects in his person both Roger Tichborne and Arthur Orton. The evidence forced one to this conclusion. Indeed, said his Lordship, I have been more than once struck with the similarity, almost rising to identity, between the descriptions given by some witnesses of Roger, and the descriptions given by other witnesses of Orton. But if a person appears, claiming to be a certain man, it is fair and necessary, in testing the truth of the claim, to ask whether he knows what has passed in the mind of the man he claims to be.

Hence no better test of the defendant's identity could be furnished than that deducible from his examination concerning his recollection of events known to have occurred in the life of the real Sir Roger. But the demands made against him in this matter must not be too strict. Trifling circumstances may well be forgotten altogether, or imperfectly or incorrectly remembered. What impresses itself upon one memory will not impress itself upon another. Different parts, different aspects, of the same transaction will remain in the minds of different persons. Half a dozen may remember what a seventh will forget. Yet there are things which a sane man cannot forget, and of which you are entitled to require that a man should display some knowledge. Though here, again, it must be acknowledged, that things of importance sometimes pass away, in whole or in part, from the mind. But if you find a multitude of things such as it seems that a man cannot forget all passing away, it is a weighty matter.

Nor should an opposite error be fallen into of believing the genuineness of the claim because the claimant remembers some apparently insignificant things. These may be acquired. Indeed some such naturally would be acquired. For no man will come forward with such a claim without some means of asserting it. He will have found out something about the man he is declaring himself to be, either from confederates or otherwise; and amid the information he collects will be small details and slight facts.

From this general introduction his Lordship advanced to the summing up of the facts in the case. Unfortunately want of space will prevent the insertion here of even a tolerably full outline of a charge which for clearness, precision, force, and exhaustiveness, probably exceeds any charge ever made to a jury. It was indeed a magnificent performance of an immense task. It is possible only to select such occasional passages as will supply points which have not been so well set forth in the preceding narrative, or which are otherwise interesting. To begin at the very beginning, the Chief Justice reminded the jurors that the "ancestors of Roger Tichborne had held the broad lands of Tichborne from a period anterior to the Norman Conquest." They had for the most part, though not uniformly, been of the Roman Catholic faith. But none were pointed out who had exceedingly distinguished themselves in history. Roger Charles was born January 5, 1829. His mother was a French lady, the illegitimate child of Mr. Henry Seymour of Knoyle, but belonging to the great French family of Bourbon-Conti.

But her fine French blood did not propitiate for her the good opinion of the Chief Justice. He paints her as ill-educated, narrow-minded, selfish in her fondness for her son, Roger, — whom she wished to bring up in an unworthy and ignorant manner, — ill-tempered, a source of misery to her husband and justly odious to all the Tichborne connection. Indeed her husband, in a very long and complaining letter to his father-in-law, gives this not pleasing sketch of his wife: —

"You would bless yourself if you were to see the figure Henriette makes of herself in a morning, generally till between two and three o'clock. It consists of an old plaid dressing-gown, extremely dirty and with several holes burnt in it, no washing or combing, a night-cap, which is frequently very dirty, and a silk handkerchief tied over it. In this disgusting costume she came to breakfast one morning when my brother Robert was with me. So different is this to our ideas of propriety and cleanliness, that I felt quite humiliated and ashamed. She does not very often wear the gowns you had the kindness to give her, her favorite dress being an old red gown, not remarkably clean, and which is my aversion. What she does with the three hundred francs which I pay her regularly every month is to me a mystery, but it is perfectly scandalous on her part to go about such a figure. Friday; I began this yesterday, but was too fatigued to finish it. My brother Robert intended remaining a fortnight with me, but was completely driven away by the brutal treatment he experienced from my wife, and quitted Paris last Tuesday."

Roger also frequently speaks of his mother's "fretting and fuming" and of the unhappy life she led his father. Once he is found saying that his mother makes his father's home a "hell" for him.

It was by something little short of a ruse that the poor father was able to get his son out of the custody, so to speak, of this doting but ill-advised mother, and to put him to school in England, at Stonyhurst. This was not accomplished till 1845. Prior to that time the boy had lived in Paris, with his parents. But the defendant had forgotten their residences and the names of the streets with which, to his sixteenth year, he had been familiar! Then he was taken over nominally to attend the funeral of a relative who opportunely died at this time, and once in England his father succeeded in prolonging his stay and continuing his education there.

In his letters from Stonyhurst the lad makes friendly inquiries after some of his old tutors, the very names of whom conveyed no idea to this defendant. At first he wrote in French, but afterward in English. Though the Chief Justice pointed out French idioms in his English letters, showing that he seemed to think in French and to *translate*, as it were, his ideas into English. His letters were read at great length. They cannot be given here; but though nowise remarkable they were in every respect the productions of an intelligent gentleman, generally free from any thing in the nature of awkwardness or inaccuracy, save only the occasional Gallicisms, and not much more deficient in the matter than in the manner. They contain occasional historical and literary references, and detail a life in which study seems to have been by no means wholly neglected. They show a lad evidently subject to fits of despondency and generally self-distrustful, but capable of being very resolute and persistent, of taking an independent course of action and of adhering to it resolutely after he had once determined upon it. The replies from friends and members of the family are constantly expressive not only of tenderness and affection but even of respect.

While upon this subject of the letters it is proper to remark the very singular error of spelling major with a g, thus "magor" committed once by Roger, and also noticeable in the letters of this defendant. Defendant also wrote "has" for "as," and the same odd blunder occurred twice in Roger's correspondence.

Of the whole school-life the defendant had been profoundly ignorant. He did not remember where he passed his long summer vacations, a lapse of memory which seemed most strange. He did not remember more than one or two of his fellow-pupils. He could not remember that he had studied Latin and Greek, and did not know that they were different. He had never heard of Julius Cæsar. Yet Roger had read the first book of Cæsar's Commentaries. And, said the Chief Justice, "the man who laid the foundations of the greatest empire which ever overshadowed and ruled the world was not altogether beyond the range of Roger Tichborne's ideas." Roger went through Euclid, though he stumbled on the Pons Asinorum. But the defendant did not know what mathematics meant, and was even oblivious of so much as the proverbial name of Euclid. Roger attended a course of chemical lectures. But the defendant confounded a science " which almost half solves the mysteries of creation with the business of a man who compounds chemicals and prepares medical prescriptions!"

The counsel for the defence said that Roger learned nothing at Stonyhurst; that the Jesuits taught nothing, and did not wish their youths to grow up in morality, virtue, and honor.

"I am no friend of the Jesuit Order," said his Lordship. "I believe that their principles and their purposes are inconsistent with the freedom, moral, intellectual, and religious, of the human mind. But to say that this order, which, whatever may be its merits or demerits, has done so much for the furtherance of education, and for which literary men ought to feel grateful to it, — to say that this order would use the opportunity of demoralizing the youth committed to its charge, and that it would do so for the purpose of those abominations to which the learned counsel referred, is in my mind one of the most hateful, most unfounded, most abominable, and most fearful accusations that ever was brought before against a body of men. Moreover, there is not the slightest shadow of a foundation for it. All that the learned counsel can point to is a foolish habit they had of mutilating the plays which were acted in the college. They omitted some scenes, and by some hocus pocus converted the relations between men and women into relations of a different kind. Because there may have been left in some of these plays a passage which the fathers in their fastidiousness or sickly sentimentality thought a little too strong for the ears of some delicate young lady, because something of that sort dropped from the lips of the Rev. Father Fitz-Simon, the learned counsel asks you to believe that these dramas were converted into something of a totally different character, and of a nature too terrible to contemplate. I never heard of such an accusation before, and I trust to God I never shall hear such another."

When it was finally settled that Roger should leave Stonyhurst and enter the army, he made a personal application for a commission to Lord Fitzroy Somerset. The document being afterward long in coming, he ventured to take what the Chief Justice remarked upon as a bold and striking step, and himself wrote directly to that distinguished nobleman, seeking to hasten matters. The whole transaction of this personal dealing with his Lordship caused much interest and gratification to Roger; yet the defendant had forgotten the very name and existence of any such individual.

In preparing for his examination he studied diligently in mathematics, his weakest point, at Gosford's office, working out great numbers of problems there.

In June, 1849, he was named a cornet in the Sixth Dragoon Guards, and was soon after duly gazetted and joined the regiment in Ireland.

It was about this time that Mr. Seymour died.

Roger went to see him just before leaving for Ireland. The old gentleman was evidently near to his end, and he had been as kind as a father to Roger. There was much to impress this parting scene upon the young man's memory. The defendant, however, had so utterly forgotten the circumstance as to say that it occurred at Knoyle, whereas, in fact, it occurred at Bath.

The defendant was extremely ignorant concerning the business affairs of the family. His counsel said it was because in all such matters he had submitted blindly and ignorantly to be guided by Gosford. What with charges and entails, life-interests and remainders, the estates were in a very complicated condition, and a scheme of much importance concerning them had been arranged in the family, to be carried into execution so soon as Roger should come of age. But at that time, when appealed to for his co-operation, which was indispensable, he refused to give his assent. He had other plans of his own, well matured and upon which he was obstinately bent. The discussion which followed was long and warm. Roger, however, held the key to the situation and finally prevailed. His numerous letters relating to this affair evinced a complete mastery of all the details, and a clear-headed understanding of his own powers in the matter, and of his own wishes. The Chief Justice said it would be for the jury to say whether so complete a forgetfulness as had been shown by the defendant in respect of all these matters could reasonably be expected to occur. Especially with regard to the Upton property Roger had the plan of making it the seat of a second family, an offshoot from the main stem, either by instating there his own second son, if he should ever have one, or otherwise his younger brother, Alfred. Defendant had not only forgotten this favorite project, but in his Australian will had quite forgotten Upton itself.

As to his love affair with Miss Kate Doughty, it began, said his Lordship, in the summer of 1849, when the cousins met after the lapse of many years, in which they had not seen each other at all. Lady Doughty seems to have vacillated much as to the matter. It was the cause of a very long and frequent correspondence between herself and Roger. The objection to his addresses chiefly lay in his propensity for drink. The Chief Justice said that this evil habit seemed to have been much exaggerated by the defendant's counsel. Roger was far from being an habitual drunkard; only two or three instances of his having taken too much were shown; he drank no more than would have been considered a virtue in the preceding generation. But it must be acknowledged that in the letters exchanged between himself and his aunt she is continually warning and chiding; he almost as frequently appears excusing and resolving. With due deference to Sir Alexander we must say that a decided alcoholic flavor hangs around the lad.

The counsel for the defendant had further stigmatized this love affair as a "humbug," a word, said his Lordship, now for the first time introduced into forensic language. It had been charged that Roger's affection was a mere low and gross animal passion. The accusation was base and groundless. Every thing known about it pointed to precisely an opposite conclusion; every word of multitudes of letters showed it to be a "noble, tender, generous, and pure" feeling, as it was certainly a most deep and ardent one. His letters are marked by equal intensity and respect.

But the course of his true love ran far from smooth. To Sir Edward Doughty the match was at first distasteful by reason of the near kinship, an important consideration in the Catholic Church. In an interview occurring January 11, 1852, Roger succeeded only in preventing this gentleman from putting an absolute veto upon his hopes. At the close of the same month, however, Sir Edward being very ill, and not wishing to leave a stern prohibition behind him in case of his death, withdrew his words, and reluctantly assented to a conditional engagement. A few weeks later Lady Doughty gave her consent. The visit to Tichborne in June (19-22) following was caused by another threatening illness of Sir Edward. Roger, who had found the previous sick-bed so opportunely favorable to him, was encouraged to repeat the experiment now, and begged to have his term of probation shortened so that an early marriage might take place. But he did himself more harm than good by the application. It was refused, and about the first of July the engagement, so far as the young lady was concerned, was broken off altogether by her parents. It was during the anxious days of that June visit that Roger gave his cousin the duplicate of the sealed packet.

All this led to a long and most confidential correspondence between Roger and Lady Doughty, which continued over many years. The letters were not of a kind to be easily forgotten; they were full of earnestness, argument, entreaty, advice, promises, negotiations; and, if the lady sometimes appears to a cold observer to have been disingenuous, the young man at least is full of ardent enthusiasm. With Gosford, also, a confidential correspondence was sedulously kept up. Yet, said the Chief Justice, as to hundreds of letters written at this time and on this subject, the mind of the defendant is an utter and hopeless blank. The jury must consider and determine whether this degree of forgetfulness passed the limits of possibility.

The dates of the letters, and their contents, too, were most important as bearing on the question of the alleged seduction. This was sworn to have occurred at the end of July or beginning of August. But from the close of the visit in June, to November, 1852, the letters are all dated from Canterbury, where the regiment was then quartered. Nor does one of them contain any trace of a visit to Tichborne. On the contrary, after the breaking of the engagement, early in July, Roger's correspondence contains the reiterated expression of his fixed resolve not to visit the Park again under any circumstances.

The same letters show that he was at Canterbury at the time fixed by the defendant for the occurrence of the much bruited "Brighton card case."

After Roger had taken up his permanent residence in England, he made three visits to Paris. The last of these was in February, 1853, when he went there to take leave of his parents before starting upon his travels. He was there at this time for three weeks, renewing all his old intimacies with the friends and tutors of his boyhood, and finally parting from them in the most friendly manner. The defendant testified that he made only one visit to Paris; that he then stayed only two or three days; and not only the parting festivities, but the very names of the friends had fled irrecoverably from his memory.

In South America, for the first time, the lines of the two lives draw near together. Roger was at Valparaiso; Orton was at Valparaiso. It is an important question whether or not Roger ever went to Melipilla. For it is admitted by himself that this defendant was there, and it may be regarded as proved that Arthur Orton was there. It does not necessarily follow, even if Roger was not there, that the defendant is Orton; though it would be evidence tending to show that identity. But if Roger was not there, then this defendant was not Roger. With the purpose of aiding the jury in coming to a conclusion on this point, the judge reviewed carefully Roger's diary and letters. From these, Roger's movements were so fully and accurately traced, that it finally appeared that his time was completely accounted for with the sole exception of a period of seventeen days. It was a possibility that he had gone to Melipilla in this space. The journey to and fro would have occupied much of the time; and it was to be remembered and weighed by the jury that the defendant had stayed in Melipilla long enough to pick up some knowledge of Spanish, to form a wide acquaintance with the people there, and to establish a quite warm and intimate friendship with the Castro family. It was further to be remarked that neither in any sentence of Roger's diary, nor in any of his numerous letters, was there the slightest trace of any such visit. Yet there was no reason for concealing it; and Roger's correspondence was uniformly very full and frank, mentioning all his wanderings and doings.

The latest letters written by Roger before his sailing from Rio indicate his intention to return home within a reasonable period of time. He was then on his way to New York, intending thence to go to Mexico. Beyond this he seems to have had no definite plans. He spoke of his coming back as of no very distant event, and requested to have his name put up at the Travellers' Club.

Then came the story of the shipwreck, an utterly incredible tale, as narrated by the defendant, and, indeed, finally abandoned by his counsel as incorrect. The theory that this absurd and incredible narrative was to be accounted for on the score of mental affliction or aberration was possible, if not probable. The jury were to consider, however, whether it was further possible that this disaster should have so utterly and so permanently changed the whole intent, mind, and character, personal habits and tastes, of the man as it must have done if this defendant was in good truth the rescued Roger Tichborne. In this connection it was appropriate to recall Roger's disposition. With all the faults of his nature and of his education, he had never shown any weakness or irresolution, any want of persistency or of stability. Certainly there was nothing in his previous career to indicate that such a cause could produce so astonishing and enduring an effect.

The silence of this young man who had been theretofore so frequent a correspondent, and who had shown to the last moment, when he was surely known to be still living, an eager desire for ample news from home, was most surprising. His counsel had accounted for this by divers absurd and some impossible theories. He had said that Roger, knowing his own unworthiness, would not come forward to claim his position so long as his brother Alfred was alive, deeming that brother a fitter head of the Tichborne family than he himself could presume to be. This suggestion found stronger confutation than its feebleness required, in the fact that when the defendant did actually proclaim himself, he had not heard of the decease of Alfred.

Defendant had been guilty of many inaccuracies and inconsistencies in his recital of the story of the wreck, and his doings thereafter. He had not told the story at all, nor had he even ventured to name the rescuing vessel or her captain, until he had been actually compelled to file his affidavit in Chancery, and in it to state these matters. When he said that he was saved by the "Themis," he said that immediately on her arrival at Melbourne he went ashore with her captain, and went to the office of the owner or consignees. When he said he was saved by the "Osprey," he said that he forthwith went ashore with the captain and proceeded straight to the Custom-house. But no entry of the arrival of an "Osprey" appeared on the Custom-house records. Neither story tallied with the testimony of the witness from the "Comet" (*ante*, p. 113).

Defendant said that he was at first anxious to make his way home from Australia, but could obtain no passage. It was shown that at the very time named by him a large ship, homeward bound, was lying at Melbourne, seeking a complement of passengers; also that another large ship sailed for England a fortnight later, and that upon either of these he could have taken passage.

He did not draw upon his bankers or write to his family for money, but lived in utter indigence; making a livelihood in various ignominious and sometimes dangerous ways. He proved a not unskilful slaughterman and butcher, and subsequently being asked how he acquired his skill in cutting meat, he said he learned it at Newgate Market, London, and he talked of that neighborhood in a manner which showed a familiar acquaintance with it. Yet it was not presumably possible that Roger Tichborne could ever have acquired such minute local knowledge, or such handiness with the cleaver.

As for the question of whether an "Osprey" was ever at Melbourne at all, the Chief Justice said the evidence was very insufficient and conflicting; and as to the important point of the time when she was there, it was totally impossible to reach any satisfactory conclusion.

In this connection his Lordship remarked that if Luie was an impostor, it was impossible that his imposition should not have been known to the defendant. The fact of such knowledge upon his part, though proving nothing against the defendant, nevertheless had a material bearing upon the degree of credibility to be accorded to him.

But even if it should be believed that the veritable Roger Tichborne was indeed rescued and carried to Australia, it by no means followed that this defendant was he. In every thing concerning that rescue this defendant had, as already noted, manifested gross and astonishing ignorance. The story of the check (*ante*, p. 34) was adverted to as improbable and almost obviously false. The forgetfulness concerning the names of the crew and of the captain, and the final suggestion of names belonging on the list of the "Middleton" were also dwelt upon at length.

A witness for the defendant had sworn that that person had once in Australia signed a receipt for him, writing the name "R. D. C. D. Tichborne," and that he had brought the receipt to England and shown it to a Hampshire farmer, but had since unfortunately lost it. Still more unfortunately, when that Hampshire farmer was called, he fully denied this statement. Defendant himself also had denied that he had ever used the name of " Tichborne " in Australia. Further, it was worthy of remark, that at the time of this receipt he had no right to use the initial " D " for Doughty.

Defendant said he was engaged to serve Mr. Foster at Boisdale in July, 1854, and traced his service at two or three other subsequent places. He was engaged, he said, under the name of Castro. It was abundantly proved that Mr. Foster did not own Boisdale till 1856, and that at the end of that year Orton was engaged in Mr. Foster's service by his own name. The periods assigned for his services at the various places named by the defendant corresponded in *length* with the periods of Orton's services at the same places. But the point of beginning was placed earlier by between one and two years. If the *dates* given by the defendant, all of them being calculated from this earliest one, were false, then, said the Chief Justice, his whole Australian narrative falls to the ground unsupported.

His Lordship then dwelt upon the singular fact that Roger Tichborne, if the defendant were indeed he, should have married a domestic servant, an ignorant woman, who was known to him to have been previously unchaste; for she had borne a child before the nuptials.

Advancing next to the time when defendant, being still in Australia, began to assert his claim,

the Chief Justice said that his statements then
made to his attorney, Gibbes, were very important.
The evidence showed that he had, at that time,
no knowledge of a great number of matters with
which Roger should have been familiar. In proof
and illustration of this, many instances of his inaccuracy and obliviousness were adduced. Among
these were enumerated the following: He said he
was born in Dorsetshire, whereas Roger was born
in Paris; he said the estates were "tied up" and
would "go to his cousin;" whereas the estates,
though subject to certain incumbrances, with which
Roger had once at least been familiar, were not
"tied up;" neither would they "go to his cousin,"
but to his brother Alfred, of whose existence defendant at this time (on the supposition that he
was an impostor) had never heard. He once even
said that "Tichborne Hall," as he called it, was in
Surrey; whereas the place was called Tichborne
Park and was in Hampshire. He said that he had
had St. Vitus's dance, and frequently repeated
the statement; of Roger this was false, nor would
every one readily accept the Dowager's explanation, that he had confused the rheumatism with
this disease; he said that his mother was large
and stout; whereas, in fact, as was ungallantly
shown in evidence, she was "leanness itself;" he
said he left Paris at the age of eleven years; Roger
did not leave till he was sixteen; he said the Tich-
bórne "dole" was three shillings in the pound of
income; it was in fact only sundry loaves of bread;
then he said the name was sometimes spelled with

a "u" before the "r," which was not the case. The name of Gosford, even the name of his mother, were both unknown; the place of his education was unknown; the number and name of his regiment were unknown; his rank, the manner of his joining, and the length of his stay in the regiment, were unknown. If defendant was Roger he had utterly forgotten all these things.

The will was then mentioned, with all its absurdities and falsehoods, especially the naming of two executors unknown, upon any possible supposition, to Roger Tichborne.

In his statutory declaration made at Sydney, defendant said that he left England November 28, 1852, in the "Jessie Miller." This was the date of Arthur Orton's departure for Hobart Town, and the "Jessie Miller" was the name of the vessel in which Arthur had come home from South America. But in November, 1852, Roger was hunting in Dorsetshire; he left England in March, 1853, for France, and sailed from Havre for Valparaiso three weeks later. There was no reasonable way in which he could be supposed even to have heard of the name of the vessel "Jessie Miller."

Knowledge, as his Lordship remarked, is far from being of equal weight with forgetfulness. The one cannot be set off against the other and a balance struck; for the forgetfulness must be genuine, the knowledge may be acquired. Such knowledge as this defendant really did at first show he had some few means of obtaining, and perhaps the extent of the means was even greater than the extent of the knowledge, *e.g.* as to his mother's name (*ante*, p. 21).

For example, he was furnished with some obituaries in the "Illustrated News;" the advertisements and letters of Lady Tichborne yielded more information; at Sydney he encountered a Hampshire man who could tell him something; and there also he got hold of Bogle. After he came to England the opportunities for coaching were immense. It was noteworthy that in Australia one or two errors in the advertisements, concerning points of personal appearance, were at first eagerly grasped at and adopted by the defendant, and were only repudiated afterward when their incorrectness became known to him from other sources.

As for Bogle, he was the old family servant. From the Dowager's letters it was learned that he was a black man, and that he was at Sydney and on the lookout for her supposed son. The defendant, thus forewarned and forearmed, came to Sydney, and there found a black man at the hotel who had been inquiring for him and was awaiting his arrival. He had the shrewdness to recognize and address him as Bogle, and at once took captive the negro's convictions and sympathy. From him the defendant got much assistance, probably not fraudulently communicated, but naturally elicited under the circumstances. Bogle, for example, is known to have furnished the defendant with a view of Tichborne, with a likeness of Sir Edward Doughty, and with the Tichborne and Doughty crests. Bogle erroneously thought that Upton had been bought by the family, and the defendant adopted the error. Though the Upton estate had been the foundation of a favorite and long-cherished scheme entertained by Roger (*ante*, p. 190). At the first trial, Bogle said that he first mentioned the name of Gosford to the defendant, but at this trial he had sworn that the defendant first mentioned that gentleman's name to him.

After the defendant's arrival at London, his expedition to Wapping, together with the sham letters, false stories, and other deceits which followed, were mentioned as utterly incomprehensible on the supposition of the defendant's honesty. There was no reason why Roger Tichborne should be found floundering in such a labyrinth of complications utterly alien to himself and foreign to all his interests. If, indeed, a friendship with Orton was at the bottom of his anxiety, there was at least no conceivable need of such haste, neither the slightest provocation for the practice of any kind of concealment or deception. But the theory of the learned counsel for the defendant, that the personality of Orton had altogether overlaid, absorbed, and destroyed in Roger his own independent personality, must be rejected as monstrous, incomprehensible, and absurd. If possible with some men, it was wholly incompatible with Roger's nature, as the same had been clearly developed in his known life and letters.

Then the covert journey to Alresford and scouting round the Park, and sending Bogle into the house with special instructions to see and report to defendant what pictures were there, and the refusal to see Roger's cousin, Mrs. Greenwood, who sent him a kindly invitation; and his false story to his mother, accounting for his not making that visit, — all these matters were recalled as most singular and unexplainable.

Then there was Gosford's testimony. The Chief Justice showed very plainly that it was much for Gosford's personal interest to have supported this defendant's claim, and intimated that Mrs. Gosford very clearly saw and appreciated this fact from the outset. Had Gosford been capable of telling a lie, never could he have been more tempted to do so. Gosford, however, though calumniously charged with the commission of a felony by the defendant's counsel, had spoken his true conviction without regard to his own interest. It was noticeable that, to all the many interrogatories put to him by Gosford at their first interview and journey together, defendant at the time had no answers ready, except the staple reply of forgetfulness. But afterward he became well posted in the matters suggested and inquired of in these memorable and important conversations. If Gosford had done nothing else, he had at least put the Claimant upon his inquiry as to many matters.

As for the evidence of Lady Tichborne, the Chief Justice bade the jury not to be led away by idle declamation about a "mother's instinct," — after all it was nothing more than *instinct*. If, before she had seen him, the blunders about the " brown mark," the " Brighton card case," and the many others heretofore recited, had not so much as shaken the lady's predetermined belief, then her *judgment* certainly was entitled to have but slight weight. The manner in which she had encountered doubts and expostulations coming from others, bore in the same manner against allowing to her opinion the full value which might otherwise be claimed for the assertion of a mother in such a matter. When she first went to see the defendant (after having thrice sent in vain for him to come to see her), she found him lying on a bed with his face turned inward toward the wall and his back to her. Even then, according to the evidence, she declared almost at once that she recognized him, saying so before she had even seén his features, and in spite of the undenied and undeniable fact that he was exceedingly changed in form and figure.

The Chief Justice then called the attention of the jury to the fact that none of the members of the Tichborne family had any material interest in opposing the genuineness of the defendant's claim. None had any estates in possession or in expectancy to lose if he prevailed. For all the lands and property belonged to the child of Alfred. Only if he should die could Lady Radcliffe take any thing. No one but he could derive any benefit from the ousting of this Claimant, and he was an infant too young to know the meaning of the battle waging in his behalf.

The Chief Justice next adverted to the interview between Mr. Henry Danby Seymour and the defendant, at which Burden, the old family servant, was present, and was mistaken by defendant for Mr. Nangle, an uncle of Roger, thirty years older than Burden. Mr. Seymour then said plainly that he did not recognize the defendant as Roger Tichborne. But the defendant made precisely the contrary statement in a letter narrating the meeting to the Dowager. At this same time also a letter written by Sir James Tichborne was shown to the defendant, but he did not know the handwriting of the person whom he claimed as his father. In the account of this interview Mr. Seymour and Burden were perfectly agreed in their testimony, which was however directly contradicted by the defendant. His Lordship remarked that similar contradictions were of very frequent occurrence. They happened in reference to matters of recent date and of sufficient importance to be remembered. They could not be accounted for as mistakes or lapses of memory. Either the defendant had told a series of falsehoods in his evidence concerning meetings and conversations similar to this with Mr. Seymour, or else a great number of the Crown witnesses had been guilty of the sin of perjury.

When the defendant and Lady Radcliffe first encountered her husband, Sir J. Percival Radcliffe, and her sister, Mrs. Towneley, were present. Mrs. Towneley was much the older of the two, and there was no resemblance between them in feature. The defendant however saluted her as Mrs. Radcliffe. His mistake was then pointed out to him and explained, whereupon he said to Mrs. Towneley,—" Oh, yes! I was wrong ; you must of course be Lucy, because you are older." Afterward defendant sought to explain his blunder by saying that the ladies had their veils down. In this however he was again contradicted by them. Even if the veils were down, however, it was a question how transparent they were and how far they permitted him to see the countenances behind them. He certainly *undertook* to make the recognition. The Chief Justice said it was for the jury to consider whether in twelve years it was possible for a man so utterly to forget the face and form of a woman whom he had passionately loved as thus to fail to recognize her.

Sir Percival requested defendant to talk with his wife about old times; but that gentlemanly person, according to his own account, refused to do so, happily remarking, as his reason, that what had passed between them in the old times was sacred and would never be known to Sir Percival. The Chief Justice commented upon the brutal vulgarity of the remark. But perhaps it was never made; Sir Percival denied that it was. It was another of the numerous list of contradictory assertions lately referred to.

At a second interview the defendant, whether from alarm, embarrassment, anger, or other cause, abruptly broke off the conversation with the remark that " this was not in the contract"!

In talking with Lady Radcliffe the defendant fell into a strange error in the matter of dates. She asked him when and where they last met. He replied that it was at Tichborne, shortly before he went away and when Sir Edward Doughty was ill. Now Roger went away from England in February, and from Europe in March, 1853; Sir Edward's illness was also in March; defendant had testified positively that he was not at Tichborne and did not see his cousin again after their meeting in the village in November, 1852, when she told him of her pregnancy; and the letters of Roger, corroborated by the evidence of witnesses for the Crown, went far towards showing, if they did not indubitably prove, that Roger was not at Tichborne after June, 1852. This was a very bad entanglement!

The Chief Justice then compared the letters of Roger and of the defendant, pointing out not only the variance of style and tone but the wide difference in accuracy and propriety. The defendant's letters were full of errors in grammar and in spelling. They were the epistles of an illiterate and of a coarse man. They were at times vulgar in matter and expression. Except such carelessness or oddity of idioms as might be fairly and readily traced to his French education, the letters of Roger had been the reverse of all this. The defendant sprinkled the phrase "my dearest mama" over his letters with a profusion equally ridiculous and boorish; but Roger's letters showed no such habit. Indeed if the truth must be told the correspondence of the real Roger with his mother did not indicate an enthusiastic affection; not unfrequently he felt called upon to rebuke her; and in speaking of her in his letters to his other relatives and friends he expresses sentiments by no means of unalloyed affection or blind admiration.

Defendant spelled the names of the Seymour

family, whom he claimed as his relatives, *Seymore*. He wrote to Hopkins, the old solicitor of the Tichborne family, referring to their "old friendship" and speaking of his "pleasure in again receiving that gentleman's advice." Whereas Roger had left home with feelings by no means especially kindly towards Hopkins, who had played such a part in the proposed arrangements concerning the family estates when Roger came of age, as had inspired the young heir with suspicion, if not with actual dislike. Hopkins had at first failed to recognize the defendant as Sir Roger; but he had by degrees been won over to a contrary opinion,—by what means, as it was remarked, did not appear.

Bogle, Carter, and M'Cann, the two last being old military servants of Roger in the Carabineers, had espoused the cause of the defendant. They had lived with him and been supported by his bounty. The two last were now both dead; but while yet alive they had borne testimony in his favor. His Lordship did not accuse them of dishonest conduct or of furnishing illicit information to the defendant. But he reminded the jury that a shrewd man might easily have gathered very much from them, without their intending or knowing it. Especially would this be easy after they had once adopted a favorable belief, ceased to observe the defendant with suspicion, and begun to speak to him with a friendly frankness and unreserve.

Captain Polhill Turner, the captain of Roger's company in the Carabineers, wrote to defendant, inviting him to make a friendly visit. Roger accepted the invitation, but with no intention of really acting upon it. He wrote to the Dowager: "I told you I was not going to Bedford, and I am not a-going."

In addition to the indirect "coaching" obtainable from so many old servants and others, it had been shown at the trial that the records at the Horse Guards had been examined to find out the places at which Roger's regiment had been quartered during his term of service; that a list of the fathers at Stonyhurst during his school days there had been obtained; and that other similar investigations had been pursued. In addition to this the Chief Justice reminded the jury that a great number of Roger's letters, and sundry journals and diaries which he had kept, had all been in the hands of his mother, and had presumably been placed by the Dowager at the disposal of the defendant. From these a great deal could be gathered. His Lordship did not say that any thing *had* been learned from them; but it was proper to state the fact of such a possibility.

In this manner might the notorious story of the snuff-box and Colonel Fraser be accounted for. The defendant said he had given to this gentleman a silver snuff-box, an old one which he carried himself; he had bought it in London, somewhere in Piccadilly, as he thought; it bore his initials, but not the Tichborne crest. This story gave rise to much comment; for, in fact, Roger had given a snuff-box to Colonel Fraser; but then it was of wood, not of silver. The circumstances attendant upon the giving were also very differently narrated by the colonel himself, and by the defendant; and the story of the latter had by no means a natural or probable appearance. He said that he offered the colonel a pinch of snuff, whereupon the colonel took the box itself, shut it up and put it into his own pocket. "Then," said the defendant, "I told him that he might keep it as his own." Now it was certainly strange that the defendant should have remembered such a gift; it was either real memory or "coaching" of some sort; for the incident was not one likely to have been invented. Neither would it have been strange if he had recalled only the fact and had forgotten the attendant circumstances, after so long a lapse of time. But he did not say that he had forgotten them; on the contrary, he professed to have a distinct and accurate recollection, and imbedded the simple fact in a minute narrative. Yet that recollection was certainly erroneous in an essential particular, and was not improbably erroneous altogether. A supposition which might explain this singular mixture of truth and error, and which had the merit of being in itself perfectly possible, was that in some diary the defendant might have found a memorandum made by Roger, of his having given a snuff-box to Colonel Fraser, without more. The attempt to be more elaborate had then betrayed him.

In one of the defendant's letters he referred to the fact that his opponents had broached the theory of his being one "Horton." But this man, he said, was living at Wagga-Wagga, under an assumed name. He was a "dark man," and "very much marked with the small-pox." The Chief Justice called attention to the inaccuracy of this description, as compared with all the descriptions of Orton, who was blue-eyed, light-haired, and, if pock-marked at all, was certainly not "very much" so.

Then the Wapping visits were again dwelt upon. Of their folly the Chief Justice could say nothing stronger than had already been said by Dr. Kenealy himself. Nor was it necessary to point out what they naturally and immediately suggested to every mind. But his Lordship remarked that the destruction of the letters written to the defendant by Orton's sisters, and especially by Charles Orton, who was receiving a weekly stipend from him, was most significant. It would have been a matter of the highest interest and importance to know upon what basis those letters were written. Were they addressed to Roger Tichborne or to Arthur Orton? In which character did they show that the writers recognized the defendant, and that he, at least in the case of Charles Orton, allowed them to recognize him? Had they borne this indirect testimony to the fact of his being Tichborne, why should they have been destroyed? Why not, rather, have been carefully preserved and triumphantly produced?

In the civil cause it was considered most desirable that the defendant should be confronted with the witnesses in South America and Australia. Commissions were issued to take evidence in these places, and at first the design was to have them proceed simultaneously. The defendant opposed this, on the ground that he wished to be present in person both in Chili and in Australia; and made the following affidavit: "I, Sir Roger Charles Tichborne, say I have made the necessary arrangements for proceeding immediately to Chili and Australia, to be present upon the examination of witnesses there under the commissions issued in this action; and I distinctly swear that it is my positive intention to carry out such arrangements, and after the execution of the commission in Chili to proceed directly from thence to Australia for the like purpose."

Accordingly it was arranged that the Chilian commission should be despatched first, and that at its conclusion the Australian commission should be proceeded with. The Claimant set forth with the parties having the commission in charge, and duly arrived with them in South America. But there, upon the plea of illness, he separated from them; and it was a remarkable fact that he returned without having encountered face to face a single one of the Chilian or Australian witnesses. Afterward an unfortunate passage in one of his letters was discovered, containing what the Chief Justice very naturally described as the "startling avowal" that he had not from the outset had any real idea of confronting these persons; nay, that he had not even intended to go so far as South America, but had resolved to leave the ship at Lisbon, and had only been prevented from doing so by some difficulty about his luggage occurring when the vessel touched there.

It was this strange shirking, and this untoward acknowledgment of his original design, which made his attorney, Mr. Holmes, throw up his case. Yet Mr. Holmes had every incentive to persuade himself of the genuineness of the Claimant, and to stand by him so long as there was a gleam of hope left in his case. For before his departure to Chili he had been induced by Mr. Holmes to make his will, in which he gave the Upton estate to Mr. Holmes, made that gentleman his executor, with an additional £500 for his services in that capacity, and also appointed him agent of the property, with a salary of £1000 *per annum*. Yet though the contingent recipient of so liberal a bounty did finally make up his mind to abandon the cause of his friend, he did not therefore escape the censure of the Chief Justice. On the contrary, that rigid conservator of professional morals read the attorney a severe lecture concerning the gross impropriety of inducing his client to execute such a testament, and a still severer lecture for his behavior in getting up his client's case. The instant that any one said or did any thing which could be shaped into a recognition of the defendant as the veritable Roger, down it had been set upon the instant in writing by direction of this Mr. Holmes, who seems never to have moved unattended by his scribe. It was then signed and sworn to, and appeared as an affidavit in the case. Next the affidavits of A and B were sent to C, and his affidavit having been elicited in this way, the affidavits of A, B, and C were shown to D, and his statement was solicited. In this unjustifiable manner no less than one hundred and eighty affidavits had been procured. Nor was this all; for it had appeared that some of these had been so dishonestly drafted as to be very far from accurately expressing the real opinions and assertions of the persons whose statements under oath they purported to be.

The letters of the defendant were particularly unhappy. We have already had occasion to comment upon several; the Chief Justice now called the attention of the jury to another. A lock of hair had been sent from Chili, which was sworn to have been cut from the head of Arthur Orton when he was at Melipilla. Donna Hayley had proved that Orton was at that place, and stayed there a year. It had not been proved that Roger had ever been there; indeed the contrary seemed probable, if not certain (*ante*, p. 193, 194). Donna Hayley's evidence was corroborated by the defendant's own letters. Now, this lock of hair, when first received, had been accepted by defendant as his own; and it was not till long after, when his blunder had become obvious, that he repudiated it, and said that he had been mistaken in acknowledging it to have been cut from his head. Yet at first he was well pleased to get it, and wrote in a manner expressive of satisfaction that his friend Castro had " sent part of my hair." The lock was laid beside a lock cut from Roger's head at nearly the same time; it was very much lighter. If, said the Chief Justice, emphatically, that hair from Melipilla had really grown on this defendant's head, then this defendant was. proved not to be Roger Tichborne.

At this point his Lordship further dwelt upon the fact that the defendant had not only at first appeared wholly ignorant of the only journey made by Roger from which he could possibly have turned aside to Melipilla, but had even positively set the visit to that place at a time when it was clearly proved to be physically impossible that Roger should have been there. These blunders he fell into in his Chancery examination in 1867. Afterward he in part amended his story at the trial in 1871. But it was noteworthy that in the interval Moore, the man who had been in attendance upon Roger in South America, had turned up, and had shed a great deal of light upon that part of Roger's career.

As for the mere opinions which had been expressed on the question of identity, especially after so long a time had elapsed, his Lordship frankly said that he thought little of most of them. Many of those advanced by the Wapping witnesses in favor of the defendant were, beyond question, nearly or quite worthless. Yet there were some few to which greater weight must be conceded; for example, that of Miss Loder. She had seen Arthur Orton daily as a lover, and she was not likely to forget or mistake him. Neither if Orton had treated her ill and jilted her, was it any reason why she should have any spite to wreak against Sir Roger Tichborne. If this defendant were Roger, Miss Loder could not satisfy her revenge against Orton by swearing that Roger, whom she never saw or knew, was her unfaithful swain.

The Chief Justice then adverted with much severity to the manner in which the defendant and his friends, agents, and supporters, had sought to accumulate evidence in his favor by creating a popular excitement in his behalf. Public meetings had been held, addresses had been made, and all for the sake of arousing so strong and wide-spread a prejudice and force of public opinion in his behalf that persons would succumb to it, and be carried away by it to believe in him. Witnesses were not left to form an unbiassed judgment, and the hope had been that even the jury could not be insensible to such a pressure of general and loudly expressed conviction. The judges had allowed the defendant exceptional immunities and privileges, because they had felt that in so costly a trial, where the Government was against him, he ought to have a full opportunity to appeal for pecuniary aid. But the liberality thus manifested by the Court had been scandalously abused, and his Lordship expressed his desire that it should not hereafter be drawn into precedent.

Nor did the Government escape uncastigated. His Lordship had in his scourge a thong for every back. The Crown had shown a disgraceful parsimony in failing to produce sundry important foreign witnesses. In a cause of the nature and magnitude of this one, when Government had once resolved to prosecute, nothing could excuse them for not prosecuting thoroughly. No consideration of expense should interfere with their making out the clearest and most indubitable case possible. They were bound to put the truth beyond a doubt, and no witness who could advance this purpose should be left unproduced, no matter what it might cost to bring him. Government had been derelict in this respect, and was blameworthy.

There was a formidable mass of testimony going to show that the defendant was not Arthur Orton. Marks had been sworn to be upon Arthur which were not upon defendant; and marks were on defendant which were sworn not to be upon Arthur. Much of this evidence, however, was wholly untrustworthy, and much more was subject to grave doubt. The Chief Justice summed it up and commented upon it with much care, but no definite result could possibly be arrived at from such confused and irreconcilable materials. Chaotic his Lordship found it, and chaotic he was obliged to leave it. Some witnesses had sworn to seeing Orton and the defendant together. But they had been sadly inconsistent as to traits of personal appearance, and as to times and places they had been worse than uncertain ; for they had positively and circumstantially stated such rencounters to have occurred when and where it was utterly and unquestionably impossible that they should have occurred. They had described Orton in a variety of ways. Yet none of the descriptions had tallied with any accurate delineation of Arthur. Supposing the testimony of these witnesses to be true, it would seem that some other person had borne the name of Orton in Australia. Arthur had several brothers, some of whom had not been heard of for years past; it was possible that one of them was in Australia. Or the habit of freely appropriating names, without much regard to the lawful ownership thereof, might account for the circumstance.

In this connection it was further a singular fact that since the defendant had left Australia there was no proof that any one had ever seen Orton there: Only one witness had presumed to furnish such evidence; and the Chief Justice was evidently far from convinced by his testimony. Yet a reward of one thousand pounds sterling had been offered for the discovery of the genuine Arthur Orton, and the news of this fact had been duly promulgated at Wagga-Wagga, where defendant said he had left that undiscoverable person. It would certainly seem that the fact of his existence, as a person distinct from the defendant, or the fact of his death, were worth enough money to have brought forward proof of either circumstance, if, indeed, either were true. It is surprising that a "claimant" for the position of Arthur Orton did not start up.

In weighing the testimony of witnesses as to the identity of Roger, his Lordship said that the opinion of nearly all who were nearest to him and most intimate with him was to be placed in the scale against the judgment of those who knew him comparatively little. Besides the Dowager, only one member of the family had appeared on behalf of the defendant, and he was a person who knew Roger very slightly. Ten or twelve officers had testified for the Crown, and only two for the defence. Of these two, one had been carefully subjected to prepossessing influence, and the other had had but indifferent opportunity for arriving at a satisfactory conclusion. The witnesses from Paris and from Stonyhurst were quite uniformly convinced of the imposition. Of the Carabineers and others, several who had testified to the identity in the first trial had not been called at this; and few had been allowed to form a really unbiassed and unprejudiced opinion. Arts had been practised to influence them before allowing them to encounter the defendant. Moreover, many of them had given the reasons upon which they had founded their belief, and most weak and insufficient reasons they often were. All this was gone into with great minuteness by his Lordship; but, of course, it is possible here to give only this gross result. Many of them had shown reluctance or embarrassment when forced to compare their memories of Roger with the likenesses of him; and some failed altogether to recognize those portraits.

Many said that defendant had "the Tichborne back," the "Tichborne face," &c.; which appear to have been upon the large and bulky scale; nor, indeed, did it seem reasonable to doubt that there were many points of resemblance of this nature. But unfortunately for their value the acquaintances of Roger said he had by no means these traits, but that he inherited the narrow face and thin figure of his mother. They nearly all agreed in attributing to Roger a weak, clear voice; whereas defendant's was coarse and husky.

Two witnesses had sworn to the initials A. O. on Arthur's arm. The scar on defendant's arm was unaccounted for, save by the story of one witness, Lewis, a linen-draper's assistant, from Alresford, who told an incredible tale about having met Roger and Miss Doughty walking in the park, of having been "introduced" by the lady to Roger, and of having thereafter been a friend and intimate associate of the young heir. He said that they used to meet in the park and indulge in sundry low and vicious practices, and that one day he accidentally wounded Roger in the arm with a stick. The wound, after healing, left a scar such as appeared on defendant's arm. The meeting and "introduction" were denied with ridicule by Lady Radcliffe, and the whole improbable and offensive tale was now dismissed by the Chief Justice quite contemptuously, as unworthy of credit. It was for the jury to consider the probability that this mark was the vestige of cauterization inflicted to remove the initials.

It was a remarkable fact, the Chief Justice said, that though people had noticed Roger's slight French accent in the defendant when he first returned to England, yet no such accent had been observable at Wagga-Wagga. Such a peculiarity might well enough have been lost by lapse of time, and have ceased to be noticeable in Australia ; but that it should return as consequent upon, or concomitant to, the return to England was quite astonishing.

In reviewing the defendant's reminiscences, his Lordship said that it was noteworthy that he recalled, professedly by an effort of memory, things which it was *impossible* that Roger should have *remembered*, but which might naturally have been told to him. Yet it must be acknowledged that he had given some proofs of memory which, if genuine, were very astonishing, and hard to explain upon any theory consistent with the imposture. But the question was, whether these pretended recollections were really such. For example, he had described the patterns on some figured shirts worn by Roger in England, and had thus fully convinced the washerwoman at Tichborne. Also, he had satisfied the regimental tailor by remembering several of Roger's suits of clothes. If unaccounted for, save upon the theory of actual memory, these circumstances were almost conclusive. But though it could not be *proved* that they were not memory, yet it could be shown that they might not be so. For the jury must remember that much of Roger's clothing had been kept and was in defendant's possession ; and that not improbably also the regimental tailor's bills might still be preserved and might have been seen by him.

The way the defendant's memory grew was also remarkable. Things which he knew nothing about at first, he afterward showed a tolerable knowledge of. Every question put to him served as a suggestion for investigation and inquiry, which had been pursued with untiring assiduity. Often it happened the things which he found that he ought to know, he afterwards came to know. He occasionally tried guessing, as if he were playing at a game of conundrums. For example, Roger had a favorite trick, which he pursued with much care and elaboration, of catching flies, placing them under a tumbler, and stupefying them with tobacco smoke. A person who was familiar with this sport had an interview with defendant for the purpose of satisfying himself on the point of identity. He suggested the fly-amusement. Defendant remembered that he used to stick pins into flies. Being told that he was wrong, he had nothing further to submit for consideration at the time, but afterward caused a friend to write a letter and ask whether the habit referred to was not that of eating flies. He did not succeed in suggesting the real custom.

A circumstance which his Lordship found especially hard to explain unless the defendant were Orton, was that when coming up the Thames, on his arrival from Australia, he asked the pilot whether he knew a river pilot by the name of Ferguson. The pilot said he knew two or three of that name. Defendant said he meant the one who used to pilot the Dundee boats. Now the Dundee boats used to bring the Shetland ponies to the Ortons; and of course Arthur knew all about them; but Roger could not be supposed to have had any knowledge whatsoever of them or their pilots.

The defendant had utterly forgotten every thing about Stonyhurst; what few statements he had undertaken to make were erroneous. He could recollect the name of only one schoolmate there, Arundell; but there were two Arundells, one of them a special friend of Roger and mentioned in his will; yet defendant did not know which one it was that he remembered. He had a list of the names of some of the fathers there, but it was significant that he did not remember those who had had charge of Roger's education, and that he did profess to remember others with whom Roger had had little or nothing to·do. The studies, the Christmas plays, the vacations, every thing in short, was a blank to defendant. He said he left in disgrace in November, 1848, whereas Roger left, under no discreditable circumstances, in the summer at the end of the regular term. It was for the jury to consider whether such forgetfulness was possible.

So likewise he had misstated pretty much every thing about his obtaining his commission. His military life in Ireland, where Roger was for two years and seven months, had been for the most part forgotten altogether; and such few incidents as he undertook to relate were grossly erroneous, and, in one instance at least, he narrated a story which was wholly fictitious. He was examined, he said, "in the landmarks of England." Being asked to explain this, he said: "The landmarks of England insinuate the formation of England at different points." The Chief Justice said this was incomprehensible nonsense, explainable only by supposing that the defendant had heard the name of the book called "Landmarks of English History." He said Roger's examination for his commission took place at London, whereas it took place at Tichborne, and that he "passed," whereas Roger did not pass, but only received a certificate of fitness in certain branches.

But the most remarkable forgetfulness was that of the correspondence with Lady Doughty. Ninety-six letters, written during his stay in Ireland, were still preserved; some might have been lost; and, supposing there were in round numbers one hundred, it made an average of one letter every fortnight. These referred to every thing that was most important and interesting to Roger, his habits of life, his love for his cousin; it was a confidential correspondence. It was all conducted between Roger and his aunt; there was not a trace of any letters being exchanged between him and Miss Doughty. Yet defendant had wholly forgotten to whom he wrote, had been very uncertain whether he wrote at all, and knew nothing of the nature or subjects of the correspondence. Gentlemen, said his Lordship emphatically, I do not know that in the whole range of the case there is any thing, to my mind, so strange as that; and the question is whether, as sensible men, you can believe that such a correspondence as that could have passed from the memory of the living man. . . . I know no better test that could be put to the memory of any one than that.

The ignorance of the defendant in military matters was astonishing. He thought a troop was the same as a squadron, though a squadron contains two troops. He said his regiment contained upwards of nine hundred men, whereas it was only three hundred strong. Could a man who had been three years in the service have been so ignorant?

Defendant's total oblivion as to the French language and literature was a most striking point. Up to the last that had been known of Roger he had spoken, written, and read French; indeed he seems to have been very familiar with the books of that nation, and he was accompanied on board the "Bella" by a French valet. Yet defendant knew not a word of the language; he even mistook Pierre for *père*, so that he was induced to say that Pierre Corneille was the father Corneille. The smattering of Spanish which had been picked up in South America had staid by the defendant. How could it be explained, then, that the so much more familiar French had totally disappeared from his memory?

The business affairs of the family had been well known by Roger. They were certainly of a most interesting nature to him, and he had paid careful attention to them, and manifested strong feeling concerning them. Defendant was not only wholly ignorant of them, but had asserted many absurdities, and not a few impossibilities in undertaking to speak of them. Could Roger Tichborne have fallen into such confusion on the subject?

As for the love affair, said his Lordship, the defendant's answers showed a state of mind which seemed inconceivable in the case of Roger. "The heart's wounds leave scars quite as deep and lasting as those which steel or fire impress upon the surface of the outward form." Yet the defendant remembered nothing. He knew that there had been an engagement and that it had been broken off, and beyond this he had no knowledge. When, by whom, for what cause, under what circumstances it had been so broken, he was unable to tell. His own feelings caused by that event, and what was said between himself and his cousin about it, he professed to be unable to recall; indeed he even pretended that the two separated lovers met and talked together without mentioning the subject at all! Was such oblivion credible if the defendant were really Roger? His love was not then a dead or dying flame. On the contrary, his subsequent letters from South America show that he was constant to his avowed affection, and still longed and hoped for a marriage with his cousin.

His Lordship came next to the discussion of the sealed packet and the seduction. It is impossible to give any abstract of what he said which would be of value in adding to the particulars already set forth. Suffice it to say that his charge was nothing less than an excoriation of the defendant! He charged him with making "crafty" statements; and assertions as to time and place which were proved to be false and could hardly be mistakes. If anybody can hereafter place the slightest faith in this story it certainly is not the fault of Sir

Alexander Cockburn. His views were undisguised, and it must be confessed that after reading what he said, it seems undeniable that the facts when brought together in a clear narrative could have been made to bear any other aspect. But if it was impossible by reason of their own nature to recite them in such a way as to appear impartial, it must be confessed that the Chief Justice did not seem to think it worth while even to make the effort. He delivered a superb argument in the shape of a "summing up," and treated the judicial function with that cavalier neglect of which no man living is so well capable as he.

The evidence concerning physical marks he brought together toward the close of his charge. There was a brown mark on defendant and abundant trustworthy testimony showed that no such mark was on Roger. The defendant's witnesses to this point had not been very satisfactory. The mark was congenital, and if Roger had it not, then this defendant was not Roger. There were only two persons who swore to any such malformation of Roger's thumb as appeared upon the thumb of the defendant; one of them was the notorious "Captain" Brown, the other a bar-maid who appeared scarcely more worthy of credit. The defendant had well developed and pendent lobes to his ears, whereas, if the daguerreotypes could be trusted, Roger had small lobes growing close to his cheeks. The defendant had the scar of a seton, and he had carefully narrated the medical treatment applied to it, which was appropriate for a seton and not appropriate for an issue. Roger had been bled at Canterbury, and the scars could not yet have disappeared. The punctures were made on both arms, both feet, and at the temporal artery. Defendant showed only scars on his ankles, and they were at a point where there was no vein, and where no skilful physician could have cut for bleeding. There was a scar on defendant's arm, which he himself could not account for; a most singular circumstance! It was where some government witnesses had sworn that the initials A. O. had been tattooed on Arthur Orton. It was not proved that it was the scar of cauterization, but it was admitted that it might be.

The evidence of Roger's having been tattooed was very strong. Witnesses had seen it at such various times, when he could not expect it to be seen, that the theory suggested by the defence that it was a mere temporary mark made by him in frolic seemed untenable. Moreover it was always the same emblems and letters in the same place. The witnesses who had not seen it had made a very discreditable appearance; some of them obviously falling either into error or falsehood. Yet if Roger was tattooed it was certain that this defendant was not Roger. Here again his Lordship made his own opinion very conspicuous.

The letters both in respect of handwriting and of style seemed to his Lordship to furnish most valuable evidence. No one could pretend that the chirography of the defendant resembled that of Roger. Moreover the free flow of ideas, the appearance of cultivation and right feeling, noticeable in Roger's letters was wholly wanting in defendant's. Roger sometimes made little slips in grammar or spelling, but rarely. Defendant's correspondence was full of such blemishes. Roger could hardly have written " worrit " and " busted."

On Saturday, February 28, having consumed eighteen working days in " summing up," the Chief Justice proceeded to sum up this summing up. He selected every point which told against the defendant, stated it with an incisive brevity which, if impressive, was also rancorous, and for the space of nearly two hours presented an appearance as thoroughly unjudicial as has been beheld upon the bench in England for many generations. The whole tone of his remarks resembled a challenge to the jury to bring in a verdict of acquittal, as he recited fact after fact, and seemed to dare the jurors to refuse to be convinced by each one of them of the prisoner's guilt. Never was a stronger belief expressed by a Judge concerning the merits of a case; never a more resolute determination manifested to control the result.

He had been accused, he said, of partiality; he had been assailed by critics who presumed to think that they knew his business better than he knew it. But he had been governed by a stern sense of duty. " Gentlemen," cried he, " I cannot invent facts, nor by the utmost effort of ingenuity can I find explanations which have no reality in point of fact. In my opinion a Judge does not discharge his duty who contents himself with being a mere recipient of evidence, which he is afterwards to reproduce to the jury without pointing out the facts, and the inferences to which they naturally and legitimately give rise. It is the business of the Judge so to adjust the scales of the balance that they shall hang evenly; but it is his duty to see that the facts, as they arise, are placed in the one scale or the other, according as they belong in the one or the other. It is his business to take care that the evidences which properly arise from the facts are submitted to the consideration of the jury, with the happy consciousness that if he goes wrong there is the judgment of twelve men, experienced in the every-day concerns of life, to set right any thing in respect of which he may have erred. If the facts make one scale kick the beam, it is the fault of the facts, not of the Judge."

His Lordship said that he and his colleagues had sought for solutions of many facts which pressed hardly upon the defendant, and if they had been unable to find such solutions it was not the fault of their desire to do strict and impartial justice. While it is the business of judicial action to protect virtue; so, on the other hand, it is the duty of the Judge to see that the guilty do not escape. In the conviction of the innocent, and in the escape of the guilty, as the old saying is, lies the condemnation of the Judge, — of the judges of the fact as well as of the presiding Judge. You must take care of the innocent, but also you owe it to society to see that the guilty man does not go free.

You have been asked to give to the defendant

the benefit of any doubt you may feel. He is entitled to the benefit of the doubt which a rational, sensible man may fairly entertain; but not to the doubt of a vacillating mind which has not the moral courage to decide, but shelters itself in a vain and idle scepticism. His Lordship could not ask one or two men who might differ from the ten or eleven others to sacrifice his or their profound and conscientious conviction; but he urged that agreement should be reached if possible. It was desirable not only for the purpose of ending such a litigation as this had been, but also in order to avoid creating in the popular mind that intense dissatisfaction which must arise if this trial should be rendered abortive by the dissensions of the jury, and which might lead to the introduction of a change in the established system, — a change which his Lordship would deprecate, though it might well be generally approved as necessary.

He further referred to the insults that had been heaped by the counsel for the defendant upon the Judges, and to the moral intimidation to which both Judges and jury had been subjected by threats that they should be handed down with infamy to posterity if the defendant should be convicted, but should be received with popular "ovations" if he should be acquitted. And now, said his Lordship, I have done; I have tried to discharge my duty. For your part, the verdict which you shall render will assuredly be received by all persons, who are not either fools or fanatics, as the judgment of twelve men who have brought vigilant attention and marked and remarkable intelligence to the consideration of the cause.

Mr. Justice Mellor added a few words justifying the action of the Court in its various commitments, fines, and reprimands inflicted for contempts of court committed chiefly by the daily press.

Mr. Justice Lush expressed his concurrence in the views of the duty of a Judge, as the same had been set forth by the Chief Justice. Some persons were of opinion that the more cogent the facts, the more should the Judge try to neutralize them. But he thought that the duty of the Judge was to assist the jury in discovering the truth, without considering whether it might make for one side or the other.

A few minutes after twelve o'clock, at noon, the jury retired. The defendant sat at his green baize table, "nervous and anxious." The densely crowded court-room was alive with most intense excitement. Every one was surprised when, at only thirty-three minutes after twelve, the jury came in and reported that they had agreed upon a verdict. The defendant stood up, "confused and abashed." The foreman read the verdict: "We find, firstly, that the defendant is not Roger Charles Doughty Tichborne; secondly, we find that defendant did not seduce Miss Catherine Doughty, now Lady Radcliffe; and, further, we find that there is not the slightest evidence that Roger Charles Doughty Tichborne was ever guilty of undue familiarity with his cousin, Lady Radcliffe, on any occasion whatsoever (applause); thirdly, we find that defendant is Arthur Orton."

A paper was also handed by the foreman to the Chief Justice, and was by his Lordship read aloud, as follows: —

The jury desires to express its opinion that the charges of bribery, conspiracy, and undue influence brought against the prosecution in this case are entirely devoid of foundation. And they regret exceedingly the violent language and demeanor of the leading counsel for the defendant in his attacks upon the conduct of the prosecution and upon several of the witnesses produced in the case.

   (Signed)   H. F. Dickens, *Foreman.*

The gratification of the old partisan who had been managing the trial and who had spared no care or pains in the training of his twelve docile jurors may be imagined. He must have felt like a schoolmaster whose pupils have made good show at a public examination. They might have been relied upon to take the same action had he not subjected them to such vigorous tutelage, but neither this fact nor the righteousness of the verdict and accompanying rebuke can in any degree justify his conduct.

Mr. Justice Mellor rose to deliver the sentence. He said that the Judges fully concurred in the verdict, and, indeed, no person free from prejudice, and who had intelligently followed the evidence, could well have arrived at any other conclusion. He addressed the defendant in terms of great severity. Wicked and nefarious as was his attempt to present himself as Roger Tichborne, and so to obtain the vast property which of right belonged to the infant heir, this crime seemed almost to sink into insignificance beside the more infamous perjury concerning Lady Radcliffe. Fortunately that cowardly calumny had been immediately and perfectly refuted, and the base charge had been shattered and exposed. The Court grieved that the sentence was much too light to constitute a proper punishment for such offences; it was seven years of penal servitude upon the first count, and thereafter, seven years more of penal servitude upon the second count.

The defendant shook hands with his counsel, Dr. Kenealy, was hurried quietly out of the court room, his person was searched, and he was then placed in the police wagon and driven to Newgate. There he was put into a cell, dimly lighted, furnished with a straw pallet and a wooden table and chair. Amid these surroundings he was left to his meditations, the place of his final incarceration not having yet been determined upon. He behaved with a perfectly tranquil coolness, not seeming surprised or disheartened, and, indeed, seldom speaking at all.

The throngs gathered in Palace Yard around the exit from Westminster Hall, though dense, manifested no propensity to become disorderly, and though they had seemed so friendly to the defendant during the trial, they appeared to have anticipated its result, and to have no fault to find therewith. It seems that in the long time that the trial had been pending, the real truth and justice of the case had had time gradually to filter down through the people, till even the ignorant rabble came at last to recognize the unquestionable fact of guilt.

THE TRIALS OF TROPPMANN AND PRINCE BONAPARTE.

I.

TROPPMANN.

THE story of the massacre of the Pantin fields must still be freshly remembered by all whom these pages are likely to reach. Neither the temptation to the act nor the act itself furnished any legitimate cause for peculiar interest. The purpose was plunder. The plan and execution comprehended only a coarse and brutal slaughter. The criminal was quickly caught, tried, convicted, and executed. Yet in spite of the threadbare vulgarity of every feature of the villany, its very monstrousness and cold-blooded ferocity awoke throughout all Europe and the United States that eager curiosity which every man calls repulsive in his neighbor, but entertains and satiates in himself.

The whole family of Kinck were slain. The father and eldest son perished separately, apart from and shortly before the rest. The mother and the five younger children were immolated and buried together in the Pantin field. The last slain were the first discovered; and while an unnatural and horrible suspicion still pointed to the father and eldest son as the slayers, Troppmann was nevertheless seized upon a vague misgiving aroused by his own confused and self-condemning appearance. He took advantage of this first shocking hypothesis to make a partial confession, to the effect that he had been an accomplice of Kinck *père* in the murder of the mother and children. This falsehood being soon exposed by the discovery of the bodies of the father and son, he next confessed that he himself was the sole executioner of all the victims. Soon after he again changed his tale, and asserted that he had accomplices in the deed, and that they had done all the worst and more active portions of the work. This remained as his last statement and was the ground which he took at the trial. Naturally all this rendered the belief in his guilt universal. The world could not disbelieve what he himself would not deny. Wherefore, though the latest form of his confession left his guilt to be formally established, yet the real questions to be determined by the jurors were only whether he was the sole murderer, or only a sharer in the crime, and in the latter case whether he was an active participant or a mere looker-on giving slight and insignificant aid. Such uncertainty as there was technically, if not substantially, did not attach to his guilt, but only to the degree of his guilt. In the contest his counsel appears to have given him but feeble assistance. In main part he did his own battle, single-handed, against the lawyers and the witnesses for the prosecution, and against the more dangerous and hostile Court itself.

The Court was opened and an immense throng pressed in. Members of the *corps diplomatique*, magistrates, highly respectable and unctious officials, especially ladies of rank in great numbers, also multitudes of fair creatures not to be elegantly named in English, crowded the benches and even dispossessed the advocates of their customary seats. The reporter for "*Le Figaro*" found himself obliged at the close of the trial to furnish an explanation or apology for grave defaults in his references to the audience. "And now," he says, "let me add a brief postscript — the farce after the drama — to defend myself from the charges preferred against me by divers of my lady readers. They are astonished that I should have been so far wanting in ordinary politeness as not to have named some of the ladies *who took part in* (*assistaient aux*) the Troppmann trial. My excuse is simple: I noticed in the audience *des dames et des femmes* (translation would involve the loss of the peculiar flavor of the words). And that I might not run the risk of placing beside a respectable name the name *d'une célébrité galante*, I chose to hold my tongue. I kept careful watch over myself all the while, in order that I might be driven into no necessity for making apologies, for which I have no taste." Such was the various but distinguished throng brought together by French tastes and French manners to witness the baiting by M. le Président of a low-born mechanic, the murderer of a family of ignorant peasants, of whom the mother at least was unable even to read. There was no element in the whole affair to excuse or palliate this morbid, and, at least in the women, odious curiosity.

Very properly did "*Le Figaro*" speak of the trial as a drama. Not only was the audience such as is wont to assemble at an opera, but the stage "properties" were likewise there, displayed with managerial art. A large table occupied a prominent position, and upon it were spread out the blood-stained garments in which the victims had been exhumed; tools found in the Pantin field, and which it was supposed had been used in digging the shallow ditch wherein the bodies had been imperfectly concealed, and divers articles belonging to the slain and found upon Troppmann at the time of his arrest. Kinck *père* was supposed to have been poisoned with prussic acid; so upon the table stood certain bottles holding chemical compounds, also a pleasant jar containing the stomach and viscera of the deceased, which had been subjected to chemical investigation. Beside these lay the broken knife with which it appeared that the mother and two of the children had been stricken down and lacerated. It cannot be denied that the *mise-en-scène* was artistic and effective.

The *acte d'accusation* was read. It was a document formidable by reason of its length, but vastly more formidable by reason of the extraordinary nature of its contents. It was a cross between an opening speech for the prosecution, and such an article as some skilled purveyor of sensational matter for the newspapers might prepare for the delectation of his readers. The circumstances attendant upon the discovery of the bodies; the shocking details of their appearance, the several contradictory confessions of the accused, the tale of his arrest, all the circumstances tending to fasten the crime upon him, were given at length. In addition to this his whole previous life was passed in review. His moral, mental, and physical development was traced. The books he had read, the pursuits he had undertaken, the wishes he had expressed, were all detailed. A thorough analysis of character, mind, and physique was made. From all this heterogeneous material conclusions were drawn, and all in such shape that one who had no extrinsic knowledge whatsoever in the premises must have seen at once that the material had been gathered and the inferences elicited by hands intentionally hostile, and with the obvious and consistent purpose of leading up to the one capital result, the commission of the murder by the accused. The moral to be drawn from a portion of this insidious narrative, a moral which at the time was not lost upon certain intelligent and observant critics, is not likely to be popular in these days. This moral was that education and a desire for knowledge are *per se* dangerous and suspicious things, and constitute proper evidence of guilty premeditation. Had Troppmann not known how to read, it could not have been recited as bearing seriously against him that he had read some books and romances not likely to have an improving influence. Had he not developed a strong taste for chemistry, it could not have been peremptorily urged that he knew how to make prussic acid, and had therefore poisoned Kinck the father. In view of his confession, his ability to make the acid might have been shown. But the books which he had read were less fitting evidence. In either case the emphatic dwelling upon these facts in the *acte*, which was properly only the indictment or bill, was inexcusable, at least according to our notions.

The *acte* having been read, Monsieur le Président entered upon his peculiar duty. This functionary has the task of cross-examining, — it might as well be said at once, the task of badgering and bullying the accused, with the view of driving him into confession, admissions, or self-contradiction. As he is by no manner of means a judge, so the French are honest enough to refrain from bestowing upon him that honorable title. They call him, in unprofessional nomenclature, " the President."

This personage now bade Troppmann rise, repeated to him his name, age, birth, and other statistical matters, and then proceeded as follows: " Your family was in troubled circumstances. Your father's affairs were in a very bad way. Your father had, for a long time, been vexed by incessant lawsuits. You yourself were a clever fellow and a very skilful mechanic. You were your mother's spoiled child. Yes, as ill luck would have it, you were the object of her especial affection. Where you were concerned, she was so weak that she always let you have your own way, and under all circumstances she took your part. Till what age did you stay with her?"

Having obtained an answer to this sudden question, M. le Président returns to his portrait-painting: "From youth your character appears to have been exceptional in a young man. You were secretive and taciturn, thoughtful, and you had no intimates. Already the violence of your temper was excessive. Your sole ambition was to acquire riches by any possible means. I find evidence of all this in the information. One day, as we hear, you quarrelled with your brother Edmond; you struck him in the forehead with a hammer, and, as the blood spurted from the wound, he cried: 'Thou art another Cain.'" The prisoner eagerly denied that there was any foundation for this story. M. le Président: "We have not summoned your brother. We felt that to do so would be too cruel. But he has spoken of you in these terms: 'My brother is a dog that bites, but barks not.'" Prisoner: "My brother never uttered such a word!"

After adding a few insignificant touches to his portrait, the president laid on one that was masterly: "Well, at Roubaix no one ever noticed in you, though you were then not twenty years old, any of those irregular habits which are usually found in young men of that age. You came in regularly at eleven o'clock every night. But still you talked constantly of your craving for riches. A girl, Sophie Mayer, whom you had for a mistress, has said so." A pregnant sentence! The presiding officer at this judicial sitting throws in the face of the prisoner the heinous charge of regular habits. But, quite *à la mode Française*, he shows his idea that a young man may be so exemplary as to become an object of suspicion, and may yet at the same time be keeping a mistress, and all at the unripe age of less than twenty years.

M. le Président continues: " When you came home to Cernay you found your parents in a destitute condition. Thereupon you devised this abominable plan for the immolation of the Kinck family."

. . . .

The president, as at one time and another he elicits from the prisoner statements contradictory of some one of the various inconsistent confessions previously made by him, is wont bluntly to say to him: " You lied, then, Troppmann, when you said so?" He uses the French verb *mentir*, which, unless we mistake, is no less insulting and offensive a word than our own " to lie : " " *vous mentiez alors, Troppmann, quand,*" &c., &c.

Though Troppmann adhered steadily to his assertion that he had accomplices who were the chief criminals, yet he obstinately refused to give up their names or to furnish any clew for their detection. M. le Président, of course, felt himself much aggrieved at this, and bound by the duties of his position to prove, if possible, that the entire story of accomplices was a fabrication. Nor did he spare any efforts to do so. The obstinacy of the prisoner in clinging to the assertion was peculiarly irritating to him and incited him to unusual exertion. Frequently he gave the prisoner the lie direct upon this point. At one time he exclaimed: "*Eh bien!* I tell you it was you, and you alone, who assassinated Jean Kinck in order to rob his family. It is all an utter fable about these persons whom you say that you accidentally happened upon in the midst of the villanous crime of highway robbery, and who joined with you to slay Kinck."

The prisoner stated that he obtained from Kinck the money to pay for certain articles which he had purchased. M. le Président broke in with: "Yes! You spent your victim's money! You displayed an ingenuity which, without extravagance, I can describe as hellish!"

. . . .

M. le Président: "So then, you assumed the name of Jean Kinck, whom you had poisoned and robbed?" Prisoner: "I killed and robbed him no more than the others. Had I sought to do what you charge me with, I need only have poisoned the whole family and not have attempted a thing so impossible, even so stupid as that." M. le Président: "There was on your part a wonderful forecast and skill in execution, which prove you to be by no means so destitute of intelligence as you would like to make out."

This persistency of the prisoner on the point of accomplices was fast driving the president beyond the power of self-control. From time to time he burst out with exclamations of disgust and disbelief, delivered with an emphasis of gesticulation which could not be photographed in the reports, but which is left to be imagined: " Miraculous circumstance!" he cried; "this extraordinary accomplice, after having committed the crime almost without assistance, leaves you to enjoy all the plunder! Come, these accomplices display such unwonted and marvellous traits that it is impossible for any one to believe in their existence."

Coming to the consideration of the entrapping by Troppmann of his victims, his meeting them in Paris, and the snares which he laid for them, M. le Président dwelt upon the drive to the Pantin field, narrated with horror the *sang-froid* with which the murderer had chatted with his victims, and told how, when arrived at the spot, he had first taken out the mother and two children, and had left the other three for a few minutes in the carriage. " We know what the other children did while they waited in the carriage. They showed their joy at again meeting their father. Yet alas for the poor little creatures! Long ago had their father been slain! Arrived at the spot, you struck the mother with a knife. She did not utter a sound. You dealt her thirty-five or thirty-six savage blows. You attacked her like a wild beast (*vous vous acharniez sur elle*). The knife was the only weapon used in killing her. Alfred also you struck in the same manner, in the neck, with the knife only. His body bore some traces of his having made resistance; that is to say, he was wounded in his hands, as if he had instinctively raised them. As for Hortense, you smashed in her head with a blow of the pickaxe. Is all this true?" Prisoner: "No, it is not true. It was the accomplices who gave the blows. . . . As for this pickaxe, I should like to see any man who could wield it so easily as you declare that I did." M. le Président: "Oh, the physicians have examined you; though you may not be a powerful man, yet there is no doubt but that you are remarkably quick and agile. Moreover, as a mechanic, you have gained an undeniable correctness of eye and precision." Well might the poor wretch despair when even his skill in his trade appeared thus to turn against him.

At last, M. le Président, having hunted his quarry to and fro over the whole ground of the anticipated testimony for the prosecution, let him drop. The witnesses were introduced. Cheerfully encouraged by the court to go as far as they could against the accused, they tried to acquit themselves satisfactorily. A butcher boy first took the stand, and told how he had made the discovery of the place of burial of the mother and children by the feeling and appearance of the sods. The president turned to Troppmann: "Troppmann, for one moment be sincere. Indulge in so much as an approach toward penitent feeling! though as yet you have by no means done so. It was you who slew Gustave?" Strange to say, this touching and persuasive appeal failed to elicit from the accused the desired confession. The trial was left to proceed in regular course.

Photographs of the corpses had been taken at the morgue, shortly after their exhumation. These hideous pictures were now produced and shown to Troppmann. The president bade him look at them, for they were his victims, and he ought to recognize them in the plight in which he had placed them. He contemplated them without visible emotion other than was betrayed by a slight smile, and answered that he did recognize them.

The sister of the slaughtered woman was next introduced, clad in deep weeds. Not that she had a syllable of testimony to give concerning the murder, but because the French mind required, for the picturesque strengthening of the lights and shades of the trial, a sketch of the domestic bliss in which the Kinck family had dwelt together. M. le Président gave her the cue by his question: " Was there not a rare degree of attachment in this household?" " Ah, yes!" sobbed the bereaved sister. She finished somewhat feebly; without the help of the president she would have failed utterly to play her allotted part. Her husband was next placed upon the stand for the same purpose, and, beneath his more vigorous handling, the colors were somewhat deepened. M. le Président opened the way by saying, " Your sister-in-law was a *profoundly* estimable woman, and an example to mothers!" to which the brother-in-law made an eloquent response. A neighbor was called to the same point. M. le Président: " You were a neighbor of Kinck. Tell us something about the family." Witness: " Jean Kinck was an extremely brave man and the best of husbands; his wife, likewise, was courageous, and a very good housekeeper." M. le Président: "They loved their children?" Witness: "They adored them." M. le Président: "And the children?" Witness: "They were models of filial affection. I knew them well; they were at my house from morning to night." The president did not stop to inquire why children so loving and so loved were wont to spend the whole day at a neighbor's house; but hastened to ask: "Kinck had a large property?" Witness: "Yes, he had a fortune earned by his own toil," &c., &c. All this matter of course had nothing whatsoever to do with the question of whether or not Troppmann had murdered the Kincks. But æsthetically such testimony was needed. The judicial drama would have been grossly incomplete without it.

Troppmann insisted upon it that he and Kinck had concocted together a scheme for making counterfeit money, expecting thereby to arrive quickly at great wealth. Beyond his reiterated statement, there was no testimony either disproving or corroborating the story. But it awoke great indignation in the mind of M. le Président, who once remarked to the accused: "Ah, this is your everlasting calumny against your victim. The jurors will not fail to appreciate it;" and again, to a witness who referred to it: "It is an odious libel on the part of the accused." Troppmann tried to prop the unsatisfactory credence which was extended to him in this particular, by deducing from the remarks of a witness that Kinck had assigned different and inconsistent causes for undertaking the journey upon which he was slain. M. le Président interrupted him: "For ever this same plan! After you have slain this ill-starred man, you slander his character." Troppmann: "I have no such plan." M. le Président: "You have brought to this hearing nothing but a string of calumnious falsehoods against your victim. In recalling such monstrous crimes, you have not a single tear, not a tone of feeling."

A female witness stated that she had sought to dissuade Madame Kinck from going to Paris in search of her husband, because her daughter was ill, and she herself was in a bad condition. M. le Président interrupted: "She was in a family way; that is not a bad condition!" whereupon the elegant audience of Parisian ladies and *quasi* ladies burst into loud laughter at his honor's little joke. There were other dashes of this species of wit to enliven the proceedings. A witness testified that he had been with Troppmann at a ball. M. le Président: "Were you alone with him?" Witness: "Oh, no, I had a woman with me, — you understand! I am not a married man." This sally was hailed by prolonged laughter, in which Troppmann, the young man of offensively regular habits, bore a hearty part.

The coachman who drove the family to the Pantin field, the scene of the massacre, was called. He was asked what they talked about on the way out, but said that he could not hear. "No matter," quoth the president, "there is no dispute about that. Troppman, while leading his wretched victims to the slaughter, had the hardihood to entertain them with talk about the beauties of the neighborhood. When Troppmann came back for the three children who were left in the carriage, what did he say?" Witness: "He said, 'come, my children, get out, we have decided to wait here.'" M. le Président: "You hear, Troppmann; there is no heart here, save only your own, that does not shudder with horror. You came to get these wretched little ones in order to slay them, and you call them 'my children!' It makes one's blood run cold. Answer me." Troppmann, upon whom the president's eloquence seems quite thrown away, coolly replied, "It is true."

A *gendarme* stated that Troppmann had spoken to him concerning Pantin and Roubaix. Troppmann positively denied it, and declared that it was a fabrication of the witness. M. le Président: "Then this witness, like all the rest of them, does not speak the truth?" Troppmann: "No." M. le Président, to the witness, ironically: "You see, witness, you also are a liar!"

A physician was called who had examined the bodies, and who was required to give a description of them. His effort to do so was extremely vivid and shocking. As he passed from one to another, he became more and more wrought up, and finally he began to sketch the whole scene, as it had established itself before the eyes of his imagination: "The little daughter, Marie Hortense, had a great gash from a knife, which laid open her abdomen so that her entrails gushed out. The knife was broken by the blow. Her skull was broken in. Her death agony must have been something absolutely terrible (*foudroyante*). But even all this did not satiate the murderer. He glutted himself (*il s'est acharné*) upon this wretched child, and mangled her with his pickaxe. Her ear was torn off; her eye was gouged out; her skull was shattered." Here the witness broke down beneath the influence of a horror which was shared by all his hearers, save only by Troppmann, who listened with perfect impassibility. The doctor recovered himself and went on, but we shall spare the reader the further recital. At the close, the Court propounded to him a "delicate question," which, however, it appears that he had already answered in the preliminary proceedings. This delicate question, certainly objectionable upon any other than the extraordinary hypothesis that this medical gentleman was judicially known to M. le Président to be an expert in murder by violence, was simply : "Do you believe that a single individual could have committed these six murders?" If the presiding functionary had felt a doubt about the propriety of the query, the doctor at least felt no modesty or hesitation in framing an answer, all-important as that answer must be to the prospects of the accused. "I need not even have recourse to suppositions in this matter. It is enough that I bethink me of the nature of the wounds. The knife was the only weapon used for despatching the first group, — a babe two years old, the mother struck suddenly, a child that scarcely defended itself. All this might have been accomplished by one man in four or five minutes. With the second group no knife was used, but they were strangled. To strangle two children is a short job." A terrible blow of the pickaxe did the work for the third." M. le Président: "You conclude, then, that the murderer was alone?" Witness: "That is my conclusion, and I am positive in it." Defendant: "I believe it is utterly impossible for a single man to have done all that; that is *my* opinion, and I am sure there are many here who agree to it."

Another physician was called. He was of opinion that "the very nature of the wounds proved that they had all been committed by the same hand." This species of testimony seems to us to leave the experts in handwriting very far in the rear. Here is a doctor who can recognize a peculiar style in a blow, that tells him by whose hand it was dealt; and not only this, but where three persons have been stabbed, two strangled, and one struck by a pickaxe, this same skilled observer can still mysteriously see that all the deeds were the work of a single hand. "In the first group, the mother was struck from behind; the babe of two years old was unable to resist; only the little boy even attempted a defence. All three were slain with the knife. The knife breaks. The murderer strangles the rest. There were two distinct processes designed by the accused to accord with the age and power of resistance of his several victims. It is my absolute conviction that there was but one murderer. I will further say, that according to my notion, Troppmann was well able to have committed, by himself, all six murders." It is open to doubt whether even the rigid doctrines of the English criminal law could have bridled the picturesque fancy and lively tongues of these emotional Frenchmen.

But there was more testimony of the same sort still to come. One of the physicians was recalled and asked if he had examined the accused. Witness: "Yes; he is weak in appearance, but he has a very strong thumb. Besides, in his profession as a mechanic he has acquired great dexterity and precision of movement. I am sure that he could have strangled the two Kinck children, one with each hand, as easily as a Hercules." Troppmann: "The two! But the third! do you suppose he would have been such a fool as to wait for me?" Witness: "The third might have been struck first of all with the pickaxe, and it was as the other two turned to flee that they were caught and strangled." A "profound sensation" was remarked among the audience as this testimony closed.

The last day of the trial came, and the elegant and distinguished personages in the audience had increased to such a number that the newspaper reporters abandoned in despair the attempt to enumerate them. A small pamphlet entitled "*Etude medico-légale sur Troppmann,*" was hawked among the benches. Some read it and found that it was an argument to prove that he was the victim of monomania at the time of the commission of the murder. Others amused themselves by looking at the defendant, and asking him, with true French politeness, how he had slept the night before. He answered that he had "slept very well, — the sleep of innocence, you know."

The proceedings of this day are not of especial interest for our purposes. A little unimportant testimony was introduced, and then the counsel delivered their arguments. M. Lachaud appeared for Troppmann. He began in a manner which may appear somewhat singular. He feared that many persons might conceive that he had done something odious and disreputable in undertaking to act as counsel for the defendant. He wished to explain clearly to such cavillers that he had done only his duty as an advocate, only what the technical honor of his office as a counsellor bound him to do. The doctrine of professional ethics was sound enough, but such deprecation of popular blame for appearing for one's client is hardly the manner in which counsel in our country are apt to enter upon an earnest defence. But the learned gentleman quickly made up for a bad beginning, by going inexcusably far in a less correct exposition of his duties, and of his fulfilment of them. "I conjure you, then, to shut the doors of your consciences against prejudice. Have the courage and the patience to hear me. Listen to me and I will seek to lay bare THE TRUTH before you; yes, THE TRUTH, such as I understand it to be, not as the accused wishes or imagines it. You do not conceive that I am here to recall and to make good all that he has said, for that would be to degrade my profession to the level of the lowest trades. It is true that I am here to defend this man, but before becoming his counsel I must also be his judge. The conduct of his defence belongs, and belongs wholly and exclusively to me. I shall present it to you like a man of honor, who speaks only according to his conscience and his belief."

It was, to a certain extent, excusable for M. Lachaud to explain that he did not propose to uphold the veracity of his client in all his statements, for it was neither possible nor desirable that inconsistent assertions, the latest of which, by the avowal of that client himself, had been put forth for the express purpose of contradicting their predecessors. But what are we to think of this declaration, that the defendant's counsel has no aim but to discover the real truth of the matter in litigation; that he does not intend to present his client's case, but impartially to extract the kernel of veracity. No lawyer intends to lie in his argument; but he intends to *suggest* every thing which is favorable to his client and unfavorable to the adverse party, and to support all such suggestions by every honest consideration, and every item of evidence which can be brought to this service. Certainly he is no judicial seeker after abstract truth. He does not examine his client's cause judicially and satisfy himself of its justice before he enters into it as counsel. To throw into an argument the weight of personal character by an expression of private opinion, is with us considered, and rightly considered, very unbecoming. Certainly the prevalence of such a habit would prove terribly demoralizing among members of the bar. But how far does this fall short of the deliberate statement of the French advocate, that he is his client's judge, and that he is resolved to make his way to the absolute truth of the matter, and to drag it forth for the enlightenment of the jury.

The argument which followed this objectionable exordium, if we may judge from the newspaper reports, was as weak as might have been expected from the difficulties of the case, though the reporters spoke of it in terms of polite praise. If it was not the promised elucidation of unalloyed truth, it was almost equally useless to the prisoner. The judge asked Troppmann if he had any thing to say to the jurors before they went out. He answered that he had not. They retired to deliberate. He proposed to his guards to play a game of cards to while away the time till their return. They were out but a short time, however, not leaving much leisure for this recreation before bringing back a verdict of guilty, without extenuating circumstances. Again the Court offered Troppmann leave to speak in his own behalf. Again he smilingly declined to say any thing. The Court retired, deliberated for five minutes, returned, and pronounced sentence of death.

It ought, perhaps, to be taken into consideration in the criticism of this Troppmann trial, that the crime was so utterly heinous as to render it impossible even for stoical men to contemplate it with entire calmness. The merciful might make due allowance for the false confessions which might conceivably have been achieved by the *peine forte et dure* of the preliminary examinations. But after mercy had been exhausted in imagining doubts, which none could seriously entertain, it remained the conviction of all men that Troppmann was the guilty creature. Something of irrepressible indignation must perhaps be pardoned in any ordinary human being brought into loathsome contact with such a wretch, the witness of his unremorseful conduct, and of his false devices for escape. But such considerations can only feebly extenuate, and by no means excuse, the conduct of the functionary who should have remembered that he filled a judicial office, and should have respected his high duties, even at the cost of a severe self-control. An English or American judge could and would have done so; but the French president probably never so much as recognized the propriety of the effort.

II.

PRINCE PIERRE BONAPARTE.

The superficial aspect of the trial of Prince Pierre Bonaparte was vastly less offensive. In his crime there was nothing to create an equally deep horror. In his rank and connections there was much to propitiate at least decent treatment. Upon the whole, he received decent treatment. The *acte d'accusation* was tempered like the wind to the shorn lamb. Troppmann's prior life exhibited nothing worse than a taste for yellow-covered literature, for chemistry, and for riches, yet in the *acte* all these traits were so grouped and colored as to resemble evidence of guilt. Prince Pierre's prior career had been "*orageuse*" in the extreme. He had even slain many men before Victor Noir dropped beneath his pistol. There was in his stormy history ample material for an *acte* which should read like the memoirs of a corsair. But no such document was concocted. That which was really read in court was quite simple, not quite so naked and technical a recital of charges as our indictment, but a narrative not very rambling, nor gravely impertinent. The *gensdarmes* who had charge of Troppmann were directed to call him *Monsieur*, a courtesy not always extended to defendants under criminal charges. But this sole mark of respect which was paid to him fell far short of the delicate consideration which was continually manifested for the Prince. Witnesses and counsel were frequently reminded that the accused was choleric, and that he was not to be provoked by censorious language, or by injurious reflections. Troppmann was continually informed by the judge that he was the sole murderer of eight persons, and was told with great precision how and why he murdered each; but when the prosecuting counsel in the latter trial so far forgot himself as to speak to or of the Prince as guilty of the murder of Noir, before the jury had determined whether the death which he had avowedly inflicted upon the deceased was murder or manslaughter, the Court interfered, and rebuked the premature use of such language. Moreover, the tribunal before which the Prince was tried at Tours, was one of extraordinary dignity. The jurors were selected by lot from among old men holding respectable official positions. It was called "*La haute Cour de Justice,*" and, at least so far as its composition was concerned, it deserved this venerable title.

But the best efforts that could be made to preserve an appearance of external propriety, so exceptional and so contrary to the traditional habits of French Courts, met with very imperfect success. The judge, or president, practised a praiseworthy self-restraint, and made attempts, which however were crowned with but limited success, to restrain the violence of the advocates and of the witnesses. For advocates, witnesses, and defendant were alike furious, and occasionally broke away from all control to indulge in wild and extravagant bursts of hostility and rage. Apart from the more superficial attributes, there were, of course, the peculiar underlying principles which control the general conduct of criminal trials in France, and which were necessarily unalterable. The judge interrogated and examined Prince Pierre, not so roughly as he might have done, but still with reasonable thoroughness. He addressed him continually with questions and remarks while the witnesses were giving their testimony. The Prince threw in his comments when and where he chose. Often there were five-handed contests, in which president, defendant, witness, and counsel for prosecution and defence took active and vigorous parts, and bandied contradiction, abuse, and sometimes even defiance, with unrestrained and graceful freedom. The prisoner's past life was, of course, considered proper material for investigation, and for free use in evidence and argument. M. le Président refrained from meddling much with it. " Mention has been made," he said, " of several occurrences in your previous career ; but I do not wish to pay any particular attention to these. If they are mentioned hereafter in the course of the trial you will then explain them. Still I must recall one affair. In 1848 you were fined 200 francs for an act of violence committed upon one of your colleagues in the national representation." The Prince : " Yes, but it was because I had been outrageously insulted, as well as my comrade, the keeper of the seals, M. Odilon Barrot." The president then read the judgment which had been rendered in this matter. The Prince : " I declared at the tribune of the Chamber that this act was not intended by me to show any want of respect towards my colleagues. This explanation was satisfactory to the Chamber and to the president."

' M. Ulric de Fonvielle, the only eye-witness of the tragedy at Auteuil, was called. It will be remembered that he had gone to the Prince's house with Noir, and that their errand was to deliver a challenge. He expressed a desire to go far back in his history, and to tell a long story in order to introduce properly the tale of the fatal day. The Court refused to allow this, and obliged him to come at once to the narration of the event itself. M. le Président, apparently taking judicial notice of the code of the duel, asked how the two came to go directly to the house with the challenge instead of seeking to be put in communication with the seconds of the challenged man, contrary to the established usage of the duel. "Mon Dieu! M. le Président," exclaimed De Fonvielle, "Many a time have I been second in such affairs of honor, and I beg to say that they are always conducted in this manner!" "Once more," replied the unconvinced president, "I must say to you that you ought never to have gone in person to Auteuil." De Fonvielle: "I had no reason for not going there. I could not anticipate such a scene of violence on the part of the Prince, although I did know very well that we were going to encounter an assassin at Auteuil!" The Prince angrily interrupted: "Assassin! Ah, you are all of a piece, you fellows! You forget all that has happened from the affair of the Rue Saint Nicaise to that of the Orsini bombs. Assassin! it is you yourself that are an assassin!" M. le Président, taking this little passage quite calmly: "Witness, you ought to have taken a more temperate young man to Auteuil on such an errand." De Fonvielle: "Though he was young, he was very governable. He was going to be married in a few days." M. le Président: "You had a revolver with you; what was that for?" De Fonvielle: "Oh! Mon Dieu! It is my habit. Being a journalist I have to be out late at night. And I have known of gentlemen being knocked over the head and beaten by the emissaries of princes and dukes." M. le Président: "Still I must say that it was a very strange thing for you to go armed to the Prince's house, when you were going as a second." It is amusing to see the Court taking judicial cognizance of the duellists' code, laying down the sound rules, and getting into a warm dispute with one who seems to have been a professor *emeritus* in such learning.

Another journalist, who was at the Prince's house just after the affray, acknowledged that he also had a pistol. But he explained to the Court that it was only a defensive, not an offensive weapon; that it had been given him by his wife, and, as the Court must know, wives never give their husbands dangerous weapons. The Prince, excitedly: "Defensive arms are only cuirasses and helmets. I hope the high-jurors will be well able to appreciate what degree of belief is due to a comrade of De Fonvielle and Rochefort, those men who in spite of my imprisonment and consequent helplessness do not refrain from insulting me in 'La Marseillaise,' and have printed a gasconade about killing me after the trial is over."

After M. Fonvielle had given his testimony, divers witnesses were placed upon the stand in order to impeach his accuracy. He had sworn that the Prince had struck the only blow that was either struck or threatened. But some of these impeaching witnesses declared that when, fresh from the adventure, De Fonvielle had narrated the occurrence, he had either actually said that Noir had struck the Prince a good round blow, or had made gestures significant of such an occurrence. The president turned to him to inquire what he had to say to all this: "M. de Fonvielle, you have heard the witnesses. They give formal testimony." De Fonvielle: "So do I. I give formal testimony." M. le Président: "They have seen a gesture made by you in giving your account of the affair." De Fonvielle: "I deny it altogether. My narration is formally made. I am the only person who saw the occurrence. I have told it just as it was and I stick to my story."

M. Grousset was next called and asked whether he was related to the Prince. He answered: Lœtitia (the Prince's mother) had so many lovers that I cannot say but that I may be related to him." The Procureur-Général objected to such language. But apparently the Court did not think it worth while to administer any rebuke, and Grousset went on with his testimony.

The famous journalist Rochefort was next introduced. He testified that he also had a duel with the Prince in process of preparation, and that he had expected to have fought him on the day following that upon which this untoward murder took place. "I had mentioned my expectation to my friend Arago, who thereupon said to me: 'Take care! the Prince has an abominably bad reputation,'—I only repeat what was said to me,—'they do say that he is a terribly low scoundrel.'" M. le Président: "Really such language cannot be tolerated. The defendant is under the protection of justice and must not be insulted." Rochefort: "I can only say that the insult is none of my own concoction. I only repeat what was said to me."

The brother-in-law of Victor Noir said that Victor had on a pair of tight-fitting kid gloves which were unbroken after his death, and was sure that had Victor struck the Prince the gloves would have been split. Upon the basis of this circumstance the witness formed and frankly stated his conclusion, that " the Prince had lied." By this time the president seems to have given over his vain and fatiguing efforts to keep the witnesses for the prosecution in order, and the remark passed unrebuked.

M. Siebecher stated that De Fonvielle wore trousers which were cut " *according to the American pattern*, that is to say, were fitted with a pocket specially shaped to carry a revolver."

Two witnesses fell into a hot dispute about a remark attributed to De Fonvielle, to the effect that the Prince had been struck by Noir. Lechantre, a butcher, swore that he had stood close by and had heard the words. Flautsch, a witness on the other side, swore that he also had been by and that the words had not been used. Lechantre stood up manfully for the truth of his assertion. Flautsch answered back that the words could not have been spoken without his hearing them. Lechantre retorted that if that was the case then obviously Flautsch was not on the spot. Lechantre appears to have had the stoutest tongue and to have come off best. Perhaps a Frenchman might fairly maintain that though such a controversy may be grossly undignified, yet it may enable the jury to weigh the respective claims to veracity of the disputants more correctly than our system does.

The counsel for the prosecution now offered some singular testimony. A Garibaldian was called, and M. Laurier, the advocate, stated that he had summoned this witness in order to answer an impeachment of character which, it was true, had not yet been made, but which must be anticipated as sure to come. The testimony thus introduced concerned the moral character of the witness, De Fonvielle, while in the Garibaldian militia. An English or American lawyer will smile with mingled incredulity and contempt when he hears that it was admitted without objection, and Kergomard, the witness, went on uninterrupted to say that De Fonvielle had been a very exemplary man; that since this trouble had arisen a story had got abroad of his having been engaged in a scandalous affair; but that a scrupulous investigation into his conduct had utterly disproved the libel; that the real sinner had been quite another person, known to the witness, but whom he did not wish at present to name; though he might be willing to do so if the charge should be pushed against De Fonvielle: that further, the real offender was well known throughout the regiment, for he had been placed under arrest and expelled from the army.

This vein of promiscuous anecdotage or scandal-mongering was found too agreeable to be checked. The court and the jury alike enjoyed and encouraged it. The next tale was in the Prince's favor, and was told by a Viscount. The narrator had been challenged by the Prince; they had actually met for the purpose of fighting. But the Prince had in the interval been convinced of his error. Wherefore he at once frankly walked up to his antagonist, held out his hand, made his reconciliation, and thereafter turned all his energy to the punishment of the false tale-bearers. The witness pointed the moral of his story with the remark that this incident might serve to give the jurors some notion of the Prince's loyal and generous nature.

Another witness told how cool and brave the Prince was in battle and danger, and how calmly he had seen him turn in the midst of foes to single out and shoot an assailant who had used insulting language to him. In testifying to his military prowess one witness had used the phrase that he had "an eagle-glance, — a natural eagle-glance." Apparently there must have been some mock-heroic air on the part of the witness, for the words, though foolish, would not otherwise have excited so much merriment. M. Laurier jeered at them and made the speaker appear in a ridiculous light. The Prince cried out warmly, "Will M. le Président allow me to say that this brave officer has been shot through the chest at my side, and that if his rhetoric is not so fine as M. Laurier's, he has vastly more courage than belongs to M. Laurier's faction!" M. Laurier: "The Court has bidden me, though needlessly, to keep myself cool. On our side it will be admitted that we have done so perfectly, throughout the trial. But

I am subjected to an unmeasured assault from the accused." The Prince: "You sneered in repeating the testimony of a brave officer." De Fonvielle, springing up from a distant seat among the audience and extremely excited: "You have simply assassinated Victor Noir." It was afterwards asserted by many, upon oath, that he added the dangerous words, "*à mort! à mort!* kill him! kill him!" A great uproar was raised at once. De Fonvielle, still more excited, continued to cry out, "You have assassinated him!—like a coward!" The tumult increased. The audience sprang upon the benches. The women gave way to terror. It seemed that there would be a hand to hand fight between the opposing partisans. M. de Fonvielle was almost torn in pieces by the *gensdarmes*, some of whom tried to thrust him into a seat, and others to drag him from the hall. The defendant was taken out. It was only by degrees, and after the *gensdarmes* had removed De Fonvielle, that order was restored and the proceedings were continued. An episode in the trial the next morning was the hearing upon this conduct of De Fonvielle. He was sentenced to ten days' imprisonment.

From this interlude the Court returned to the conduct of the trial, that is to say, to a farrago of all sorts of extraneous matters. The president read the proceedings relative to a caning inflicted once upon a time by the witness Rochefort upon a printer, for which the offender had been punished by law. He also stated that Victor Noir was with

Rochefort when the chastisement was inflicted. Next he read the proceedings concerning an insult given and a blow threatened by Noir to a soldier. Laurier: "But no prosecution grew out of this." M. le Président: "The truth is explained in a letter from the Procureur-Impérial of Bordeaux. The magistrate of the town declined to follow up the complaint, because he had good proof that Victor Noir was at the time very drunk and did not know what he was about. But the magistrate took Noir into his private room and gave him a severe lecture."

The evidence was at last declared to be all in, though the story-telling might have been continued till the Arabian Nights had been rivalled. The counsel for the prosecution then began his speech. He had not made much progress in it before he touched upon the past life of the Prince. He began to tell stories of previous affrays and murders done by this same violent hand. He told of a violent blow dealt to an aged man in the Assemblée; of another assault; of a condemnation to death pronounced against the Prince for having slain an officer of the Pope's *gensdarmes* and wounded several of the soldiery, in an affair which appeared to have grown out of still another murder previously committed by the Prince; of the expulsion of the Prince by the British government from the Ionian Isles. "So," he said, "you see that when Pierre Bonaparte was Victor Noir's age he had already three murders upon his conscience. Yet, Prince though he always remembers himself to be, many who have written of his life have called him an adventurer!" The Prince broke in, "You see, M. le Président, there is a conspiracy to drive me beyond the bounds of self-control!" But the President only reminded him that the turn of his own counsel was coming, and that he ought to disappoint the schemes of his adversaries by maintaining the self-restraint which they sought to disturb.

So the counsel continued to say what they pleased. M. Laurier drew a picture of Noir as the most amiable of men, "as gentle, faithful, and affectionate as a Newfoundland dog," — such was his unique simile. "But on the other side," he said, "we have Pierre Bonaparte; wherever he has gone you find his path marked in tracks of blood. He has been a murderer in America, at New York; in Albania. In Africa he has broken the rules of military discipline. In Paris he has assailed an old man." All this passed unchallenged. It was only when once more, toward the close of his speech, the advocate again spoke of the defendant as the murderer of Noir, that the president interrupted him and bid him not use such language before it had been authorized by the verdict of the jury.

The accused said only a few words in his own favor at the close of the arguments of counsel. The jury retired and brought in a verdict of acquittal. It was understood that it was by a majority of one only; for a majority was sufficient; unanimity was not required. We have no comments to make upon the political aspects of the trial.

These descriptions of two famous trials are intended, as the reader must have seen, not so much to present an abstract of evidence from which the guilt or innocence of the accused can be determined, as to give a tolerably correct idea of the temper and of some of the rules prevailing in French criminal practice. But bad as the trial itself seems to those accustomed to the English practice, the worst part of the system is found at an earlier stage. So soon as the accused is arrested he is shut up in a solitary cell; his sole visitors are his gaoler and the *juge d'instruction*. This latter functionary is free to visit him at any time, by day or night, and to cross-interrogate, torment, and harass him without measure, for the purpose of extorting confession in full, or such admissions and statements as may aid in securing conviction. At the same time the witnesses are separately examined and their testimony is not communicated to the accused, so that he can have no light from this quarter to aid him in framing his answers. The moral effect of this process, when brought to bear by an experienced and heartless official, upon a terrified or dull-witted prisoner, is easily to be imagined. Utterly false results must be, and are known often to have been, obtained. The trial itself, ludicrous, uncouth, and often unjust, as it seems to us, is yet by no means grossly unfair, at least provided the accused be reasonably clever. The president is too often not impartial, still less judicial, in conducting it. Neither is the counsel for the defence allowed to cross-examine the witnesses. He can only state to the president what inquiries he wishes to have made, and the president then puts them in such shape as he sees fit. Still it is a sort of free fight; the prisoner can not only tell his story in answering the president's interrogatories, but he is left free, in practice at least, to interrupt the witnesses with contradictions or explanations; and, before the jury goes out, he may address them in his own behalf. The counsel for the defendant is partially shackled, and furthermore the odds against the defendant are usually increased by the wonted hostile proclivity of the president. Still the defendant has a chance, if he be able, to fight his own battle, and that is a privilege which many an accused man would value beyond all others, and which it is utterly impossible for him to enjoy even distantly under our laws and regulations.

The French system, with divers modifications, but with the preservation of its substantial principles, prevails over the continent of Europe. In France efforts are now making, or were making prior to the interruption of the war, to introduce certain reforms, intended to effect an approximation towards the English mode of procedure. M. Prévost-Paradol was an urgent advocate for changes of this nature; and not long since M. Ollivier, in his report to the Emperor, sketched an outline for a new scheme. It is not intended to adopt the English system altogether, but only portions of it; thus making, as it were, an amalgam. If this shall prove possible, it will probably also be wise. For, though the French system is so grossly harsh towards the accused, who must after all often not be the criminal, that it seems abhorrent to us, yet, upon the other hand, our own system is so grossly unjust toward society that the French are certainly not wrong in rejecting it as only half fulfilling the acknowledged ends of criminal justice. The extreme length to which fear of conviction can go in deterring from the commission of crime, must be reached under the French system. The famous answer that so discomposed Choate could never have been given in France: "Oh," the accused said, "never mind: let us kill him, and if we are caught when we get home, Choate will get us off." Choate, in the fetters of the French code, would have been only a Prometheus bound. The extreme length to which society can safely go in allowing criminals, whom all the world knows to be criminals, to escape by the aid of technical rules, is reached, and perhaps is exceeded, in English law. It is the custom with us to take it for granted that our system is as nearly perfect as can be, and the pending or recent efforts of the French to borrow from it have been triumphantly pointed at as proof of that fact. But this evidence does not go quite to the desired length. It proves only that the French think their system can be improved by an admixture from our own. But if they thought ours, as it stands in its entirety, to be the best conceivable or practicable system, they would adopt the whole instead of laboriously borrowing a part. We are at the end of a long article, and cannot plunge into a discussion. Yet perhaps we may venture to suggest, as a topic for reflection, whether the French are not right in thinking that our criminal law is very far from perfect, that it could be made much more just to society without being really unjust to the criminal, and that this demoralizing plan of giving a man whom all the world knows to be guilty, not only every natural but also many artificial avenues for escape, is an error as needless as it is dangerous.

Already it has been found necessary in England to approach, though only by a single and a short step, towards the French system. The recent Habitual Criminals' Act, 1869, throws upon those members of the law-breaking community, whose previous record of convictions and misconduct brings them within this description, something beyond even the ordinary burden of proof, — the burden of averting suspicion. They are placed under the surveillance of the police, and, if found without visible means of honest support, or otherwise in suspicious circumstances, they may be apprehended, taken before a magistrate, and in default of satisfactory explanations, committed to gaol. The passage of this act was the result of a stern public necessity. Just as it was in theory, logical in law, and practicable as it has since appeared to be in execution, it was yet moved in Parliament with much timidity and reluctance, and was supported by arguments which, sound as they were, seemed to be weighed down by the profusion of explanation and apology. The strong common sense and thorough knowledge of its advocates seemed to quail before the supposed force of a venerable but antiquated hostile prejudice. Their fears were needless, however, for the people at large welcomed the act which all could see to be intrinsically reasonable, and which all felt to be practically necessary. Regarded as matter of principle, it was a grave and important innovation upon the established and time-honored fundamental doctrine of English criminal law. But it was an innovation for which the minds of Englishmen had become prepared by an advance in a sound knowledge of real justice, and by observation of the social facts surrounding them.

THE TRIAL OF MRS. WHARTON.

It may be a subject of doubt whether a criminal trial, resulting in an acquittal, can be justly regarded as a *cause célèbre*. The *dénouement* is, perhaps, inadequate to sustain this dignity. There is a certain sense of bathos when the elaborate prosecution ends in a verdict of "Not Guilty." The default of a tragic end is an æsthetic failure. In this respect only does the trial of Mrs. Wharton fall short of attaining the highest distinction.

Whenever there is a prosecution upon a charge of sufficient magnitude to interest the people at large, there are usually two trials going on collaterally. The one is conducted in the court-room, and is decisive concerning the life or liberty of the accused; the other is conducted at the bar of public opinion, and has to do only with the more shadowy matters of reputation and good name. Not unfrequently the two proceedings have very different results. In the court-room a vast mass of testimony is never heard, which nevertheless the public greedily listen to, and make the basis of an ultimate, irreversible verdict. We have no desire to asperse the established law of evidence in criminal causes, which is doubtless capable of being defended in the most logical manner; yet though public curiosity is often fed with monstrous falsehoods and outrageous hypotheses, which could never penetrate the legal sanctuary, on the other hand it has the benefit of much information which would be indispensable to any intelligent man who might wish to arrive at an honest, though perhaps a strictly illegal, belief in the premises. Never was this double process better illustrated than in the case of Mrs. Wharton; and it is worth while, therefore, briefly to tell the tale which passed from mouth to mouth among her fellow-citizens, and which created such a suspicion and prejudice against her as could not be wholly allayed by the verdict of acquittal, rendered by jurors who were bound to give the prisoner the benefit of their possible doubts.

General W. S. Ketchum, of the United States army, the deceased, was a man somewhat past the prime of life, but still apparently sound, strong, and vigorous, perhaps to an unusual degree. Mrs. Wharton was the widow of an army officer, and was upwards of fifty years of age. The two were intimate friends. They had had some money dealings together, in which the general, who had led a frugal life and amassed a modest competence, had lent sums, amounting to $2600, to Mrs. Wharton. She was generally believed to be poor, though boasting of property and expectations which the defence did not even seek to establish upon the trial, though the evidence would have been pertinent and important. She was preparing to go to

Europe, though here again it was currently reported that she was short of funds and unable to procure her letter of credit.

On the 23d of June, 1871, General Ketchum came from Washington to her house, to bid her farewell, and also, as he stated, to collect the amount of her indebtedness to him, viz., the $2600. He was in good health when he left Washington, in good health when he came within her doors. Soon afterward he was taken ill. He rallied, but again relapsed, and on the 28th of June he died. In this series of events there was nothing more extraordinary or suspicious than is often attendant upon the somewhat sudden decease of apparently robust men. But other matters aroused suspicion. The disease of which the general died was, at least in the opinion of his physician and attendants, singular and obscure. Whilst he lay dying another gentleman was also strangely and unaccountably prostrated by a sudden and violent illness in the same house, and narrowly escaped death. This was a Mr. Van Ness, a near friend of Mrs. Wharton, a clerk in the banking-house of Alexander Brown & Sons, of Baltimore, and said to have an accurate cognizance of the accounts of the suspected lady. No symptoms of the maladies which attacked these two victims displayed themselves in any other persons among the household or guests of Mrs. Wharton.

After the death of General Ketchum, his waistcoat was missing, and the note of Mrs. Wharton for $2600 has never yet been found. Mrs. Wharton asserted that she had paid the sum to the general, received the note from him, and, in accordance with his advice, had destroyed it, there being no witness present during the transaction. So far from being indebted to him, she alleged the fact to be precisely the contrary, and she claimed from his estate four thousand dollars in United States bonds, which she asserted that he had in his custody for her. She had no voucher for the money or the bonds. No memorandum or entry in any of his books showed that the general had received either the money or the bonds. Yet he was a man of unquestionable integrity and of the most unusual scrupulosity in the matter of accounts, going in this respect to the verge of pettiness, so that he was even said to have entered in his books the gift of one cent to a beggar. In all this the public might have found ground for suspicion, but not an iota of proof.

What was, or seemed to be, proof, however, was furnished by the following facts: that tartar-emetic, a substance containing an antimonial poison, was said to have been found, by chemical analysis, in the sediment of a tumbler of milk-punch prepared by the accused for the general; that twenty grains of the same poison were said to have been discovered, by a post-mortem examination, in the stomach of the deceased; that fifteen grains of the same poison were reported to have been found in a tumbler of beer offered by the accused to Mr. Van Ness, but not drunk by him; that Mrs. Wharton bought and was possessed of tartar-emetic during the week when these singular illnesses occurred in her household.

In these few facts people easily found the motive and the means of the crime, and the belief readily became rife that Mrs. Wharton had poisoned General Ketchum, and had tried to poison Mr. Van Ness. She meanwhile was continuing her preparations to leave for Europe, and was to have departed from Baltimore on the evening of Monday, the 10th of July, 1871. But upon that day a warrant for her arrest was issued, and the deputy-sheriff, armed therewith, visited her and prevented her departure. It will be seen that in the trial which followed much of what has been already narrated was necessarily ruled out as incompetent evidence. Upon the trial for the murder of one man, the evidence of an attempt to kill another man, though at nearly the same time and by the same means, was inadmissible. The corroboration to be found by the public in the story of Van Ness was totally wanting to the jury in the prosecution for the poisoning of General Ketchum. The question of the poisoning was tried as if no other person had been ill in Mrs. Wharton's house. Otherwise the facts, substantially as above narrated, were alleged and in great part were established by the attorneys for the prosecution. By reason of the eagerness of public opinion in Baltimore, it was feared that a fair trial could not be had there, and it was judged expedient to change the venue to Annapolis, whither the prisoner was brought on the 2d of December, 1871.

We come now to the history of the trial itself. Mrs. Chubb, a lady employed in the treasury department, and who came from Washington with General Ketchum to the house of Mrs. Wharton, testified that he was ill and vomiting on Saturday night, after his arrival; that he continued too ill to go to church with her on Sunday, though he went out on that day; that he was ill again Sunday night, and on Monday morning complained of a sick stomach and giddiness. Sunday evening he and Mrs. Chubb each drank a glass of lemonade prepared for them by Mrs. Wharton. Monday afternoon he still complained of nausea, and sent for a physician. Mrs. Wharton came from his chamber soon after the physician had prescribed for him, and said she had accidentally broken his bottle of medicine. Mrs. Chubb went to the druggist's to replace it, and at the same time, by Mrs. Wharton's request, bought for her a parcel of tartar-emetic, to be used, as she said, for her breast. Later in the evening Mrs. Chubb saw Mrs. Wharton shake this package over a mustard plaster, throw the paper into the slop jar, and apply the plaster to her breast.

On Tuesday the general felt better; he had dismissed and paid his physician, and expected to go to Washington in the eleven o'clock noon train. But in the afternoon he was vomiting again, and by Wednesday morning he was still at Mrs. Wharton's, and sicker than ever. The doctor prescribed for him, administered a dose of medicine to him in the presence of Mrs. Hutton, a sister of Mrs. Van Ness, and gave directions as to administering a second dose at one o'clock. Before half-past twelve o'clock Mrs. Wharton appeared, saying that she had dropped the medicine, and was anxious to give it to him. She manifested no small degree of haste to give it before the appointed hour, stating as her reason that the previous dose had appeared to do him so much good. The dose prepared by Mrs. Wharton was larger than that prepared by the doctor, but she said she had added more water, and insisted somewhat strenuously upon giving it. The cup and spoon in which the medicine was mixed and administered were retained by Mrs. Wharton. About fifteen minutes after the dose was taken by the general, he manifested symptoms of pain and uneasiness. He clutched at the back of his neck, at his throat, chest, and stomach with such violence as to abrade the skin upon the throat. He made convulsive efforts to raise his body, from his head to his legs. When he was moved, his legs appeared to be stiffened. He uttered inarticulate cries, and had a series of convulsions. A witness, who saw the dose prepared by Mrs. Wharton, stated that it was unlike in color to a dose which was made up in the court-room according to the doctor's prescription. The dose given was of a grayish or leaden color, and turbid, which was not the case with the yellow jasmine, or the mixture of yellow jasmine and chloral, which were the doses ordered by the physician. But this witness further stated, that in view of the suspicion in this case, he had added tartar-emetic to the yellow jasmine, and the product had not resembled the dose prepared by Mrs. Wharton.

Evidence was adduced showing that some milk-punch was prepared on Wednesday by Mrs. Van Ness, that she gave a glass of it to her husband, and it was admitted that he experienced no ill effects from it. The remainder was poured into a tumbler and left in a little refrigerator. This tumbler, which was destined to play a significant part in the trial, next appears in the hands of Mrs. Van Ness. The sister of Mr. Van Ness entered the dining-room and found Mrs. Van Ness standing with a wineglass in her hand, into which she had poured the fluid from the tumbler; the tumbler stood upon the table with a peculiar-looking deposit in it. The conversation between the two ladies was of course incompetent, but Mrs. Loney, the sister, understood that there was a suspicion of something wrong about the sediment in the tumbler. She tasted it, and found that it left a metallic taste in her mouth and a grating sensation in her throat. The ladies took pains to conceal their suspicions from Mr. Van Ness, and Mrs. Loney put the tumbler in her pocket, first tying her handkerchief tightly over it to protect the moist contents, and kept it until it could be safely handed by her to Dr. Chew. Mrs. Helen Van Ness, the wife of the sick man, testified that she made this punch in the presence of Mrs. Wharton, Mrs. Hutton, and Mrs. Van Ness; that Mrs. Wharton suggested making a double quantity; that she did so, — took half to her husband and left the other half in the refrigerator; that some time afterward, coming back to the refrigerator and pouring the punch from the tumbler into a wineglass, she noticed a sediment in the tumbler. She tasted this sediment, and it tasted like a brass pin. She made a fresh punch for her husband. She drank some of the milk after making the punch, without ill effect. The ingredients of the punch were milk, whiskey, and one lump of sugar.

The testimony concerning the indebtedness between the parties, given by the sons of General Ketchum, showed that soon after his decease Mrs. Wharton called upon the son and demanded the $4000 in United States bonds. She then stated that she had paid the $2600 in two instalments, to wit: On July 1, 1870, she had paid $130 interest, and $1300 on account of principal; on January 17, 1871, she had paid $65 interest and the balance of the principal; but she had destroyed the note at the general's advice; had taken no receipts for principal or interest; had paid in cash, received from rents and other sources, and had mentioned to no one that she had so much money in her possession. The son afterward produced his father's pocket diary, and read from it to Mrs. Wharton the following memoranda: "Interest on E. G. W.'s note, 17 January, 1870, $130." "Interest, ditto, 17 July, 1870, $130." "January 25, 1871, interest from E. G. W., $130." Mrs. Wharton interrupted, saying she had paid that money, and that the last entry of interest should have been $65. She also said that she had noticed of late that General Ketchum's memory had sometimes appeared blurred. In the course of the testimony of this witness, it was made to appear that General

Ketchum had said that he was going to Baltimore to collect the note which Mrs. Wharton owed him. It was carefully explained to the jury that this evidence was not entitled to the weight of evidence of the fact of indebtedness. The books of General Ketchum were offered in evidence by the state's attorneys, but were not admitted. The son testified that he examined his father's clothing in Mrs. Wharton's presence, looking for the note, but that he did not find it. At the time of this investigation the missing waistcoat had again reappeared. The son stated that it was his father's habit to carry his valuable papers pinned up in his inside waistcoat pocket.

Marshal Frey testified that when he first called upon Mrs. Wharton he intimated suspicions against other persons, suggesting some servant in the house as the probable criminal. She strenuously repudiated the idea; said that she had bought tartaremetic while the sickness was in the house, but had made the purchase herself; had put the parcel into her portemonnaie, and had only taken it thence at the time of applying it to her breast, so that no one else could by any possibility have got at it. Twice Mrs. Wharton offered money to the marshal, on the ground that he must be at a great deal of trouble in her case, for which she wished him to receive compensation. She was emphatic in refusing to suspect any of her servants of the alleged poisoning.

On Tuesday Mrs. Wharton bought some brown stout, and prepared some sangaree for General

Ketchum. She took it to him, and on her return said that he drank it. She was not particularly observed while mixing it.

Mr. Van Ness was called by the attorneys for the state. They proposed to prove by him that he lay sick at Mrs. Wharton's house all the while that General Ketchum also lay sick there; that his symptoms were the same with those of the general; that tartar-emetic was found in the vessels in use in Mr. Van Ness's sickness; and that Mrs. Wharton knew of the deadly character of the medicine. After listening to an elaborate argument by counsel, the Court ruled out this testimony on the obvious ground that it belonged to another case. The state then proposed " to introduce evidence to show that whilst the deceased lay languishing in the prisoner's house, certain articles of food and drink, to wit, milk and beef tea, were taken to the house; that when taken there these articles were free from all noxious or poisonous qualities; that after they had been a short time in the house, and in places where the prisoner had knowledge of them, these same articles were found to be impregnated with poison, as far as that fact can be shown by the taste of the poison, and the symptoms of those affected by it; and further, that the symptoms of those who had occasion to make use of the milk and beef tea, indicated the presence of tartar-emetic." Had they been allowed to show these facts, the counsel for the prosecution would have had little difficulty in bringing substantially within the knowledge of the jury the main circumstances concerning the illness of Van

Ness, and the poison found in articles appropriated for his use. The strength of their case would have been increased by all the corroborative suspicion inevitably to be derived from this source. The decision of the Court was of grave moment for the defence, and fortunately for them it accorded with the spirit of the ruling already made. The chief judge said that the Court would admit a part only of the proffered testimony. It was competent to show that tartar-emetic had been found in Mrs. Wharton's house, and it could be proved by persons who tasted it, but not by the symptoms of those affected by it. If any person could aver that he had tasted poison in Mrs. Wharton's house, that would be admissible in order to prove the existence of that article at that place. The fangs having been thus drawn from the proposition, the prosecuting officers refrained from advancing the mutilated residue; and all prospect of bringing in any of the facts connected with Mr. Van Ness was evidently at an end.

The counsel for the prisoner made an effort to show that if the deceased died from the administration of any noxious drug, it was from laudanum, with which he secretly dosed himself. This attempt was, however, lamentably weak and ill-sustained; nor indeed did it accord with the testimony even of those medical experts who were called by the defence. It seemed that Mrs. Wharton had already, before the charge had been preferred against her, sought in a quiet way to convey this opinion to a few persons nearly interested in the general. The conversations in which she had made remarks to this general effect were repeated in the course of the testimony. The defence tried to show that the general had been in the habit of dosing himself, but they made poor work of it. The only substantial evidence was that of Susan Jacobs, a colored cook in the employ of Mrs. Wharton. How this witness may have appeared upon the stand we are unable to say, but the impression which the printed narrative of her testimony conveys is by no means favorable to its perfect credibility. Her faithful zeal in behalf of her mistress, and her mistress's eager rejection in the first instance of the idea that the poisoning could have been done by her servants, are suggestive of the two sides of an equation. This servant stated that on Tuesday, in the early part of the day, she found General Ketchum in a kind of drowsy sleep. He bade her let him alone, and he would soon sleep it off and feel better; he further said that he did not think the doctor had dosed him enough, and he had taken a dose of his own medicine which he knew was sufficient. Later in the day the same servant — Mrs. Wharton and the general being present in the room — made up his bed, and in so doing, according to her statement, a little vial rolled from the bedding on to the floor. This she picked up, smelt laudanum in it; saw only a drop or two left in it, and gave it to Mrs. Wharton. The bottle was produced, and a Baltimore druggist, a member of a firm whose name appeared on the cork of the bottle, examined it. He said that if the vial had been purchased from him on June 24, it would not now have the incrustation which he saw upon it. It would require fully six months or a year for the substance to assume its present look and collect the present sediment.

Testimony was introduced by the defence as to the good character of Mrs. Wharton, but it was remarked that the majority of the witnesses came from some other place than Baltimore. The question put to one of the witnesses: "From your knowledge of Mrs. Wharton's general reputation as to the qualities of humanity, kindness, and amiability, as you have testified to, would you or would you not believe her capable of committing the crime of murder?" was objected to. A long argument ensued between counsel, and the Court ruled the question out. The testimony which was admitted was of a vague character, meaning little more than that she was a pleasant, amiable, kindly-seeming lady, about whom none of the witnesses remembered to have heard disagreeable gossip.

Dr. P. C. Williams, a physician who had been in practice for eighteen years in Baltimore, was called to attend General Ketchum on Monday, June 25th, in the afternoon. He described the symptoms which he observed, and the remedies which he applied, as follows: The patient was much nauseated, vomiting every few minutes; his pulse was weak and rapid. The first notion of the doctor was that the complaint was cholera-morbus. The prescription was two drops of creosote and a table-spoonful of lime-water, to be repeated every two hours until relief. The next morning, Tuesday, about ten o'clock, the doctor called again; found the general sleeping and roused him. He seemed better; professed his intention of returning to Washington that day, and paid the doctor for his services. Both were of opinion that no further dosing was necessary. The witness was next summoned again on Wednesday morning, about ten o'clock, and found the sick man lying on a sofa upon his right side, having his face to the back of the sofa. His head and face were very much congested; the face was red, of a shade suggesting a purple tinge. He made no reply when the doctor sought to rouse him by speaking to him and touching him, but the touch caused a slight convulsive tremor to pass over him from head to foot. When he was finally aroused and asked how he was, he said, "tolerably;" muttered replies to some other commonplace questions, and relapsed into the same condition already described. With the aid of Mr. Hutton, the doctor got the patient from the sofa to the bed, noticing as he did so that the arms and legs were stiff and rigid, so that it was necessary to slide his feet along the floor and lift them up on the bed. The prescription was for an application of ice to the head, and a dose of forty drops of the tincture of yellow jasmine, to be given every two hours in two table-spoonfuls of water. It was the second of these two doses which should have been given at one o'clock, and which, as has been already narrated,

Mrs. Wharton prepared and was so anxious to administer before that hour arrived. The doctor then left the room and was shown the laudanum bottle and heard the story of its discovery. With reference to this the physician testified that he told Mrs. Wharton that he was glad it had been found, since it explained the patient's condition, who, if he had taken nothing but laudanum, would recover. The doctor said he had seen many cases of opium poisoning, but that in this case he found no evidence of a dangerous amount of opium having been taken; the contraction of the pupils of the eyes which would have followed such a dose was not present; the breathing was not of the slow and laborious character to be expected in such a case, nor was there the customary muscular relaxation. The pulse, also, though feeble, was much too rapid. After a short absence the doctor returned to the sick-room. He found the sick man in a semi-comatose state; the pupils of the eye were of a natural size, but almost wholly insensible to light. The doctor prepared the first dose of the medicine, and found the general's teeth so clenched that it was matter of considerable difficulty to get the spoon into his mouth. Having sat for some few minutes by the bedside to watch the effects of the medicine, and seeing that it was evidently working well, the color and eye of the patient manifestly improving, the doctor left, giving directions for the second dose at one o'clock. But about one o'clock he was called again, and found the general was in convulsions. His first impression in the morning had been that the general had apoplexy; this was dissolved by the appearance of rigidity in the limbs; and next he feared paralysis. Now the idea of urinic poison suggested itself. He accordingly administered chloroform, and used the catheter; but upon testing the urine he found it perfectly healthy. The convulsions were peculiar, the patient seeking apparently to throw himself from side to side. The doctor noticed the abrasions on his throat, forehead, and stomach. Not wishing to allow chloroform to be administered by inexperienced persons, he prescribed thirty grains of chloral.

The doctor remarked to a Mr. Snowden, before his last visit to his patient, about two o'clock, that he feared the general had been poisoned. While his suspicions were thus aroused he had a conversation with Mr. Hutton, which, of course, he was not allowed to repeat. But the result was that he had an interview with Mrs. Loney, the lady in whose charge the suspected tumbler then was, and the tumbler was shown him. He tasted a particle of the sediment, and found it had a strong metallic taste and burnt his tongue. Thereafter he returned to General Ketchum's room with his doubt very much changed into conviction, and found the general growing rapidly worse. A few minutes after death occurred. The doctor immediately searched the dead man's clothing, but could find no waistcoat and no note signed by Mrs. Wharton.

At eleven o'clock the next morning Dr. Williams, assisted by Drs. Chew and Miles, made a post-mortem examination at the undertaker's. They examined the brain, liver, kidneys, and spleen, and found them all apparently healthy; though in the brain there were minute little red points, spoken of in the books as punctiform congestion; but there was no effusion of blood or serum, and the points might naturally follow a prolonged death-struggle. The bowels were opened, and no noteworthy appearance found, save occasional points of congestion. The heart and lungs were not now examined, but afterward, when the grand jury had found the indictment, the same physicians went to Washington, had the body exhumed, examined those organs, and found them sound and healthy. About two inches of the spinal column were examined and found healthy. A ligature was applied above and below the stomach, which was then taken carefully out, placed in a clean glass jar, and sent by the hands of Dr. Chew to Dr. Aikin.

With regard to the poisonous action of tartar-emetic, Dr. Williams testified that the symptoms were pain and constriction in the throat; a metallic taste in the mouth; pain and griping in the stomach; usually extreme relaxation up to a certain point, and then a stiffness or tetanic condition, especially about the neck, arms, and legs; a reddish-bluish livid appearance about the surface, resulting from the weakening force of the poison upon the heart, producing a passive congestion throughout the venous system; a stupor, more or less profound; an increase, rather than a diminution of urine; sometimes profuse vomiting, but sometimes none at all.

Dr. Samuel P. Chew, of Maryland University, summoned by the prosecution, enumerated substantially the same symptoms, adding that the pulse was generally depressed; that giddiness might be caused, but actual insensibility he had never known to follow even excessive doses of the poison. There was a striking similarity between some of the symptoms of poisoning by tartar-emetic and cholera-morbus. He regarded the case as a very obscure one, as to which he would give no fixed opinion, but from Dr. Williams's description of the case, and from what he had seen in the post-mortem examinations, he thought death did not supervene from natural causes.

Professor Miles, also of Maryland University, from the narration of the symptoms and from what he saw at the post-mortem examination, was of opinion that General Ketchum did not die from natural causes.

Dr. Chew did not think that those specific particles of tartar-emetic which were found in the stomach caused the death. The poison which produced this effect would have been found in other organs, the kidneys, liver, or alimentary canal; for tartar-emetic only becomes fatal after being absorbed into the system.

Dr. Miles also said that before the tartar-emetic could act to produce death it must be absorbed, and would thereafter be found by an analysis of the liver or kidneys. The information obtained from the post-mortem examination would not alone suffice to explain the death.

Dr. Donaldson said that the tartar-emetic must be absorbed and pass into the system in order to produce death. But the process of absorption was a very rapid one. Thereafter it would of course be in the blood or other organs rather than in the stomach. He thought the case, as described, a very obscure one, resembling in certain particulars divers known diseases, yet wanting some of the chief symptoms of each. The symptoms certainly corresponded substantially with those of poisoning by tartar-emetic, as given in the medical authorities. From the symptoms alone, or from the post-mortem examination alone, he would not have given an opinion as to the cause of death. He must base any opinion on the two together.

Dr. J. Harry Thompson had had some actual experience with patients who had been dosed with tartar-emetic. The symptoms he recited were very like those of General Ketchum. He did not think the general died from natural causes.

From the testimony of the various physicians in this case, it would appear that yellow jasmine was a somewhat unusual drug, though not by any means unknown in its operation, or dangerous in doses no greater than were taken by General Ketchum. It appeared to be a rather favorite recipe with Dr. Williams. Its action was to relax the nerves. The solution was prepared by macerating four ounces of the root in twelve ounces of diluted alcohol. The symptoms of an overdose would be a wide dilation of the pupils of the eyes, and a consequent impairing of the vision; a paralysis of the eyelids, so that the patient could not open his eyes: a profuse perspiration, caused by the relaxation; the breathing and the action of the heart natural in the earlier stages, but afterward becoming hurried and quick. None of these symptoms were noticed by Dr. Williams in the case of General Ketchum. On the contrary, the action of this medicine should have been to prevent convulsions. Eighty drops would not be an overdose; forty drops was the amount ordered for General Ketchum.

The stomach was delivered by Dr. Williams to Dr. Aikin, with the statement only that poison was suspected. Dr. Aikin, also of Maryland University, understood that he was desired, as a chemical expert, to examine the contents of the stomach, and report whether or not he found there any thing of a poisonous character. His first thought was of strychnine, then of arsenic. He failed to find indications of either of these. In searching for strychnine the doctor used in the first instance tartaric acid, and afterward bicarbonate of soda. The original matter, with the addition of these ingredients, was then separated into two parts, and one of these parts was used for the purpose of searching for arsenic. The result showed no arsenic, but aroused the suspicion of antimony, and the doctor had recourse to the other part to search for antimony. His description of his process was as follows: He added an excess of tartaric acid, filtered it, and examined the filtrate with sulphuretted hydrogen. This examination was made by passing through the material a stream of sulphuretted hydrogen gas, to ensure the action of which heat was applied to the vessel containing the material, and while the gas was passing through, the temperature was raised; it was then allowed to stand and cool for twenty-four hours; the operation was repeated a second time. The result was an abundant brownish red or reddish-brown precipitate. There seemed no necessity for destroying the organic matter, and the chemist did not use muriatic acid and chlorate of potash. The precipitate, when separated and dried, was dissolved in muriatic acid. Muriatic acid was not used in preparing the material. The hydrochloric solution, when dropped into water, gave a white precipitate; upon treating this with sulphide of ammonium it became orange-red. It was also soluble in a solution of tartaric acid. This, Dr. Aikin said, completed all that was necessary to satisfy him that he had been dealing with some preparation of antimony; he knew of nothing else which could yield such results. The only compound of antimony used in commerce, with which he was acquainted, was tartar-emetic, whence he inferred that tartar-emetic had found admission into the stomach. But the only certainty was that antimony was present.

Upon the question of amount he was not willing

to testify accurately; but by approximation he estimated it at about twenty grains. His theory was that ten grains of sulphide of antimony would imply not exactly but very nearly twenty grains of tartar-emetic.

The same physician investigated the character of the sediment in the tumbler. He tasted a fragment of white arsenic, a crystal of tartar-emetic, and the sediment, in order to compare the respective tastes. The resemblance was between the sediment and the tartar-emetic, and he accordingly sought for antimony. He used the same process as already described, with the addition of one more test; for where tartar-emetic is not mixed with organic matter, it has the property, when acted on by a drop of hydrochloric acid, of giving a white precipitate which is soluble in an excess of the acid. This experiment he made, and it sustained his suspicion. He then treated a portion of his material, as before, with sulphuretted hydrogen, and procured a precipitate of orange-red sulphide of antimony. This precipitate was collected, dried, and heated with boiling hydrochloric acid. The solution yielded a white precipitate, which was soluble in tartaric acid, and which, when treated with sulphide of ammonium, became orange-red. This again satisfied the professor of the presence of an antimonial poison, doubtless tartar-emetic.

With a view to determining the quantity present he weighed out one grain of the sediment from the tumbler. The dried sulphide of antimony obtained therefrom weighed four-tenths of a grain;

the amount of tartar-emetic present would, therefore, be about eight-tenths of a grain. In his judgment about fifteen grains of the compound were present, and therefore, to be within bounds, he should say there were at least ten grains of tartar emetic in the sediment.

After tartar-emetic has passed into the stomach it ceases to exist precisely as such. It becomes dissolved, and cannot be found in the shape of tartar-emetic. But the antimony, which is a constituent of the tartar-emetic, cannot be thus destroyed, and it is that which must be sought for, and which alone can be found. The professor further said that all the chemical agents used by him were pure. He had unfortunately neglected to preserve any of the results of his processes. When making the examination he had no knowledge as to what medicines had been administered to the deceased, and had not heard of the doses of yellow jasmine and chloral. All he did was to satisfy his own mind of the presence of antimony by the use of tests which he deemed sufficient and conclusive. Having thus made up his own mind, he took no further trouble, regarding his duty as performed. He might have obtained the metallic antimony, provided, of course, that it was really present. He had the necessary means, to wit, Marsh's test, at hand, but he did not use it, and did not seek or obtain the metal.

Professor William P. Tonry, an analytical chemist, was requested to examine the liver and kidneys, which were removed from the body after exhumation by Drs. Williams and Chew. He was requested to search only for antimony. It is but just to him to say that his examination was conducted with the most scrupulous care. He protected with sealing-wax, impressed with his private seal, both the room and the receptacles used by him, whenever he was obliged to leave them. A full description of the chemical processes resorted to by him would be lengthy, tedious, and useless. It suffices to say that he brought his examination to the same point to which Dr. Aikin had already conducted his processes in the examination of the contents of the stomach. The same tests which satisfied Dr. Aikin also satisfied him. He did not get the metal antimony, nor did he try to get it, except in so minute a quantity that it was impossible to say with absolute certainty that it was the metal. He was satisfied to stop short of this point, because the same reactions procured by Dr. Aikin were also procured by him, and were considered by him to be proof sufficiently positive of the presence of antimony.

The testimony of the chemical experts summoned by the defence was so voluminous that it is impossible to do more than state its general character and bearing. Their first, and perhaps their best, witness in this portion of their case was Professor R. S. McCulloch. In his opinion the tests used by Professor Aikin to establish the presence of antimony were insufficient, and the analysis made by that gentleman was radically defective. The results obtained by him established a probability, but by no means a certainty, of the presence of antimony. A large number of other tests could and ought to have been tried. The metal antimony could have been easily obtained, and no test which failed to produce it could be regarded as at all conclusive. Even after the metal was obtained it should be carefully tested. Especially in examining the contents of a stomach in a search for metal, where organic, animal, or vegetable matter is present, it has been held for many years that the reactions described by Professor Aikin may prove entirely fallacious. This witness further stated that he had made experiments with reference to this particular case. He had tried the reaction of sulphuretted hydrogen on chloral, and had procured from it a precipitate which might readily be mistaken by its color for one of sulphide of antimony. A similar experiment with yellow jasmine likewise gave a precipitate easily to be mistaken by its color for a precipitate of antimony. The same result was produced with a combination of chloral and yellow jasmine. The witness then prepared a mixture containing the white of an egg, whey from milk that had soured, beef tea, a drop of lactic acid, a drop of hydrochloric acid, and a little pepsin. The object was to reproduce as nearly as possible the probable contents of General Ketchum's stomach. Trying the same experiments with this material, a red precipitate was obtained, closely resembling that which antimony would give. Another important experiment tried by this gentleman gave the following results: The red precipitate thrown down by sulphuretted hydrogen in tincture of yellow jasmine, dissolves in hydrochloric acid, as that from antimony does. When this solution in hydrochloric acid is dropped into water, it also gives a white cloud, just as the same preparation of antimony does. That white cloud is soluble in an excess of hydrochloric acid, as is also the same preparation of antimony. This solution, with sulphuretted hydrogen, again gives a precipitate which might be mistaken for one of antimony. The resemblance of the reactions, the witness said, was truly remarkable, and had very much astonished him. The same fault which was to be found with Dr. Aikin's examination of the contents of the stomach was also to be found with his analysis of the sediment in the tumbler. Here also he should have found the metal antimony.

Professor McCulloch was likewise dissatisfied with the sufficiency of Professor Tonry's tests. Professor Tonry had also fallen into the fatal error of not producing and proving the metal. Supposing certain spots, found by him and mentioned in his testimony, to have been antimony, they were so minute that their presence might have arisen from impurities in some of the chemical agents used. For example, hydrochloric acid is liable to contain impurities; it often contains arsenic, and may contain antimony. The tests of the purity of his sulphuric acid, which Professor Tonry stated that he had applied, were insufficient to establish the fact of that purity.

Some of the precipitates produced by the experiments of this witness in the court-room, in illustration of his statements, were kept until the following day, when they were found to have become dark, and no longer to resemble antimonial precipitates. The witness ascribed this change to some alteration in the organic substance. Upon cross-examination the witness acknowledged that, if a tablespoonful of brandy or whiskey, white sugar, and fresh milk had been the only contents of the tumbler, he did not think that the sediment could have yielded the results obtained by Professor Aikin. These results certainly created the basis for a suspicion that antimony was present.

Dr. Genth, an analytical chemist from Philadelphia, gave substantially the same testimony as that of Professor McCulloch. Dr. John J. Reese, a toxicologist, followed, with corroborating testimony. Professor Harry C. White, of Annapolis, made the like statements, and had tried similar experiments with jasmine and chloral, obtaining like results.

Dr. Reese thought, from the symptoms, that General Ketchum might have died from cerebro-spinal meningitis. Dr. Edward Warren was of opinion that he did die of cerebro-spinal meningitis. He based his opinion on the symptoms, and found no cause for changing it in the revelations of the analyses. This witness had seen two cases of antimonial poisoning. He expressed a decided opinion that General Ketchum's death was not due to this cause. Going through the several days, and showing reasons why he could not have died from this poison if administered on Monday or Tuesday, because all the symptoms of such poisoning were absent on those days; he concluded by saying that the deceased could not have been poisoned by a dose of tartar-emetic swallowed on Wednesday; for when he was lying in a semi-unconscious condition, and the physician's hand was merely placed upon him, a shiver passed over his frame, demonstrating the existence at that time of cutaneous hyperæsthesia, a symptom never observed in any case of antimonial poisoning, but a characteristic phenomenon in cases of meningial fever. The additional circumstances, that he tried to get out of bed, slapped the shoulder of an attendant, and applied his hands at will to various portions of his body, thus showing the existence of normal contractile power in such of the voluntary muscles as were not rigid or convulsed, and the ability to employ it at discretion, form another stable link in the claim of proof, which associates the morbid condition then developed with the operation of a natural cause, and a wide hiatus in the connection which is sought to be established between it and the action of this or any other poisonous agent.

It was also testified that opisthotonos and pleurosthotonos, signifying respectively a muscular bending of the body backwards and sideways, were noticeable in General Ketchum's case, and were symptoms of cerebro-spinal meningitis.

Professor Harvey L. Byrd testified that, from the recital of symptoms, he thought General Ketchum died from natural causes. He was unable to identify the disease, though many of the symptoms resembled cerebro-spinal meningitis.

Dr. Goolrick, judging from the symptoms and post-mortem examination, thought the general might have died from natural causes.

Dr. John R. McClurg had no hesitation in saying that he thought the death resulted from natural causes, and he inclined to attribute it to cerebro-spinal meningitis. This gentleman had seen many cases of poisoning by tartar-emetic, though none of them had been fatal. But this witness said that if antimony had been found in the stomach, liver, and kidneys of the deceased, he should be unable to say whether death resulted from antimonial poisoning, cerebro-spinal meningitis, or apoplexy from congestion.

Dr. Wm. H. Baltzell was inclined to attribute the death to cerebro-spinal meningitis. The operation of tartar-emetic would have been too rapid to accord with the progress of General Ketchum's disease.

Dr. Josiah Simpson attributed the death to natural causes.

Dr. Abram Claude, from the symptoms and the post-mortem examination, thought the death due to natural causes, and thought the disease resembled cerebro-spinal meningitis.

In rebuttal, the state attorney called some half-dozen medical gentlemen, who expressed the opinion that General Ketchum died from non-natural causes, and, of course, not from cerebro-spinal meningitis. Dr. Aikin was also recalled. He had made further experiments, and wished to state the result of them. After an eager argument by counsel, the Court admitted his testimony. It was not extremely valuable. He simply said he had tried the experiments described by Professor McCulloch, and had obtained results of a different character from those described by that gentleman. He was sure he had been correct in his previous statements, and that the mistakes concerning the character of the precipitates, regarded by the experts for the defence as very easily to be made, were not such as any intelligent man could make, and of course had not been made by himself.

Cerebro-spinal meningitis appeared by the testimony of nearly all the witnesses to be a rather obscure disease. In older days it was known as "Death by the grace of God," but in time this name gave place to the present learned appellation. It varied a good deal in its symptoms in different cases. An effort was made to show that it was epidemic in Baltimore about the time of General Ketchum's death. Though in this attempt the defence was only partially successful, yet they showed that it was at least a disease of not unfrequent occurrence in that city.

Many of the physicians summoned by the defence were of opinion that cerebro-spinal meningitis in its fulminant form, as they were pleased to call it,— signifying by this alarming adjective only the qualities of violence and rapidity in the development and progress of the disease,— would leave behind no lesion of any of the organs which would be discoverable in a post-mortem examination. Thus they explained away the inferences drawn from the soundness of all the vital parts of the general's body. Whereas some of them testified that poisoning by antimony should have left traces upon some of the organs.

Throughout the trial the newspaper reporters, after the fashion of their tribe, kept their lynx-eyed watch upon the prisoner, and duly described, for the benefit of the public, every movement, every expression, so far as they could penetrate the concealment of her veil, and every article of dress; even commenting on the fit of her kid gloves. By their account, which may be trusted as accurate, she exhibited the most rigid and unvarying self-control. She sat inscrutable and impenetrable from the beginning of the long trial on Dec. 4, 1871, to its close on Jan. 24, 1872. When all others were moved she alone was immovable. When others grew excited at some significant piece of evidence, she remained passive. None of the varying phases of the criminal process, now tending in her favor and now against her, stirred any apparent emotion. It would be cruel to judge of a person's guilt or innocence by such signs as these. No one of us knows how an unfounded charge and a trial for life and fame might affect his character and bearing. It might strike one to a statue. But it was impossible not to reflect that in this wonderful unbroken composure of Mrs. Wharton, there was the token of that mental force and power, which, could conscience once be mastered, would have enabled her to contemplate with equanimity and to perform without flinching, crimes even so atrocious as those which she was accused of, and for which she could undergo so impassively her dubious trial.

The jury brought in a verdict of "not guilty." Yet the result of the trial, if the prisoner were really innocent, must have been far from satisfactory to her. It was obvious that the verdict, known to the Scotch criminal law, "*not proven*," would have more accurately expressed the result of the proceedings. Mrs. Wharton's counsel had not established her innocence. Indeed, they made no very strenuous effort to do so. They were content to emancipate their client from the clutches of the law. Suspicion was not silenced. None of the facts which induced suspicion were encountered and overthrown. In respect of the money transactions, neither side absolutely proved any thing, but the prosecution established a strong case, and the defence presented an eminently weak one. The defence did not even attempt to account for the absence of General Ketchum's waistcoat immediately after his death, and its subsequent reappearance. They did not undertake to show any cause why Mrs. Wharton should have applied tartaremetic to her breast. They weakened the probabilities of their case extremely in the minds of all intelligent men by the futile effort to show that General Ketchum had dosed himself with laudanum. Mrs. Wharton's reputation would have stood better with the world at large this day if her counsel had not shown that they felt obliged to grasp at so absurd an hypothesis in order to save her.

She probably was acquitted because the testimony of the chemical and medical experts, especially the former, called by the government, was so unsatisfactory. It was not enough, and it ought not to have been enough, that Dr. Aikin and Dr. Tonry had satisfied their own minds by producing a very high degree of probability. Their failure was a warning to experts in all future time to rest content with no amount of investigation which leaves any known test untried. Had they gone on with their analysis and actually produced the metal antimony from the contents of the stomach, liver, and kidneys of General Ketchum, Mrs. Wharton might at this time have been under sentence of death. It is impossible not to speculate on the probability that the extension of the search by further tests might have had this result. It is impossible to be blind to the effects upon the trial of such a result had it been obtained. It must be supposed that Mrs. Wharton owed her escape to the fact that the chemical experts called by her counsel, men of eminence and respectability, were not satisfied beyond the possibility of a reasonable doubt that antimony had been found in the vital organs of General Ketchum. If the government did not establish this, they did not establish their case. Then the medical experts were able to say that the deceased apparently died from some natural cause, probably from cerebro-spinal meningitis.

They could not say he died from the administration of poison, when no poison had been proved to be present in his system. They, or at least most of them, considered the symptoms and the absence of any proof, satisfactory to their minds, of the presence of poison, and they were obliged to attribute death to that known disease whose symptoms, obscure and variable at best, most closely resembled the developments of the general's illness. What their expression of opinion might have been had they been satisfied that a deadly poison was lurking in vital organs in the body, it is impossible to say.

It was thought by the members of the legal profession that much valuable light upon the subject of expert testimony might be obtained from this case. We cannot see that it was peculiarly useful in this way. It was a simple instance of disagreement between experts upon a difficult and obscure subject, wherein the witnesses who were obliged to sustain the burden of proof did not succeed in doing so. Had Professors Tonry and Aikin gone a little further before desisting from their analyses, it is possible that there might have been very little disagreement of experts. Either these learned gentlemen would have been satisfied, by the failure of some sure test, of the non-existence of antimony in the material furnished to them for examination, or they would have proved its existence so absolutely that no intelligent chemist or physician could have doubted it. Either alternative would probably have determined these criminal proceedings. The need for the very highest conceivable degree of thoroughness in his preparation to testify, both out of regard to the value of his testimony and to his own reputation, is the lesson which every expert witness may draw from the cause. But the lawyers have little to learn from it as to the intrinsic character or value of such evidence.

NOTE. — At the time of this trial another indictment was also pending against Mrs. Wharton, charging her with an attempt to kill Mr. Van Ness by administering poison to him. But some months later the counsel for the State entered a *nolle prosequi*, for what reasons it was never generally or distinctly known.

THE METEOR.

On the 23d January, 1866, the steamship "Meteor," lying at her wharf in New York, was seized by the United States Marshal, by virtue of a warrant filed by the United States District Attorney, in the District Court for the Southern District of New York. The libel charged that the "Meteor" had, within the jurisdiction of the Court, been furnished and fitted out, or attempted to be fitted out, by persons to the District Attorney unknown, with the knowledge and intent that she should be employed in the service of the government of Chili, to cruise and commit hostilities against the subjects and property of the government of Spain (with which power we were then at peace), contrary to the third section of the Act of Congress approved, April 20, 1818, commonly called the Neutrality Act.

On the 14th March following, Mr. Evarts, of counsel for the owners, moved to have the vessel appraised and released to them on bond, according to the custom in causes in admiralty on the instance side of the Court. He supported his motion on the ground that it was matter of ordinary right in such causes. He adduced the analogy in the practice under the Slave Trade Act, and the Piracy Act; and urged that a privilege never withheld from the nefarious traffickers in human beings ought not, certainly, to be refused to men of the well-known high standing and integrity of the owners of this vessel, constructed, as she had been, upon the most patriotic motives. The District Attorney, in reply, argued that the Neutrality Act was a complete whole in itself, which in some cases directly authorized bonding, and in others by a necessary implication withheld the privilege. He suggested that to bond the vessel was simply to set her free at once to depart upon her illegal cruise. He further insisted that even if the Court had power to bond the ship, it was, at least, a matter of judicial discretion; and as a consideration, which in this view would be "fatal to the motion," he read and "made part of his argument" certain letters from the state department, embodying "instructions" to himself. Probably no error can be committed in construing the contents of these letters as the District Attorney himself construed them; that is to say, as imperative exhortations to use all the machinery of the law for the purpose of securing the forfeiture of this vessel. In the same connection, he argued strenuously, as a fact which "ought to have some bearing on the question now before the Court," that an application had been made to the state department to release the vessel, and had been refused. This matter and the "instructions" of the letter were dwelt upon at length and emphatically; and thus, at this early stage in the proceedings, the government counsel, with a faint deprecation, took the ground, which they afterward deliberately and distinctly assumed, that the whole matter was an affair of state, rather than a question of law, and that the judge was, for the purposes of this cause, not so much a judicial magistrate as a political subaltern.

Mr. Evarts replied. He said that the Court had no precautionary power which could be exerted to prevent any further offence by the vessel; that such power, in an ample degree, was lodged with the executive. That the bonding was matter of obligation, not of discretion; but, if it should be held matter of discretion, he stated facts which he thought should induce the Court to grant his motion. In reference to the application stated to have been made to the state department, he explained that it was only an application for the entire discontinuance of the suit and absolute release of the vessel, grounded on the belief of the owners that the government, "in plain view of the rights and purposes of the owners, could not seriously intend to make it a matter of judicial inquiry;" that the request was properly preferred to the executive, within whose province lay the duty of deliberation and the power of control as to whether the suit should go on or be discontinued; that the owners had never "asked the government, by any intimation of its wishes, to affect the Court's direction and conduct of questions arising in the prosecution;" that if the prosecuting attorneys insisted upon having the Secretary of State and the President "heard on questions touching the due administration of justice, except by argument and in methods for which the law provides," then they "introduced an impropriety into the administration of justice," not justified by the Secretary's letter, and which the "judiciary of the United States would not submit to tolerate for a single moment."

On the twenty-third of March the opinion of the Court was rendered, refusing the motion. The position taken was, that the statute itself was conclusive to the effect that "the vessel, while held under seizure by process in favor of the United States for the violation of that statute, *cannot* be discharged on bail by order of a judge of the United States under the authority of the common rules and practice of this Court." . . . That the "clear purport and intent" of the statute was that "the vessel [should] herself be detained, so that the forfeiture, which is the penalty, &c., may be enforced against her specifically in case of condemnation." The Court thus decided that it *had not the power* to bond the vessel at this time when she had in her favor the legal presumption of innocence. Soon afterward the trial upon the merits was had, and the Court pronounced a decree of condemnation. Thereupon the vessel became tainted with guilt, and the necessity of enforcing the forfeiture "*against her specifically*" seemed then to be in a fair way to be executed. But just at this juncture the judge reversed his former decision, and the decree of condemnation was promptly followed by an order that the "Meteor" should be appraised and bonded, if her owners so wished. It was accordingly done, and she was released. No opinion was delivered, either at the time or afterward; no reasons or explanation were vouchsafed for this astonishing contradictory action. The record simply remains thus: On the twenty-third of March the Court had no legal power to bond the vessel which was then presumably innocent; on the twentieth of July, it bonded her after she had been adjudged guilty. We of the outside world are remitted to our own cleverness to account for this strange series of incongruous acts. No new law, no new legislation, occurring between March 23 and July 20, aids us.

To take up again the thread of the history of the case, we will go back to the twenty-eighth of March. On this day the trial of the case began. The vessel was then still in the custody of the United States Marshal. The substance of the evidence adduced by the government was briefly as follows: The "Meteor" was a swift sea-going steamship; she was built by a number of public-spirited citizens, with the intention of offering her to the United States Government for the purpose of pursuing and destroying the "Alabama;" to this end she was capable of carrying a moderate armament; but her chief merit lay in her speed, to which every other consideration had been made subordinate. Before she was finished, the need for such vessels had ceased. She had since been used by government as a transport ship for troops, and afterward had been employed as a freighting vessel, in the merchant service, between home ports. Originally two Parrott guns had been placed on board her, which had been subsequently removed; and, beyond this, she had received no warlike equipment whatsoever. She had on board 750 tons of coal, being about twelve tons per day for the shortest voyage to Panama, and provisions for six months, a portion of which were marked "reserved stores." She was for sale for several months. There was war between Spain and Chili, pending which a certain accredited agent of Chili, in New York, wished to buy stanch sea-going steamers; the "Meteor," among others, attracted his attention (though through no act of her owners), and suited his purpose. Three "adventurers," of that nondescript hand-to-mouth occupation which furnishes a mysterious livelihood to so many inhabitants of large cities, sought to get a handsome commission by bringing about a sale of the "Meteor" to this Chilian agent. One of these men was an army and navy claim agent, interested in petroleum and mining stocks; the other sometimes "speculated in oil stocks," and had been a "bounty broker." For want of ready money, their efforts ended only in egregious failure, as they themselves very freely acknowledged. The owners, the Messrs. Forbes, were ready and willing to sell the vessel to this Chilian agent; but she was to be sold and delivered in precisely the condition in which she was then lying at the wharf, for the full price in cash down. This money could not be thus raised. The whole plan, for this reason, fell through, and the negotiations conclusively ceased. The vessel, with the coal and provisions before named, was cleared or about to clear for Panama, when she was seized under the libel. The informer was one of the three disappointed adventurers. The evidence was explicit to the effect that in the negotiations with the Messrs. Forbes, nothing was for a moment contemplated, save an outright sale of the vessel as she lay, for cash down in full. It was further explicit and consistent, to the effect that the negotiations concerning the sale were understood by all parties to have been finally and totally abandoned, without having accomplished any thing, a long time before the seizure. The only connection between the three middle-men, or "runners," as they were called on the trial, and the owners of the vessel, consisted in two or three visits of inquiry made by the middle-men, to a shipbroker, who communicated the offers made to him for the ship to the New York agent of the owners, and who received authority from him to sell her upon the terms above stated.

To breathe into these historical facts, in themselves apparently innocent, a guilty life, the District Attorney and his associate counsel relied upon testimony which they were permitted to introduce contrary to the strict rules of law; because, as they frankly stated, unless this permission was accorded to them, they should be quite unable to make out their case. The evidence which was admitted through the door of this cogent necessity was as follows: One witness testified that a man who looked very like a stevedore, but who might, nevertheless, have been some other species of laborer, told him that the ship was going to Chili. The same witness was allowed to add that "*stevedores were apt to know*" the destination of vessels. One Conkling, the man who had stated himself to be an "oil speculator" and "bounty broker," was even permitted to state that one man had said to another man, that "*he believed*" the arrangement for the sale of the vessel had been completed by a third individual. It was further shown, that when the vessel was seized, with her steam up, Captain R. B. Forbes was on board; that he said he was sorry to lose his trip down the Narrows; called for his carpet bag, received from the errand boy a small black hand-bag, and went ashore; that afterward, as he was crossing on the ferry-boat, he encountered a seafaring man. This man was placed on the stand, and stated substantially, that when he met Mr. Forbes, he "wanted to talk;" that he had himself been actively urging some of the third parties to put him in command of the ship, if they should succeed in buying her, and that he was disappointed at the non-success of his demands. In other words, this "captain" was an American citizen, who had been disappointed in the laudable design of becoming a Chilian privateersman. In a loud tone the "captain" said to Mr. Forbes, that he thought the "Meteor" was going to Chili; Mr. Forbes said she was bound or cleared for Panama; the other responded, that if she had gone to Chili, he had supposed that he should have gone in command of her. The folly of this speech, which, however harmless for others, might have been damaging to the speaker, was rebuked by Mr. Forbes, with the admonition that the captain had better not make such remarks in so high a tone. Further, it was stated that Captain Kemble, in command of the "Meteor" when she was seized, and previously, had been heard to say that if she was sold, he should take her out to Panama and there deliver her over to a "fighting captain." Besides this, the tale of the fiasco of the three disappointed adventurers was narrated in full. In the course of the narration, hearsay testimony was introduced by wholesale, when the very witnesses who could have given it at first-hand were sitting in the court-room. Neither was any link established between this story, which was a thing of the past, that had found its death and burial in empty words and nothing more, and the subsequent condition and history of the vessel. On this ground, the defendants' counsel took exception to the admission of that part even, which was not hearsay; objecting that it related wholly to a separate, distinct, and completed transaction, having no bearing upon or connection with any fact that could be proved, or had been offered, or attempted to be proved, against the vessel under the libel.

Upon this evidence the government rested its case. Mr. Evarts then rose and stated that it was not his intention to introduce any testimony, inasmuch as he was fully satisfied with that given by the witnesses called by the government. We do not propose to dwell upon the arguments at any great length. The ground assumed by the government counsel was double: they urged that, under the law as it stood, the facts warranted a decree of forfeiture. The strongest point which they made in this branch of their argument ought, perhaps, to be briefly suggested, for it was so subtle and ingenious, though withal so weighty and pregnant, that it might escape the attention of the reader, and fail to meet that consideration which it deserves, and which Judge Betts awarded to it. As oaks from acorns grow, so this theory in all its completeness sprouted from the little piratical-hued carpet-bag of contents unknown, or at least unproved. It was suggested that this bag contained the muniments of title of the ship; that Mr. Forbes was going with her outside of Sandy Hook; that there he was going to make formal delivery of her, with all the legal documents, to certain agents of the Chilian Government, who were to turn up from somewhere and be outside Sandy Hook; that then Mr. Forbes would return, and from some source not known, or at least not named by the government, an armament would be put on board the vessel; that she would then hoist the Chilian flag and begin her career of destruction. The whole story had the incontrovertible force of being a physical possibility. If true, it would certainly have plunged the owners deep into a guilty collusion with a belligerent purchaser. While the ingenuity of the conception challenges admiration, the question, whether or not this elaborate plan, with all its minute details, could be considered as reasonably proved to the conviction of an ordinary mind, by the appearance of the carpet bag, with its peculiar traits of size and color, is a matter on which each of our readers must make up his own mind. Whatever each one may decide, none will fail to draw the obvious moral against carrying small black hand-bags.

The second ground of the government counsel was purely diplomatic. In this branch of their argument they urged, that, if the law had been previously against them, yet the necessities of the nation now required that this law should be changed. Referring directly to the Anglo-rebel cruisers, they said that "public reasons" demanded "an interpretation" of the act, such as would make their case good. The leading case on the subject is that of the "Santissima Trinidad." The famous ruling of Judge Story, in his opinion delivered in that case, has always since been assumed by judges, lawyers, and publicists, as laying down what had before been supposed to be the sound law in such matters, and what could never, after the publication of that opinion, be doubted. This obstacle it was thought more advisable to crush beneath the juggernaut car of the state department, than to seek to undermine or circumvent by legal subtlety. The language used in discussing it was as follows:—

"If the Supreme Court maintains the broad dictum of the 'Santissima Trinidad,' after the late positive utterances of the department of state on that very point, there will be a conflict of opinion between the executive and judicial departments of the government, on a matter of international law, not at all creditable to the United States, which, since its peremptory demand on England for indemnity for losses occasioned by Anglo-rebel cruisers, cannot well change its attitude."

From this pregnant text issued a long, urgent, elaborate, politico-diplomatic argument, crammed full of the various phases of the "Alabama" discussion, and the present position and real or supposed needs and wishes of the Secretary concerning the same.

In speaking thus of these diplomatic features of this trial, we are advancing no novel views. Severe animadversions upon them have been reiterated again and again in other quarters. But we do not wish to be understood as undertaking to utter such animadversions. Neither do we wish to be understood as making any unreasonable imputation against the motives of either the counsel or the judge. There can be no question that they were actuated solely by a regard to what they supposed to be the public good. They conceived that they had the best authority for believing that the condemnation of the vessel would be a national advantage, that it could almost be called a national necessity, in view of the great aid which this condemnation would furnish in the negotiations with England. Their patriotic anxiety probably blinded their eyes to the obvious impropriety of introducing such arguments as those which we have narrated above, into legal proceedings which could properly deal only with the facts in evidence and the law bearing upon them. But it would seem to be shown by the history of this case that the question, whether or not it is justifiable to seek to change the established interpretation of a statute, and to overrule decisions, on the ground of public utility, is one of legal ethics on which honorable members of the profession are able to differ.

When the case came upon appeal before Mr. Justice Nelson, it was for the first time stripped of such foreign accompaniments, and was tried by that eminent judge upon the sole basis of its legal merits. It is at this stage that the case becomes very valuable to the profession. Judge Nelson is probably the first authority in the land upon questions of marine and commercial law. His rulings in this case were clear and decisive, and were given without any expression of doubt. It was a piece of great good fortune that the cause fell within his circuit.

The evidence which we have above commented upon as hearsay, and a part of which we have narrated, had been admitted by Judge Betts on the ground that it was the testimony of some of several co-conspirators against others. Judge Nelson disposed of it briefly in the statement, that "the principle that Judge Betts lays down is all right; but it does not cover the evidence that was allowed." Referring to the evidence of Conkling, above stated, he suggested, with a certain satirical humor, that "if you want to prove what a person has said, you cannot prove it by one man saying that another said he had said it."

On the matter of the sufficiency of the proof offered, Judge Nelson stated that he regarded it as absolutely indispensable for the government to show some outfit of a warlike nature; some furnishing which had prepared, or aided in preparing, the vessel for belligerent use. Coal and provisions, to the amount which she was shown to have had on board, he did not consider as constituting such a furnishing or fitting out as was contemplated by the use of these phrases in the act. If a simple sale was legal, he said, and that it was so was admitted by the government counsel, then fuel and provisions were a necessary concomitant to enable the vessel to leave the port. The naked right of sale, unless it included these indispensable privileges, was an utter nullity. It was *ex necessitate rei* that if she could be legally sold, she could be legally delivered, and if coal and provisions were requisite to make delivery possible, they could be legally placed on board her. The judge said, " These owners had a right to sell the ship, and the government must make out that she has been fitted and equipped for a military or naval expedition. . . . It must be an arming or fitting out for war purposes. . . . I do not see any evidence of that fitting out.' . . . I agree that if the agents of a hostile government should make a contract to build a ship for service in war, then suspicion would commence in the origin of the contract, and very slight circumstances might go to make out the purpose and the intent. But this vessel was built as a war vessel for our own government. [Being no longer required for that use] the owners had a right to sell her; and therefore, having that right, the mere fact that stores were put on board of her, that were necessary to convey and transfer her abroad to the parties to whom she was sold, forms no ground of suspicion at all; because the right to sell carried with it the right to put on board these provisions and stores. In order to make out that there was a hostile purpose intended, as an expedition against a country with which we were at peace, in violation of this law, you must show there was some fitting out, in the military or naval sense, with intent to commit this hostile act against a government with which we were at peace. . . . I do not see that you have made out any thing. No munitions of war on board, and no evidence that any were to be put on board. . . . There was nothing illegal in the furnishing of stores and supplies, — nothing in the act to forbid it You must connect this with the military or naval expedition, which you have not done. . . . *I cannot decide this case on conjecture or suspicion.* . . . I have been waiting for you to show any naval equipment, either in fact or intention." The judge proceeded to say, that, since the prosecuting counsel acknowledged that the vessel might be legally sold to the Chilian Government, he thought, with their evidence, " they might as well give up their case." The want of any proof even that there had been a sale, the judge stated, was one of his " troubles in the case." It was his own impression, from the evidence, that there had been no sale; an opinion which, later in the progress of the cause, he stated decisively. But at any rate, he said, it was a "transparent" fact that there was "no evidence of fitting out within the sense of the act."

Much extraneous matter having been thus cleared away, the judge came to the consideration of the important point of the intent. He said, "I think the only question in the case is one of intent." He considered that the vessel had undoubtedly been furnished with stores and fuel by the owners, with the intent to carry her to Panama, and there or elsewhere to sell her "to the Chilian Government, if they could, or anybody else; *knowing, if* they sold her to the Chilian Government, that she would be employed in the war between Chili and Spain." If this knowledge of the result to be expected upon the fulfilment of a contingency was a breach of the act, the government had made out its case. Judge Betts had declared that it was so. In other words, he had declared that a *knowledge of the use to which she would be put* was equivalent to, and identical with, *an intent that she should be put to that use*, as the phrase "*intent*" was to be construed in the act. That is to say: A sale is legal; but if the seller knows that the thing sold will be used for the purpose for which it is made, and to which it is adapted, the sale is illegal. The *reductio ad absurdum* is evident. It was well put by Judge Nelson: "I cannot imagine a sale to a government at war that can be upheld upon that doctrine; because, while as a mere commercial transaction the sale of a war vessel is conceded to be legal, yet if you connect with it that the vessel is *known to be used* by the belligerent against his enemy, then it is illegal. That I understand to be the doctrine of Judge Betts. I do not see, therefore, but that he virtually annuls the right to sell."

This point is, doubtless, the most important in the case. It is the point of divergence between the case of the "Meteor" and the cases of the rebel cruisers. It is the distinction which leaves the former innocent, and makes the latter guilty. The correctness of Judge Nelson's views seems obvious almost to the degree of an axiom. To say that a man may sell a knife, but that he shall not do so if he knows that it will be used to cut with, is an imbecility. Yet the legality of simple sales of war vessels to a belligerent is a privilege which Congress has insisted upon preserving to all American citizens. The history of the legislation on the subject is at once instructive and conclusive. The first Neutrality Act was passed in 1794. The case of *The Mermaid*, Bee, Adm. 69, and the case of *Moodie* v. *The Alfred*, 3 Dall. 307, which was probably the same case under a different name, decided that under this act a sale of a war vessel to a belligerent was legal. The further legislation in 1797, subsequent to both these decisions, made no change in the act in this respect.

In 1816, during the long war between Spain and her South American colonies, the Spanish minister to this country was anxious to have the sale of war vessels wholly prohibited. President Madison consulted Attorney-General Rush concerning the force of the existing law. In the opinion which Mr. Rush returned, he said:—

"I am aware of no law of the United States that can prevent a merchant or ship-owner selling his vessel and cargo (should the latter even consist of warlike stores) to a citizen or inhabitant of Buenos Ayres or of any part of South America, nor will it, do I think, make any difference whether such sale be made directly, in a port of the United States, with immediate transfer and possession thereupon; or under a contract entered into here with delivery to take place in a port of South America." (1 Opinions of Attorney-Generals, p. 190, July 27, 1816.)

Thereupon the President called the attention of Congress to the subject, that they might, if they thought expedient, legislate afresh in the matter. The debates which followed were long, warm, and animated. There can be no question but that the matter was thoroughly discussed, and the conclusion was the deliberate judgment of Congress upon the policy which it behooved the United States to maintain. The history of the debate is important. A bill was introduced, entitled, "A bill to prevent citizens of the United States from *selling* vessels of war to the citizens or subjects of any foreign power, and more effectually to prevent the arming and equipping vessels of war in the United States, intended to be used against nations in amity with the United States." The first section of this bill enacted, "That if any citizen of the United States shall, within the limits of the same, fit out, &c., any private ship or vessel of war, to sell the said vessel or contract for the sale of the said vessel, to be delivered in the United States or elsewhere, to the purchaser with intent or *previous knowledge*, that the said vessel shall or *will* be employed to cruise or commit hostilities, &c.; such person so offending shall, on conviction thereof, be adjudged guilty," &c. This bill emerged from the hands of our national legislators so wonderfully shorn of its important features as to be scarcely recognizable. Congress did not propose to take away, or in any degree to trammel, the full right, as it then existed, of dealing in vessels of war. So the phrases about " selling vessels of war" disappeared equally from the title and the body of the act which was finally passed in 1817. Neither did it escape the keenness of the statesmen who were engaged in the discussion, that this right of sale would be, as Judge Nelson said, a " mere nullity," if the "*previous knowledge*" of the seller that the vessel " *will* be employed" to cruise, &c., were allowed to remain a part of the law. They were resolved to retain the right of sale as a practical right. So when they struck out the words which forbade a sale, they also struck out these words about " knowledge" which would otherwise have been potent wholly to frustrate an essential object of the legislation. The codification in the following year, 1818, constituting the present law, left this matter unchanged.

In 1822, the whole subject being still freshly remembered, Judge Story delivered the famous opinion in the case of *The Santissima Trinidad*, 7 Wheat. 283. This sustained the legality of sales of war vessels to one of two belligerents, with the other of whom we were at peace. This has ever since been considered the leading case on the subject. Ten years later, in 1832, it was followed and affirmed in *United States* v. *Quincy*, 6 Pet. 445. Since then there has been no adjudication until this " Meteor" case arose.

In comparing the case of the " Meteor" with those of the Anglo-Confederate cruisers in connection with this principle, that a naked sale is legal if unaccompanied with circumstances showing an illegal intent, we must again seek for a clear exposition of the law, in a quotation from Judge Nelson. He said, " It is impossible to say that these owners [of the " Meteor"] took any interest in co-operating with or aiding the Chilian Government in war with Spain, or are connected with that idea." Also, we would refer again to his remark previously quoted, that if a vessel were built under a contract made with the agents of a belligerent government, then suspicion would rest upon her from the very inception. In these words of the learned Justice, the whole distinction lies as in a nutshell. Precisely those essential circumstances indicative of an illegal intent which were absent in the case of the " Meteor," were notoriously present in the cases of the rebel cruisers. Some, at least, of these were built by contract, with agents of the Confederate Government, and according to specifications furnished by these agents. The English builders, owners, and sellers of all of them, certainly "took an interest in co-operating with and aiding" the rebels "in war with" our government, and were "connected with that idea." It was by their aid, or rather by their sole action, that the armament and munitions of war, the stores and supplies, were placed on board, and the crews were enlisted and shipped. It is on these very facts that we base our demands.

The "Alexandra" was built in pursuance of a contract with, and according to directions furnished by, Confederate agents.

The "Alabama" sailed from Liverpool to a small port near Holyhead; there took in a part of her fighting crew, which had been enlisted in Liverpool; thence sailed to the Azores, and there took in her armament, which was brought to her by two vessels from Liverpool. The "Georgia," or "Japan," sailed from Greenock, to a small French port in the Channel, whither her armament, officers, and crew were brought out to her from Liverpool. The "Shenandoah," or "Sea King," sailed from London to Funchal, and there received her armament and crew from a steamer which brought them to her from Liverpool; sailing from that port at the same time that she sailed from London. It seems hardly necessary to point out the particulars in which the facts in all these cases transcend the facts in the "Meteor" case. In each one of them, the guilty intent is clear. In no one of them did the transaction bear any resemblance to a simple matter of outright bargain and sale. There was "co-operation," — active, essential, and important "co-operation" and "aid," — furnished by the sellers to the buyers, up to the very moment when these vessels were completed fighting ships of the Confederate "navy." The English parties *intended* to do, and actually did, more than merely dispose of ships for cash, after the fashion of the ordinary and innocent sale which was at one time projected by the owners of the "Meteor;" but which Judge Nelson found that they failed to accomplish. The English vendors lent active, efficient, and indispensable assistance to the rebel vendees, up to the very point of cruising in the vessels themselves. They only stopped short of becoming actual combatants. They were *partners in the proceeding* up to the very moment when the vessels began to burn and destroy. They took the active part in all the previous undertakings. They built the ships by contract and under directions; they made the arrangements for their departure, and for the simultaneous departure and safe transportation and sure transfer of the munitions and crew, upon receipt of which the vessels were at once in fighting trim. If these circumstances do not constitute proof of an "*intent*" such as that designated in the statute, then the United States has no case against England; and if they do not show an intent utterly different from an intent to sell outright for cash a wholly unequipped ship, long since built for most honorable purposes, and there to drop all connection with her, then there is no precision or intelligibility in language.

We have forborne to criticise the opinion rendered by Judge Betts, because we have not intended so much to criticise as to narrate. But it is a suggestive fact, that at the trial before Judge Nelson, the District Attorney put it in as his brief in the case, because, as he said, it "puts it in a better manner than I can do." Judge Nelson simply rendered a short decree reversing that of Judge Betts, on the ground that the evidence did not sustain the allegations of the libel. The government gave notice of their intention to appeal to the Supreme Court of the United States, but, have since withdrawn their appeal. So the case is closed with the decree of Judge Nelson. Under these circumstances it is to be regretted that his honor did not see fit to write an elaborate opinion discussing both the law and the facts in the case, which must have been of very great value, by reason of the peculiar fitness of Mr. Justice Nelson to adjudicate in causes of this nature. The quotations which we have made, are from his rulings at the hearing before him, and are, of course, much less elaborate than could have been expected in an opinion.

Judge Betts suggested a melancholy consolation for the owners, when he refused to bond the vessel. He said, in case of acquittal, Congress might see fit to compensate them for their injuries and losses unjustly incurred. It is not a cheerful prospect for men who have lost money enough to ruin a prosperous merchant, to be remitted to the uncertain success, and the certain vexation, labor, expense, and delay, attendant upon the effort to secure reimbursement by a private bill in Congress. A rich man might well be utterly ruined if his vessels are to be kept rotting at the wharves, while his case is slowly passing through the many stages of litigation which precede the final judgment. The power of the informer to levy black-mail in such a case is enormous, and wholly disproportioned to the power which it has been deemed safe to allow him in any other class of government prosecutions.* We should incline, as a question of law, to consider the argument of Mr. Evarts as conclusive to the effect that bonding is, at least, a matter of discretion, if not of obligation. But the point is a doubtful one, and the first action of Judge Betts certainly affords a precedent for holding that bonding is not even permissible. These facts seem to suggest the advisability of some supplementary legislation which should place this important matter upon a certain and a just ground. It would be easy to declare that bonding shall be either obligatory or discretionary, as shall seem good. Also, it would seem quite worthy of a fatherly government to provide some better means than the alarming prospect of an appeal to Congress for reimbursing a citizen whom the law declares innocent, and who has, in the course of the litigation which has led to this conclusion, lost, it may be, some hundreds of thousands of dollars. The hardship in these

* It must be remembered that this sentence was penned before the name of Mr. Jayne had acquired its present ignoble prominence.

cases is not only vastly greater in degree, but it is entirely different in kind, from the hardship suffered in ordinary cases of governmental prosecution of men, finally found innocent; and seems to admit and to demand some recognized method of restitution, at least, for the injury inflicted upon their property. Such restitution would still leave them, like other men acquitted in government suits, to bear their own costs of court and counsel fees; a rule which is equally unjust and universal, and which it would be hopeless to try to change. But if a ship, worth $200,000 or $300,000, had grown so unseaworthy, that, at the close of the trial, she was worth only $50,000 or $25,000, her innocent owner ought certainly to have a surer and an easier remedy than the privilege of lobbying a private bill through Congress.*

* At the time of this printing (March, 1874), the claim of the owners of the "Meteor" for restitution is still pending in the Court of Claims.

[*Law Review,* July 1871. *Book Notice.*]

LAURA D. FAIR.

Official Report of the Trial of Laura D. Fair, for the Murder of Alexander P. Crittenden; including the Testimony, the Arguments of Counsel, and the Charge of the Court, reported verbatim, and the entire Correspondence of the Parties, with Portraits of the Defendant and the Deceased. From the short-hand notes of Marsh & Osbourne, official Reporters of the Courts. San Francisco: Printed by the San Francisco Co-operative Printing Company. Pamphlet, 8vo. 1871.

ON the third day of November last (1870), Mrs. Laura D. Fair shot Mr. A. P. Crittenden, on board the steam ferry-boat "El Capitan," in the Bay of San Francisco. Her trial was begun at San Francisco, on the twenty-seventh day of March, and continued without intermission until the twenty-sixth day of April, when it was closed by the verdict of "Guilty of murder in the first degree." The cause has attracted much attention, but its interest is rather psychological than professional. Mr. Crittenden was a distinguished lawyer, a daring speculator, a man of cultivation and intellectual vigor, a member of the famous Kentucky family of that name. Counsel in describing him found prose unequal to the emergency, and sought adequate expression in nearly two pages of poetry, quoted from Pollock's Course of Time, and certainly depicting a man of very uncommon moral and intellectual traits. But these astonishing qualities did not suffice to prevent him, though he was a married man, from being caught in feminine toils. Mrs. Fair was apparently not more than tolerably good-looking; but she was of a vehement and passionate disposition, and it was probably her character rather than her face that proved so attractive to a man of Mr. Crittenden's calibre. She had two ruling tastes; namely, for money and for men. She had, in her brief career, gratified each with great success. She had managed to lay by some $10,000; and she had been married four times, and if all that was said at the trial was true, she ought for the sake of her own fair fame to have been wedded even oftener.

These two pursuits went hand in hand pretty harmoniously upon the whole, though at times somewhat ludicrously. Thus, while she was trying to separate Mr. Crittenden from his wife, she writes: "It seems to me that you might have made her choose between you and the furniture; and then, if she insisted upon despoiling my house of almost every thing in the shape of furniture, which I held sacred, then you ought to have remained mine, — all mine." The same letter concludes with a paroxysm, for which we must refer the reader to the original report. But we must do Mrs. Fair the credit to say that her correspondence does not contain many passages "*de hault goust.*" There is a little maudlin sentiment, and a good deal of fleshly passion thinly covered by the language of love, but rather less stuff than might be expected. Wrath and jealousy finally got the better in the conflict with worldly prudence. She had long been expecting and demanding that Mr. Crittenden should procure a divorce from his wife and marry her. She could not bear, as she often wrote to him, to think that he was sleeping with another woman. She hounded him on ceaselessly, and he met her with promises. Finally, when his wife came on from the Eastern States to join him, Mrs. Fair could bear it no longer. She talked to him in her usual strain; but the apparent effect of her arguments and entreaties was unsatisfactory. Unknown to him she followed him to watch his meeting with his wife. She saw him kiss that lady, and her vindictiveness culminated. She walked up to him, and shot him through the chest, dead.

At the trial she set up the thread-bare defence of insanity. It was obvious that she was not insane a little while before or a little while after the event. But she sought to make out that when she fired the fatal shot she knew not what she was about. It was that form of transient lunacy known as the "emotional." Her testimony concerning this was extremely clever. She began by giving a clear narrative, which as she neared the actual moment of the murder grew more and more indistinct, until at last she appeared like one absolutely bereft of memory. She would not say that she could remember nothing, that she looked back upon an utter blank. Far better than this was her testimony. Certain facts seemed to whirr backwards and forwards before her mind's eye with an uncertain motion, and an indistinct outline. She could not fasten them or describe them definitely. They danced like will-o'-the-wisps, in what was otherwise a black void of forgetfulness. It may be that her evidence here followed the precise truth. The intense excitement of the moment may have left such singular traces in her mind. It does not impress us so. But whether it was genuine or false, it was put in admirable shape.

The trial was conducted in the main thoroughly and well, with somewhat less regard for the decorum of the court-room than is customary in most Eastern cities, though far in advance of the practice in New York City in this respect. The following sketch of a scene will illustrate the laxity and the tendency to a free and general fight, which was sometimes manifested: —

Mrs. Fair (in the witness-box). I am sure he was the only friend I had in the world. I would not have desired to have harmed him, and if he had been living now, gentlemen, when Mr. Campbell insulted me the other day, he would have made Mr. Campbell on his bended knees apologize for it. [Here there was considerable applause in the court-room.]

The Court. Silence! The officers will bring the parties forward immediately that applauded. Bring them forward at once and have them sworn.

An Officer. [After a search had been made among the crowd outside.] We cannot find anybody who applauded.

The Court. Bring them all forward and have them all sworn.

Mrs. Fair. Judge, it was my fault, probably.

The Court (to the witness). Just answer the questions, madam. Of course you are not to blame for the disturbance.

Mrs. Fair. Well, Judge, human nature could not stand it.

Francis M. Hughes is brought forward by the officers and sworn by the clerk.

The Court. Did you applaud?

Hughes. No, sir.

The Court. Did you see any one applaud?

Hughes. No, sir; I did not see any one.

The Court. You did not see any one, and you did not applaud?

Hughes. No, sir.

The Court. The officers will bring forward some one who did, then.

Emily Pitt Stevens is here pointed out by an officer in the court-room, and rising, advances towards the judge and says: "Judge, I was not aware that I could not applaud in Court."

The Court. Did you applaud?

Emily. I said " Good."

The Court. What is your name?

Emily. Emily Pitt Stevens.

The Court. You did applaud in the Court, did you?

Emily. I said " Good," and I put my hand down on the desk so [showing].

The Court. Did you make any noise?

Emily. I made no noise with my feet.

The Court. Did you with your hand?

Emily. With my hand I did.

The Court. You are fined $25.

Mrs. Fair. I will pay it.

Emily. Thank you.

Mrs. Booth is here pointed out by some party as having applauded, and says: "I did not applaud."

A Voice. You did.

Mrs. Booth (rising and addressing the Court). "Judge, I was not aware that I could not applaud."

The Court. What is your name?

Mrs. B. Mrs. Booth.

The Court. Did you applaud?

Mrs. B. I stamped my foot: I was not aware that it was against the rules.

The Court (to the clerk). Enter a fine of $25.

Mrs. Fair. I will pay it.

Mrs. Booth. Thank you.

The Court (to Mrs. Fair). You will have to draw heavily on your bank if you pay the fines of all of them.

Mrs. Fair. I do not think, your honor, these ladies understood the rules of the Court.

The Court. Well, they will understand them now. I wish the officers now to keep a careful lookout, and arrest any person guilty of applauding on either side.

The arguments of counsel were long and elaborate, somewhat picturesque and high-strung, yet withal vigorous and effective. But the element of humor seems to be somewhat singularly developed among the barristers of the Pacific Coast if the following outburst may be taken as an example. It was proved that Mrs. Fair had procured the pistol used by her, several days before the murder. She accounted for this by saying that uproarious and impertinent boys were wont to haunt the door-way and staircase of the house in which she had rooms. She feared them, and wished a means of protection in case of need. Counsel dealt with her explanation as follows : —.

"It will not do for this lady to declare, either now or at the time of the purchase, that she procured this pistol, this instrument of death, in order to shoot boys. Boys, as a general rule, are not shot. It is not necessary, nor is it customary, in this or any other civilized community, to shoot boys. It is not necessary for women living in San Francisco to employ pistols for the purpose of shooting boys; because we have a very large and a very useful and energetic and vigilant police."

Certain exceptions taken at this trial on behalf of the defence having been sustained, a second trial became necessary. This took place at the close of the year 1872, and resulted in an acquittal. The verdict was far from satisfactory to the public, and gave rise to some forcible utterances of opinion concerning the present manner of impanelling juries in criminal causes. In making up the jury in this case hundreds upon hundreds of persons were rejected upon the score of preconceived opinions. Practically, nearly everybody who had read the newspapers, who had any knowledge of passing events, or any intelligence to apply to that bare knowledge, was ruled out as incompetent. It began to seem that it would be impossible to have a trial at all because it would be impossible to find in or around a thriving and active city like San Francisco twelve men sufficiently ignorant and stupid to fulfil the requisitions of jurors. Nothing but an idiot asylum could be reasonably expected to furnish such a panel as the learned judges insisted upon having. At last, after a long period and careful search, a dozen men were brought together, presumably the most unintelligent creatures in California, so exceptionably imbecile as to be unexceptionable! These worthies sat solemnly in the box, listening to the harangues and theories of the learned and eloquent counsel for the accused lady, until it may be supposed that their mental condition became even more confused than hers was represented to have been at the time of the commission of the deed of killing. Indeed it is not satisfactorily shown that they had even been educated up to the comprehension of the idea that to shoot a human being is really an objectionable act. Their finding was only what should naturally have been anticipated, and after all it was the law or the administration thereof which insisted upon having such men for jurors, rather than the men themselves, that ought justly to be held answerable for their action.